THE KEY
STUDENT STUDY GUIDE

Biology 20

THE KEY student study guide is designed to help students achieve success in school. The content in each study guide is 100% curriculum aligned and serves as an excellent source of material for review and practice. To create this book, teachers, curriculum specialists, and assessment experts have worked closely to develop the instructional pieces that explain each of the key concepts for the course. The practice questions and sample tests have detailed solutions that show problem-solving methods, highlight concepts that are likely to be tested, and point out potential sources of errors. **THE KEY** is a complete guide to be used by students throughout the school year for reviewing and understanding course content, and to prepare for assessments.

Rao, Gautam, 1961 –
THE KEY –Biology 20
      Alberta

   1.   Science – Juvenile Literature. I. Title

Published by
Castle Rock Research Corp.
2340 Manulife Place
10180 – 101 Street
Edmonton, AB T5J 3S4

   4 5 6 FP 13 12 11

Publisher
Gautam Rao

Contributors
Richard Klinger
Chris Dambrowitz
Christine Farag
Rob Hill
Karen Kline
Simonne Longerich
Susan Ferbey

Dedicated to the memory of Dr. V. S. Rao

THE KEY—Biology 20

THE KEY consists of the following sections:

KEY Tips for Being Successful at School gives examples of study and review strategies. It includes information about learning styles, study schedules, and note taking for test preparation.

Class Focus includes a unit on each area of the curriculum. Units are divided into sections, each focusing on one of the specific expectations, or main ideas, that students must learn about in that unit. Examples, definitions, and visuals help to explain each main idea. Practice questions on the main ideas are also included. At the end of each unit is a test on the important ideas covered. The practice questions and unit tests help students identify areas they know and those they need to study more. They can also be used as preparation for tests and quizzes. Most questions are of average difficulty, though some are easy and some are hard—the harder questions are called *Challenger Questions*. Each unit is prefaced by a **Table of Correlations**, which correlates questions in the unit to the specific curriculum expectations. Answers and solutions are found at the end of each unit.

KEY Strategies for Success on Tests helps students get ready for tests. It shows students different types of questions they might see, word clues to look for when reading them, and hints for answering them.

Practice Tests includes one to three tests based on the entire course. They are very similar to the format and level of difficulty that students may encounter on final tests. In some regions, these tests may be reprinted versions of official tests, or reflect the same difficulty levels and formats as official versions. This gives students the chance to practice using real-world examples. Answers and complete solutions are provided at the end of the section.

For the complete curriculum document visit http://education.alberta.ca/teachers/program/science/programs.aspx

THE KEY *Study Guides* are available for many courses. Check www.castlerockresearch.com for a complete listing of books available for your area.

For information about any of our resources or services, please call Castle Rock Research at 780.448.9619 or visit our website at http://www.castlerockresearch.com.

At Castle Rock Research, we strive to produce an error-free resource. If you should find an error, please contact us so that future editions can be corrected.

TABLE OF CONTENTS

KEY Tips for Being Successful at School

KEY TIPS FOR BEING SUCCESSFUL AT SCHOOL

KEY FACTORS CONTRIBUTING TO SCHOOL SUCCESS

In addition to learning the content of your courses, there are some other things that you can do to help you do your best at school. Some of these strategies are listed below.

- **Keep a positive attitude:** Always reflect on what you can already do and what you already know.

- **Be prepared to learn**: Have ready the necessary pencils, pens, notebooks, and other required materials for participating in class.

- **Complete all of your assignments:** Do your best to finish all of your assignments. Even if you know the material well, practice will reinforce your knowledge. If an assignment or question is difficult for you, work through it as far as you can so that your teacher can see exactly where you are having difficulty.

- **Set small goals for yourself when you are learning new material:** For example, when learning the parts of speech, do not try to learn everything in one night. Work on only one part or section each study session. When you have memorized one particular part of speech and understand it, then move on to another one, continue this process until you have memorized and learned all the parts of speech.

- **Review your classroom work regularly at home:** Review to be sure that you understand the material that you learned in class.

- **Ask your teacher for help**: Your teacher will help you if you do not understand something or if you are having a difficult time completing your assignments.

- **Get plenty of rest and exercise:** Concentrating in class is hard work. It is important to be well-rested and have time to relax and socialize with your friends. This helps you to keep your positive attitude about your school work.

- **Eat healthy meals:** A balanced diet keeps you healthy and gives you the energy that you need for studying at school and at home.

HOW TO FIND YOUR LEARNING STYLE

Every student learns differently. The manner in which you learn best is called your learning style. By knowing your learning style, you can increase your success at school. Most students use a combination of learning styles. Do you know what type of learner you are? Read the following descriptions. Which of these common learning styles do you use most often?

- **Linguistic Learner**: You may learn best by saying, hearing, and seeing words. You are probably really good at memorizing things such as dates, places, names, and facts. You may need **to write and then say out loud** the steps in a process, a formula, or the actions that lead up to a significant event.

- **Spatial Learner**: You may learn best by looking at and working with pictures. You are probably really good at puzzles, imagining things, and reading maps and charts. You may need to use strategies like **mind mapping and webbing** to organize your information and study notes.

- **Kinaesthetic Learner**: You may learn best by touching, moving, and figuring things out using manipulative. You are probably really good at physical activities and learning through movement. You may need to **draw your finger over a diagram** to remember it, **"tap out" the steps** needed to solve a problem, or **"feel" yourself writing or typing** a formula.

SCHEDULING STUDY TIME

You should review your class notes regularly to ensure that you have a clear understanding of all the new material you learned. Reviewing your lessons on a regular basis helps you to learn and remember ideas and concepts. It also reduces the quantity of material that you need to study prior to a test. Establishing a study schedule will help you to make the best use of your time.

Regardless of the type of study schedule you use, you may want to consider the following suggestions to maximize your study time and effort:

- Organize your work so that you begin with the most challenging material first.
- Divide the subject's content into small, manageable chunks.
- Alternate regularly between your different subjects and types of study activities in order to maintain your interest and motivation.
- Make a daily list with headings like "Must Do," "Should Do," and "Could Do."
- Begin each study session by quickly reviewing what you studied the day before.
- Maintain your usual routine of eating, sleeping, and exercising to help you concentrate better for extended periods of time.

CREATING STUDY NOTES

MIND-MAPPING OR WEBBING

Use the key words, ideas, or concepts from your reading or class notes to create a *mind map* or *web* (a diagram or visual representation of the given information). A mind map or web is sometimes referred to as a knowledge map.

• Write the key word, concept, theory, or formula in the centre of your page.

• Write down related facts, ideas, events, and information and then link them to the central concept with lines.

• Use coloured markers, underlining, or other symbols to emphasize things such as relationships, time lines, and important information.

• The following examples of a Frayer Model illustrate how this technique can be used to study scientific vocabulary.

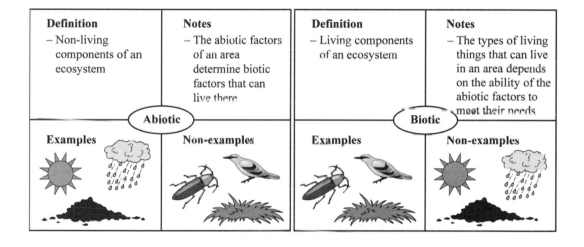

INDEX CARDS

To use index cards while studying, follow these steps:

- Write a key word or question on one side of an index card.

- On the reverse side, write the definition of the word, answer to the question, or any other important information that you want to remember.

> What is the difference between
> heat and thermal energy?

> What is the difference between
> heat and thermal energy?
>
> Thermal energy is the total energy of the
> particles in a solid, liquid, or gas.
> Heat is the amount of thermal energy
> transferred between objects.

SYMBOLS AND STICKY NOTES—IDENTIFYING IMPORTANT INFORMATION

Use symbols to mark your class notes. For example, an exclamation mark (!) might be used to point out something that must be learned well because it is a very important idea. A question mark (?) may highlight something that you are not certain about, and a diamond (◊) or asterisk (*) could highlight interesting information that you want to remember.

- Use sticky notes when you are not allowed to put marks in books.

- Use sticky notes to mark a page in a book that contains an important diagram, formula, explanation, etc.

- Use sticky notes to mark important facts in research books.

MEMORIZATION TECHNIQUES

- **Association** relates new learning to something you already know. For example, to remember the spelling difference between *dessert* and *desert*, recall that the word *sand* has only one *s*. So, because there is sand in a desert, the word *desert* only has on *s*.

- **Mnemonic** devices are sentences that you create to remember a list or group of items. For example, the first letter of each word in the phrase "**E**very **G**ood **B**oy **D**eserves **F**udge" helps you to remember the names of the lines on the treble clef staff (E, G, B, D, and F) in music.

- **Acronyms** are words that are formed from the first letters or parts of the words in a group. For example, **RADAR** is actually an acronym for **Ra**dio **D**etecting **A**nd **R**anging, and **MASH** is an acronym for **M**obile **A**rmy **S**urgical **H**ospital. **HOMES** helps you to remember the names of the five Great Lakes (**H**uron, **O**ntario, **M**ichigan, **E**rie, and **S**uperior).

- **Visualizing** requires you to use your mind's eye to "see" a chart, list, map, diagram, or sentence as it is in your textbook or notes, on the chalk board or computer screen, or in a display.

- **Initialisms** are abbreviations that are formed from the first letters or parts of the words in a group. Unlike acronyms, initialisms cannot be pronounced as a word themselves. For example, **BEDMAS** is an initialism for the order of operations in math (**B**rackets, **E**xponents, **D**ivide, **M**ultiply, **A**dd, **S**ubtract).

KEY STRATEGIES FOR REVIEWING

Reviewing textbook material, class notes, and handouts should be an ongoing activity. Spending time reviewing becomes more critical when you are preparing for tests. You may find some of the following review strategies useful when studying during your scheduled study time.

- Before reading a selection, preview it by noting the headings, charts, graphs, and chapter questions.
- Before reviewing a unit, note the headings, charts, graphs and chapter questions.
- Highlight key concepts, vocabulary, definitions and formulas.
- Skim the paragraph and note the key words, phrases, and information.
- Carefully read over each step in a procedure.
- Draw a picture or diagram to help make the concept clearer.

KEY STRATEGIES FOR SUCCESS: A CHECKLIST

Review, review, review: review is a huge part of doing well at school and preparing for tests. Here is a checklist for you to keep track of how many suggested strategies for success you are using. Read each question and then put a check mark (✓) in the correct column. Look at the questions where you have checked the "No" column. Think about how you might try using some of these strategies to help you do your best at school.

KEY Strategies for Success	Yes	No
Do you attend school regularly?		
Do you know your personal learning style—how you learn best?		
Do you spend 15 to 30 minutes a day reviewing your notes?		
Do you study in a quiet place at home?		
Do you clearly mark the most important ideas in your study notes?		
Do you use sticky notes to mark texts and research books?		
Do you practise answering multiple-choice and written-response questions?		
Do you ask your teacher for help when you need it?		
Are you maintaining a healthy diet and sleep routine?		
Are you participating in regular physical activity?		

Energy and Matter Exchange in the Biosphere

ENERGY AND MATTER EXCHANGE IN THE BIOSPHERE

Table of Correlations				
Specific Expectation	**Practice Questions**	**Unit Test Questions**	**Practice Test 1**	**Practice Test 2**
Students will:				
A1 *Explain the constant flow of energy through the biosphere and ecosystems.*				
A1.1 explain, in general terms, the one-way flow of energy through the biosphere and how stored energy in the biosphere, as a system, is eventually "lost" as heat	2	1, 3		
A1.2 explain how energy in the biosphere can be perceived as a balance between both photosynthetic and chemosynthetic activities and cellular respiratory activities; i.e., energy flow in photosynthetic environments, energy flow in deep sea vent (chemosynthetic) ecosystems and other extreme environments	1, 4, 9	5	3	
A1.3 explain the structure of ecosystem trophic levels, using models such as food chains and food webs	5, 6	9	3, WR1	
A1.4 explain, quantitatively, the flow of energy and the exchange of matter in aquatic and terrestrial ecosystems, using models such as pyramids of numbers, biomass and energy	8, 18, 20	4, 10,	10, 22, 25	
A2 *Explain the cycling of matter through the biosphere.*				
A2.1 explain and summarize the biogeochemical cycling of carbon, oxygen, nitrogen, and phosphorus and relate this to general reuse of all matter in the biosphere	3, 10, 11, 12, 13, 19	6, 7, WR2		1
A2.2 explain water's primary role in the biogeochemical cycles, considering its chemical and physical properties; i.e., universal solvent, hydrogen bonding	16	11, 12		
A3 *Explain the balance of energy and matter exchange in the biosphere, as an open system, and explain how this maintains equilibrium.*				
A3.1 explain the interrelationship of energy, matter, and ecosystem productivity (biomass production)	7	13		20
A3.2 explain how the equilibrium between gas exchanges in photosynthesis and cellular respiration influences atmospheric composition	14, 17	8, 2, WR1		
A3.3 describe the geologic evidence (stromatolites) and scientific explanations for change in atmospheric composition, with respect to oxygen and carbon dioxide, from anoxic conditions to the present, and describe the significance to current biosphere equilibrium	15	14	2	

ENERGY AND MATTER EXCHANGE IN THE BIOSPHERE

A1.1   explain, in general terms, the one-way flow of energy through the biosphere and how stored energy in the biosphere, as a system, is eventually "lost" as heat

ENERGY FLOW IN THE BIOSPHERE

Most of the energy on Earth comes from the sun as light. Some of this light is reflected back into space, which is why Earth is visible from space. The reflection of light off of reflective surfaces, such as snow, ice, and water, is known as the albedo effect. Most of the light that is not reflected back to space is absorbed as heat, especially by darker surfaces, such as soil.

A small percentage of the sun's light arriving at the Earth is captured by plants in **photosynthesis**.

The energy that is stored in **autotrophs** can be passed to **heterotrophs**, but eventually most energy taken into organisms by photosynthesis is freed in the form of **heat**. You can feel the heat leave your body during physical activities. Once energy leaves an organism in the form of heat, it is lost to the atmosphere and space. For this reason, it is said that energy flows in a one-way direction and is not recycled the way matter is. New energy must continually enter the biosphere as solar energy for ecosystems to continue.

Practice Question: 2

A1.2   explain how energy in the biosphere can be perceived as a balance between both photosynthetic and chemosynthetic activities and cellular respiratory activities; i.e., energy flow in photosynthetic environments, energy flow in deep sea vent (chemosynthetic) ecosystems and other extreme environments

ENERGY BALANCE

Energy flows through the biosphere in a one-way direction from solar energy to work or heat. The transfer of energy through living things depends on the interdependent processes of photosynthesis and cellular respiration.

Because the sun by itself is not a useful form of biological energy, photosynthesis is needed to capture solar energy within the chemical bonds of glucose. Photosynthesis is an **endergonic** reaction, meaning it requires energy to occur. The sun supplies this energy, but only green plants have the chemical and structural machinery to harness the sun's energy into the useful form of glucose. The bonds between the atoms of carbon (C), hydrogen (H), and oxygen (O) found in the abundant and low-energy molecules of carbon dioxide (CO_2) and water (H_2O) act as a storage medium for this solar energy, creating the high-energy molecule glucose ($C_6H_{12}O_6$).

When an organism needs energy from adenosine triphosphate (ATP) for its metabolic activities (e.g., moving, thinking, growing), it will turn to the glucose found in its food or stored in its body as a source of energy. The **exergonic** (energy releasing) process of cellular respiration tears the bonds of glucose apart, releasing the energy stored there. It is this energy that is used to make ATP. Because solar energy is transferred to glucose, then to ATP, and is then used for cell activities, it is possible to think of organisms as being solar powered. When cellular respiration is complete and the energy contained in glucose is released, the low-energy molecules of CO_2 and H_2O are left behind and can be used again for photosynthesis.

All life on Earth depends on the chloroplast's ability to capture the sun's energy through photosynthesis. The only exceptions are bacteria that undergo **chemosynthesis** rather than photosynthesis, such as those living at ocean depths where light cannot reach them. Instead of using sunlight as a source of energy to make glucose, these bacteria (called **chemoautotrophs**) use the energy of oxidation of hydrogen sulfide or methane.

The processes of photosynthesis and cellular respiration are dependent upon each other and play key roles in the transfer of energy through the biosphere.

Practice Questions: 1, 4, 9

A1.3   explain the structure of ecosystem trophic levels, using models such as food chains and food webs

A1.4   explain, quantitatively, the flow of energy and the exchange of matter in aquatic and terrestrial ecosystems, using models such as pyramids of numbers, biomass and energy

ENERGY FLOW MODELS

The biosphere is composed of all the areas of Earth that can support life. This includes the land and water on Earth's surface and extends slightly into the atmosphere. Energy constantly enters the biosphere in the form of light and leaves the biosphere in the form of heat. In contrast, the amount of matter on the planet does not change— the atoms that make up the earth's matter are recycled over and over.

The organisms present within an ecosystem form simple food chains and complex food webs that display the flow of energy and matter through an ecosystem.

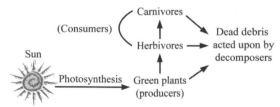

Bacteria convert complex organic substances back to inorganic salts and minerals absorbed by green plants.

A predator that eats a producer is consuming the producer's matter. When the predator dies, this matter is taken up by decomposers. Decomposers, such as bacteria and fungi, are vital to the recycling of matter because they release atoms back to the soil and air where producers will use them again in photosynthesis.

Energy flows through food chains from producers (which initially capture light energy during photosynthesis), to consumers, and finally to decomposers.

At each trophic level, most of the energy is lost from the system as heat. That is why there are more producers in an ecosystem than there are herbivores and more herbivores than there are carnivores. This concept can be shown as a **food pyramid.**

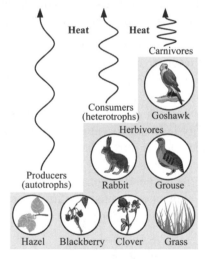

The triangular shape of an ecosystem's energy pyramid, biomass pyramid, and numbers pyramid all reflect this concept.

A numbers pyramid can be used to illustrate how toxins can accumulate in a food chain. Each top predator needs to eat many lower-level consumers. Each lower-level consumer eats large numbers of producers. As a result even small amounts of a toxin in the producer levels can accumulate to very toxic levels in top predators. This phenomenon is called **biological magnification.**

Practice Questions: 5, 6, 8, 18, 20

A2.1   explain and summarize the biogeochemical cycling of carbon, oxygen, nitrogen, and phosphorus and relate this to general reuse of all matter in the biosphere

BIOGEOCHEMICAL CYCLES IN NATURE

Unlike energy, matter used by living things is continually recycled. The atoms of matter exchanged during **photosynthesis** and **cellular respiration** are cycled between the two processes. During photosynthesis, an autotroph takes in carbon dioxide and water, produces food (glucose), and releases oxygen into the air. During cellular respiration, organisms take in food (glucose) and oxygen and release water and carbon dioxide into the air. The products of photosynthesis are the reactants for cellular respiration and vice versa, illustrating that matter cycles.

Each ecosystem in the biosphere is characterized by limiting abiotic factors that determine what organisms can survive there. The availability of important elements, such as carbon, water, phosphorus, nitrogen, and oxygen, depends on biogeochemical cycling mechanisms that have been present since Earth was young. Because of these cycles, matter is continually moving from the biotic to the abiotic worlds and back again.

In the biotic world, carbon is found in the form of organic molecules, either as food (carbohydrates, fats, proteins, and nucleic acids) or fossil fuels. In the abiotic world, carbon is found in the form of atmospheric CO_2, CO_2 dissolved in water, and carbonates.

Cellular respiration, decomposition, volcanic activity, and the burning of fossil fuels release carbon dioxide into the atmosphere. Atmospheric carbon dioxide is removed from the atmosphere by photosynthesizing plants, where it is incorporated into glucose. If the rates of cellular respiration and fossil fuel burning exceed the rate of photosynthesis, carbon dioxide will build up in the atmosphere. An increase in carbon dioxide concentrations will trap more heat in the atmosphere, causing the global temperature to increase.

Nitrogen is required by plants to synthesize protein, ATP, DNA, and other organic compounds. The atmosphere is about 78% molecular nitrogen gas (N_2), which plants cannot use. Nitrogen must be in the form of nitrate (NO_3^-) or ammonia (NH_3) in order for plant roots to absorb and incorporate it into protein. The more nitrates in the soil, the more fertile the land and the better the crop.

Many species of beneficial soil bacteria participate in the **nitrogen cycle**. These bacteria convert nitrogen in animal and plant wastes into forms that can be used by plants.

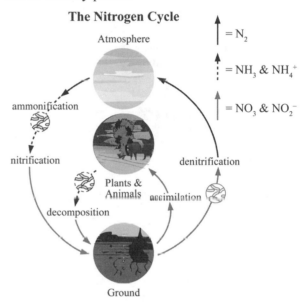

The Nitrogen Cycle

Atmosphere

ammonification

nitrification

Plants & Animals

decomposition

denitrification

assimilation

Ground

$= N_2$

$= NH_3$ & NH_4^+

$= NO_3$ & NO_2^-

Ammonifying soil bacteria convert dead matter and wastes into ammonia (NH_3), and **nitrifying** soil bacteria convert ammonia into nitrite (NO_2^-) and finally nitrate (NO_3^-). The nitrate is absorbed by plant roots and made into proteins, completing the cycle.

Denitrifying bacteria thrive in hard-packed or water-logged soils. They reduce soil fertility because they convert useful nitrates back into ammonia. Legumes (peas, beans, lentils) are said to be nitrogen fixing plants. Special **nitrogen-fixing** bacteria in the nodules of their roots convert normally unusable atmospheric nitrogen (N_2) into ammonia (NH_3). Nitrifying bacteria in the soil then quickly convert the ammonia into useful nitrates that the plant can use to make protein. For this reason, legumes are higher in protein than other plants and are an excellent alternative to meat.

Sewage and agricultural fertilizers containing nitrogen compounds that increase plant productivity can run off into rivers and lakes. This produces excessive plant growth and algal blooms in a process called **eutrophication**. The extra plant growth dies and sinks to the bottom where decomposer bacteria carry out cellular respiration on the dead matter, using up the oxygen in the water. This often results in the death of the fish in the water or the creation of an anaerobic swamp.

The **phosphorus cycle** is simpler than the nitrogen cycle. Plants need phosphorus to make DNA, ATP, and special fat molecules that make up cell membranes called **phospholipids**.

The Phosphorus Cycle
Ground

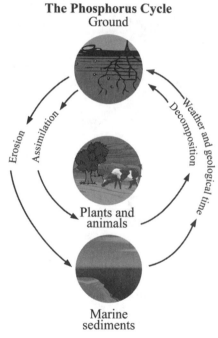

Soil phosphorous may come from the underlying rock sediments or from decomposing organisms. Phosphorous returns to marine sediments through run-off from the land, completing the cycle as sediments become rock over time. Phosphorous is a limiting factor to aquatic plant growth. As such, run-off from phosphorous-rich agricultural fertilizer and the use of phosphate detergents are contributors to eutrophication of lakes and rivers.

Practice Questions: 3, 10, 11, 12, 13, 19

A2.2   explain water's primary role in the biogeochemical cycles, considering its chemical and physical properties; i.e., universal solvent, hydrogen bonding

THE ROLE OF WATER

In the hydrological cycle, plants take in liquid water through their roots to be used in photosynthesis, and then release it back into the atmosphere as water vapour from cellular respiration and **transpiration** from stomata. Animals obtain water by drinking and release water in their breath, perspiration, or urine. Because most of Earth's surface is water, **evaporation** from oceans returns water to the atmosphere where vapour cools, undergoes **condensation** in clouds, and returns to Earth as **precipitation** in the form of rain or snow. Precipitation either permeates the soil to plant roots and the **water table** or returns to the oceans as run-off. Solar energy from the sun drives the water cycle in that its heat causes the evaporation of water from the oceans and transpiration of water from trees.

The Hydrologic Cycle
Atmosphere

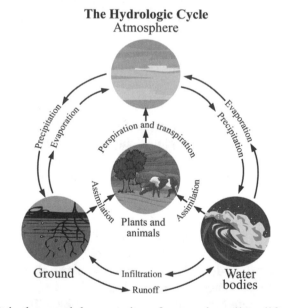

It is the special properties of water that allow life to exist on Earth. **Hydrogen bonds** between water molecules cause water molecules to stick together. These strong **cohesive** properties mean water does not change phase easily, having higher freezing and boiling points than would be expected for such a small molecule.

Water also has a high **specific heat capacity**, meaning it does not change temperature quickly. This affects nature in several ways. For example, Earth's surface is mostly water, so oceans store heat in the summer and release heat in the winter, moderating the temperature of the atmosphere seasonally. Earth's water has the same role in moderating day and night temperatures. This is also true in living things. This high heat capacity means body temperatures are also slower to change, remaining stable regardless of changes in environmental temperature.

The strong cohesive properties of water give it high **surface tension** allowing organisms such as insects to live on the surface of water.

Cohesion of water is also responsible for **capillary action** which allows water to move from plant roots, up xylem tubes, and out of stomata through transpiration. If water did not return to the atmosphere through transpiration, a great quantity of water would remain locked in the soils and rock strata of Earth.

Because water is a **universal solvent**, many compounds can dissolve in it, forming the ions that participate in biological reactions. Gases, such as oxygen and carbon dioxide, can also dissolve in water, making photosynthesis and cellular respiration in aquatic ecosystems possible. Water is also essential for the erosion that carries minerals from one part of an ecosystem to another, as seen in the nitrogen or phosphorous cycles.

Practice Question: 16

A3.1   explain the interrelationship of energy, matter and ecosystem productivity (biomass production)

ENERGY AND BIOMASS

The energy that arrives at Earth's surface is finite, being defined by the amount of solar radiation received through the atmosphere. This averages to a solar constant of about 1 360 W/m^2 (watts per square metre). Energy is constantly arriving at that rate, and it is also leaving at the same rate, obeying the laws of thermodynamics.

FIRST LAW OF THERMODYNAMICS

Energy cannot be created or destroyed, but it can be converted from one form to another.

Biologically, this means that solar energy can be trapped into the chemical energy of glucose bonds during photosynthesis, which can then be converted to ATP, kinetic energy, and heat.

SECOND LAW OF THERMODYNAMICS

As energy is converted from one form into another, some energy is always lost as heat.

In terms of biology, this means that with every step up the food chain, most of the energy (approximately 90%) in each level is lost as heat, with very little energy transferred to the next level. The reason for this loss is that cellular respiration is very inefficient. For example, when a carnivore eats a herbivore, the flesh is digested and becomes glucose, which is sent to the carnivore's cells for cellular respiration. Unfortunately, only a small amount of useful ATP energy will be recovered from cellular respiration. Most of the energy of glucose is lost as waste heat. Another reason for the loss of energy between levels is that a lot of food that is eaten is indigestible. For example a coyote that eats a rabbit will excrete the indigestible hair, bone, and connective tissue in its feces. Most of the rabbit's flesh that is digested and absorbed into the coyote will be burned in cellular respiration to produce ATP and heat and will not remain as part of the coyote's body. Therefore, if a coyote eats a rabbit that has 100 J stored in its body, only 10 J will be incorporated into the coyote. A bear that eats the coyote will receive only 1 J. Because of the second law of thermodynamics, very little energy reaches the top predators, limiting their numbers and the length of the food chain. Many people believe that humans should eat lower on the food chain (eat more plants) in order to prevent this waste of energy and resources that occurs between trophic levels. For example, 100 J of corn plants will produce 10 J of human tissue. However, 100 J of corn produces 10 J of beef, which produces only 1 J of human tissue. For this reason, perhaps humans should be eating corn instead of beef.

Biomass is a measure of the entire mass of living material within an ecosystem, including all producers, consumers, and decomposers. The total biomass making up the producer level of a food chain, called **biomass productivity**, is determined by the amount of solar energy available for photosynthesis in that biome.

Available solar energy depends on latitude. Equatorial biomes receive more intense solar energy than polar ones and do not have seasonal changes in the amount of light they receive. Because of Earth's tilt, biomes closer to the poles, such as those in Alberta, have seasonal changes in the amount of light received. The biomass productivity of a biome is also limited by the availability of inorganic matter and minerals, such as nitrates and phosphates. Photosynthesis requires water in abundance, and water is a limiting factor to productivity in terrestrial biomes.

Practice Question: 7

A3.2   explain how the equilibrium between gas exchanges in photosynthesis and cellular respiration influences atmospheric composition

METABOLISM AND ATMOSPHERIC COMPOSITION

Since the chemical processes of photosynthesis and cellular respiration are opposites of one another, the carbon dioxide and water released from cellular respiration provide the reactants for photosynthesis. The oxygen and glucose released from photosynthesis are the reactants needed for cellular respiration. Normally, the production of carbon dioxide by cellular respiration, decomposition, forest fires, and volcanic activity is balanced by the amount of CO_2 removed from the atmosphere by photosynthesizing plants.

This delicate balance has been maintained for most of the history of Earth, but it has now been altered by human activity. Technological advances since the Industrial Revolution have given the rapidly growing human population access to long-buried fossil fuels (coal, oil, and gas). When fossil fuels burn, they release the same products as cellular respiration, including carbon dioxide, which traps heat in Earth's atmosphere. At the same time, the rapidly increasing human population has cut down most of the world's forests in order to grow crops for food, obtain lumber for shelter, and fuel for heat and cooking. This massive deforestation has greatly reduced photosynthesis, meaning that carbon dioxide is not being taken out of the atmosphere as quickly as it once was.

The combined effect of fossil fuel use and **deforestation** is that atmospheric carbon dioxide levels have risen. Because CO_2 and other greenhouse gases trap heat normally released into space, the average temperature of Earth's atmosphere is rising.

The effects of **global warming** predicted by computer models include an increase in extreme weather, melting of the polar ice caps, a rise in ocean temperatures and sea levels, increased precipitation and coastal flooding, and reduced precipitation and drought in mid-continents.

Changes in these abiotic conditions have resulted and will continue to result in a loss of habitat for natural populations. It remains to be seen which species will be able to adapt to the rapid rate of environmental change and which will become extinct.

The effects on human food supply, disease, global migration patterns, and economics are the subject of much speculation. Political solutions aimed at addressing the imbalance include reducing CO_2 production, increasing forestation, and developing technologies to replace fossil fuel combustion.

Practice Questions: 14, 17

A3.3 describe the geologic evidence (stromatolites) and scientific explanations for change in atmospheric composition, with respect to oxygen and carbon dioxide, from anoxic conditions to the present, and describe the significance to current biosphere equilibrium

CHANGES IN ATMOSPHERIC COMPOSITION

Earth's first atmosphere was mostly hydrogen and helium. Later, volcanic activity added carbon dioxide, hydrogen sulfide, and nitrogen. The first oxygen appeared when water droplets were split into H_2 and O_2 gas by ultraviolet light. It was not until the first photosynthesizing bacteria, called **cyanobacteria**, appeared that oxygen accumulated in the atmosphere to a significant degree.

Cyanobacteria precipitate calcium carbonate out of the water in which they live. As calcium carbonate was laid down in domed layered columns called **stromatolites**, fossilized cyanobacteria were trapped within. Stromatolites are seen today as evidence of the appearance of these bacteria, which began to change Earth's atmosphere from an **anoxic** one to an oxygen-rich one that is able to support the great diversity of life seen today. Today's atmosphere is 78% nitrogen, 21% oxygen, 0.9% argon, and about 0.034% carbon dioxide.

Practice Question: 15

PRACTICE QUESTIONS—ENERGY AND MATTER EXCHANGE IN THE BIOSPHERE

Use the following information to answer the next question.

The Gaia hypothesis, named after the Greek goddess of Earth, was first proposed by James Lovelock. The hypothesis suggests that Earth's biosphere possesses a self-regulated feedback mechanism, like that of biological organisms.

1. Which of the following statements summarizes Lovelock's original Gaia hypothesis?

   A. The climate and habitat of Earth are controlled by life itself.

   B. The abiotic factors in the environment are constants to which all life on Earth must adapt to survive.

   C. The process of natural selection is responsible for the evolution of modern forms of organisms.

   D. The first life forms evolved in the oceans, followed by the evolution of photosynthetic organisms, which led to formation of an ozone layer.

Use the following diagram to answer the next question.

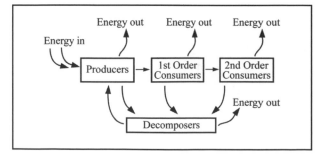

2. This diagram represents the idea that

   A. both matter and energy form a cycle

   B. neither matter nor energy form a cycle

   C. matter cycles, but energy does not cycle

   D. matter does not cycle, but energy does cycle

Use the following information to answer the next question.

In 2004, approximately 86.5% of all of the world's power consumption was provided by fossil fuels, such as oil, natural gas, and coal. Fossil fuels provide energy through combustion reactions that release carbon dioxide into the atmosphere.

3. The **most likely** impact that carbon in the atmosphere from fossil fuel combustion has on the biosphere is that

   A. Earth's albedo is increasing

   B. Earth's climate is growing warmer

   C. the ocean tides are becoming erratic

   D. the hours of sunlight per day are decreasing

4. Which of the following substances is a product of photosynthesis?

   A. Water

   B. Glucose

   C. Mitochondria

   D. Carbon dioxide

Use the following information to answer the next two questions.

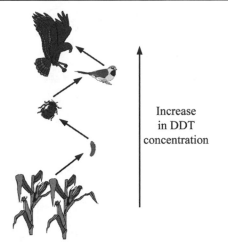

Increase in DDT concentration

When it was first introduced, DDT was considered to be a miracle pesticide because it killed insects but did not appear to harm other animals. Unfortunately, the concentration of a small amount of DDT sprayed on crops becomes higher in herbivorous insects that consume the sprayed crops. Carnivorous insects that consume the crop pests acquire an even higher DDT concentration, and birds that consume the carnivorous insects acquire an even higher concentration. High DDT concentration in some birds weakens egg shells, causing a drop in reproductive rate. Peregrine falcons, which prey on small birds, almost disappeared as a species in the 1960s because of high DDT concentrations in body tissues.

5. The idea that a toxin can increase in concentration as it passes through trophic levels is called
   A. predation
   B. a pyramid of biomes
   C. a pyramid of numbers
   D. biological magnification

6. In this food chain, the peregrine falcon is
   A. the primary autotroph
   B. a fourth-order consumer
   C. a second-order consumer
   D. at the fourth trophic level

Use the following information to answer the next question.

The amount of energy entering into an ecosystem is equal to the amount of energy passing out of that ecosystem, although it changes form as it moves through the ecosystem.

7. The given statement illustrates the
   A. pyramid of energy
   B. law of conservation of mass
   C. first law of thermodynamics
   D. second law of thermodynamics

Use the following information to answer the next question

A group of people were shipwrecked on a tropical island. Without appropriate equipment, catching fish was impossible for the stranded group. Fortunately, the group was able to salvage some chickens, goats, and a variety of seeds from the ship. Growing conditions on the island were good, but the island was very small. In fact, it was far from certain that the area would be large enough to support everyone. Therefore, the group had to decide on the most energetically efficient way to maximize the yield of food.

8. According to the concepts contained in a pyramid of numbers, a means of maximizing food yield would be to

   A. eat a little bit of everything

   B. grow grain crops to feed the goats and chickens and then eat the meat

   C. grow grain crops to feed the animals while living off eggs and goat's milk

   D. kill and eat the goats and chickens and then survive on the crops from the seeds

Use the following information to answer the next question

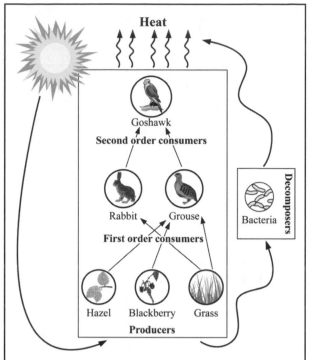

The quantity of energy decreases at each successive trophic level because energy is lost at each step.

9. In this ecosystem, the energy entering and the energy leaving are in the forms of

   A. light and heat

   B. ATP and heat

   C. light and motion

   D. ATP and motion

Use the following information to answer the next question

Environmentally friendly soaps now available for home use are phosphate-free. Regular soap contains phosphates that are rinsed down drains, releasing phosphates into the environment.

10. Which of the following statements **best** explains why excess phosphates are harmful to the environment?

   A. Phosphates destroy the ozone layer.

   B. Phosphates are poisonous to plants and animals.

   C. Phosphates react chemically to form phosphoric acid, a component of acid rain.

   D. Phosphates promote explosive growth of plants in bodies of water.

11. Because a bog is acidic, most bacteria cannot survive in bog soil. Without bacteria in the soil, which of the biogeochemical cycles would be **most** affected?

   A. Water cycle

   B. Carbon cycle

   C. Nitrogen cycle

   D. Phosphorus cycle

Use the following information to answer the next question

Many conservationists agree that producing electricity from a hydroelectric dam has less impact on global warming than producing electricity by burning coal.

12. Burning coal has a greater impact than the hydroelectric dam on global warming because burning coal releases which of the following gases as waste?

   A. O_2

   B. CO_2

   C. SO_2

   D. H_2O

13. The carbon and nitrogen atoms found on Earth today

   A. were produced by consumers using the process of cellular respiration

   B. are the same as those that were present on Earth three billion years ago

   C. were produced by plants using the process of photosynthesis

   D. are the result of a flow of matter into and out of Earth

Use the following information to answer the next question.

Cellular respiration and photosynthesis are the major chemical reactions in animals and plants, respectively. Animal cells rely only on cellular respiration for energy production. Plant cells, however, contain both mitochondria and chloroplasts. Therefore, they undergo both cellular respiration and photosynthesis.

14. Some hospitals used to remove plants from patients' rooms at night time. The theory behind this policy was that plants alter the atmospheric composition by

   A. contributing nitrogen to the atmosphere

   B. producing more oxygen than carbon dioxide at night

   C. producing carbon dioxide and consuming oxygen at night

   D. removing carbon dioxide from the surrounding atmosphere

Use the following information to answer the next question.

Currently, scientists are concerned about the balance of carbon dioxide in the atmosphere. In the earliest history of Earth, the atmosphere also had high concentrations of CO_2.
The bacteria responsible for changing this atmosphere were trapped in stromatolites that contain embedded colonies of these early life forms.

---

15. It is thought that the biochemical activities of these bacteria served to convert carbon dioxide to

   A. oxygen

   B. nitrogen

   C. methane

   D. carbon monoxide

16. The reason that water is a universal solvent is that

   A. no substances dissolve in it

   B. many substances dissolve in it

   C. water covers a large portion of Earth

   D. water exists naturally in all three states of matter

17. Which of the following statements about cellular respiration and photosynthesis is **false?**

   A. CO_2 given off during cellular respiration is required for photosynthesis.

   B. Photosynthesis produces glucose, which is required for cellular respiration.

   C. Photosynthesis produces oxygen, which is required for cellular respiration.

   D. Cellular respiration produces oxygen, which is required for photosynthesis.

18. In respiration, the energy **not** captured by ATP is

   A. released as heat

   B. eliminated along with oxygen

   C. transferred to organic compounds

   D. transferred to the next level of the food chain

19. The process of nitrogen fixation occurring in the root nodules of legumes is the conversion of

   A. nitrates to protein

   B. ammonia to nitrates

   C. atmospheric nitrogen into ammonia

   D. nitrates to useful atmospheric nitrogen

20. Which trophic level has the **greatest** amount of biomass?

   A. Producers

   B. Herbivores

   C. Top predators

   D. Secondary consumers

ANSWERS AND SOLUTIONS—PRACTICE QUESTIONS

1. A	5. D	9. A	13. B	17. D
2. C	6. B	10. D	14. C	18. A
3. B	7. C	11. C	15. A	19. C
4. B	8. D	12. B	16. B	20. A

1. A

The Gaia hypothesis was proposed as a model for the maintenance and regulation of life-supporting conditions on Earth by life itself. The abiotic conditions (temperature, climate, atmospheric gas, and soil composition) present on Earth today are maintained and regulated by life on Earth. For example, plants perform photosynthesis, which releases oxygen into the atmosphere and removes carbon dioxide. Cellular respiration achieves the opposite: oxygen is removed from the atmosphere and is replaced with carbon dioxide.

2. C

Matter consists of all the atoms on the planet, including solids, liquids, and gases. These atoms have been on Earth since its origin and are continually recycled into living or non-living forms. The biogeochemical cycles are the mechanisms of recycling. Energy, on the other hand, comes into the biosphere as solar energy, which is then converted to chemical energy by photosynthesis and released to organisms in cellular respiration as ATP. Any energy not used for cell activities escapes as heat, which is eventually lost to space. For ecosystems to continue, the energy lost as heat must be continually replaced by the sun as new solar energy entering the system. For this reason, energy is said to flow in a one-way direction only.

3. B

The burning of fossil fuels (coal, gas, and oil) releases CO_2, H_2O, and energy the same way cellular respiration does. The CO_2 released to the atmosphere acts like a blanket, insulating Earth against heat loss in the same way glass in a greenhouse prevents heat loss. Other gases, s uch as CH_4 (methane), CFCs, and water vapour, have the same insulating effect.

Albedo is reflection of light off any surface. Ice and snow have a high albedo. High carbon dioxide levels from burning fossil fuels will heat the atmosphere, causing the polar ice caps to melt. This reduces the albedo effect. Tides are caused by the gravitational pull of the moon, so they would not be affected. The hours of sunlight per day have to do with the rotation of Earth and the tilt of its axis, so they would not be affected.

4. B

Photosynthesis uses carbon dioxide and water to form glucose and oxygen within plants. Mitochondria are the cell organelles that produce metabolic energy, not a product of photosynthesis.

5. D

Biological magnification illustrates that a small concentration of a toxin in an autotroph population accumulates in a greater concentration in first-order consumers and in an even greater concentration in second-order consumers.

Biomes are large biological regions, such as coniferous forests or tundras. A pyramid of numbers shows that the plants are abundant in a community, herbivores are less abundant, and carnivores are far less abundant. Predation involves the capture of food by carnivores and does not necessarily have anything to do with toxins.

6. B

The peregrine falcon is an organism typically found at the top of its food chain, preying on other organisms but not having any natural predators itself. In this food chain, the crop plants are the primary autotrophs, the pests are the first-order consumers, the carnivorous insects are the s econd-order consumers, the small bird is the third-order consumer (also at the fourth tropic level), and the falcon is the fourth-order consumer.

7. C

The first law of thermodynamics states that energy can neither be created nor destroyed. Living systems also obey this law, although there are many energy transformations that take place. Plants convert light energy to food, and consumers convert food energy into the energy of motion or produce body heat.

8. D

The survivors should kill and eat the goats and chickens and then survive on the crops grown from the seeds. The shape of the energy food pyramid indicates that with every step up the food chain, 90% of the energy of the previous level is lost as heat. If any animals are kept for food (meat, eggs, or milk), when the animals eat the seeds, 90% of the energy in the crop is lost as heat in the conversion to meat. When the humans eat the animals (as second-level consumers), 90% of that energy is also lost as heat in the conversion of meat to human flesh. If humans eat the producers directly (as primary consumers), energy is lost only once as heat during conversion. By eating producers instead of consumers, more energy an be derived by humans from the food chain. This will help to support the maximum number of survivors.

9. A

Solar energy (light) is captured by the producers and then transferred to the first-order consumers. The first-order consumers (herbivores) eat the plants, gaining some of the chemical energy stored in them. The remaining energy is lost as heat.

10. D

In living organisms, the element phosphorus is an essential component of a number of important molecules, such as DNA, RNA, ATP, and ADP. Organisms can use phosphorus in the form of phosphates (e.g., PO_4^{3-}). Plants obtain phosphates from the soil, and animals obtain phosphates from the plants and animals they consume. In addition, both phosphates and nitrates (NO_3^-) are components of fertilizers used to promote plant growth. Therefore, excess phosphates in soil and water could cause an overgrowth of plants.

Phosphoric acid is not a component of acid rain. Both nitric and sulfuric acids are found in acid rain. CFCs (chlorofluorocarbons) are responsible for the destruction of the ozone layer.

11. C

Since nitrifying bacteria in the soil are responsible for the availability of nitrates that plants absorb to make proteins, the nitrogen cycle would be most affected by the absence of bacteria.

The water, carbon, and phosphorous cycles are not as dependent on bacteria as the nitrogen cycle.

12. B

Global warming is largely caused by increased concentrations of CO_2 (carbon dioxide) in the atmosphere. CO_2 contributes to the greenhouse effect, in which the temperature at Earth's surface increases because the atmosphere is insulated by a thick layer of atmospheric gases surrounding Earth. As a result, energy (travelling at a short wavelength that can enter the insulating layer of gas) from the sun enters but does not escape (because the energy released by Earth is of a longer wavelength). Instead, energy is reflected back to Earth. Water vapour and greenhouse gases make up the atmospheric insulating layer. Other greenhouse gases include methane (CH_4, produced from decay by bacteria and released by animals), chlorofluorocarbons (CFCs, plastics), and nitrous oxide (N_2O, present in fertilizers and released by animals).

Although H_2O (water) is a greenhouse gas, it is not released as a major waste gas from burning coal. O_2 (oxygen) does not contribute to global warming, and SO_2 (sulfur dioxide) contributes to the formation of acid rain.

13. B

The atoms that make up Earth are the same ones that were present when Earth formed.

Atoms (apart from meteors) do not enter Earth's atmosphere because space is a vacuum devoid of atoms. Atoms (apart from spacecraft or satellites) do not leave Earth because of the pull of Earth's gravity. Photosynthesis does not produce matter, but rather it converts matter (atoms of C, H, and O) from inorganic forms, such as CO_2 and H_2O, to organic forms, such as glucose ($C_6H_{12}O_6$). Cellular respiration does the opposite.

14. C

In the absence of light, plants do not photosynthesize but continue to respire, removing oxygen from the air and adding carbon dioxide. This was thought to be potentially damaging to patient health, so plants were ordered to be removed from patients' rooms when the sun went down. Current medical thinking is that, overall, the plants contribute more oxygen than they consume, and the minor negative consequences at night are not serious enough to warrant their removal.

15. A

The cyanobacteria found fossilized in stromatolites were photosynthesizers that introduced oxygen into the early atmosphere of Earth.

16. B

Water is called a universal solvent because many substances dissolve in it.

17. D

In photosynthesis, carbon dioxide gas, water, and solar energy are used by green plants to produce glucose and oxygen gas.

$$6CO_2 + 6H_2O + \text{solar energy} \rightarrow C_6H_{12}O_6 + 6O_2$$

In cellular respiration, glucose and oxygen gas are utilized in the mitochondria of all organisms' cells to release carbon dioxide, water, ATP energy, and heat.

$$C_6H_{12}O_6 + 6O_2 \rightarrow 6CO_2 + 6H_2O + ATP + \text{heat energy}$$

Photosynthesis supplies cellular respiration with glucose and oxygen. Cellular respiration provides photosynthesis with carbon dioxide and water.

The balance between photosynthesis and cellular respiration partly determines the amount of free atmospheric oxygen and carbon dioxide present on Earth. As such, the two processes regulate each other, comprising a major portion of the regulatory mechanism that controls life-supporting conditions on Earth. Decomposition is simply cellular respiration done by bacteria and fungi, using dead matter as the source of glucose.

18. A

When cellular respiration occurs in the mitochondrion of a cell, high-energy glucose is torn apart, releasing energy. About 40% of that energy is captured in ATP as a high-energy bond that can be used to power cell activities. The remaining 60% of the energy in a glucose molecule is not trapped and escapes as heat. This waste heat is useful in heating warm-blooded organisms but is not used for anything else and is eventually lost to space. For this reason, cellular respiration is considered to be inefficient in transferring energy.

19. C

Biological nitrogen fixation refers to the process by which specific bacteria living in the root nodules of legumes (peas, beans, lentils) convert unusable atmospheric nitrogen (N_2) into ammonia (NH_3). Although most plants cannot use NH_3, nitrifying bacteria in the soil will complete the conversion from NH_3 to useful nitrates (NO_3^-). The plant then absorbs the nitrate from the soil and uses it to make protein. Nitrogen-fixing plants have a more dependable source of nitrates than other plants and will have better yields than other plants given the same fertility of soil. Legumes, such as alfalfa, are often grown and ploughed under just to improve the nitrate fertility of the soil.

20. A

In a biomass food pyramid, the producers have the greatest amount of biomass. The reasoning for this has to do with the inefficiency of cellular respiration. When a herbivore, such as a cow, eats grass, some of the grass is not digestible and is excreted. When the digested and absorbed portion reaches the cell, cellular respiration will only be able to extract a small amount of useful energy from it; the rest is lost as heat. Each trophic level assimilates only about 10% of the energy from the level below it. The remaining 90% is lost as heat.

UNIT TEST—ENERGY AND MATTER EXCHANGE IN THE BIOSPHERE

1. Most of Earth's energy is derived from the sun. Solar energy reaching Earth is
   A. stored only in fossil fuels
   B. mostly reflected back to space
   C. stored in water, plants, and fossil fuels
   D. entirely absorbed by the Earth's surface

2. What gaseous product of cellular respiration is also a necessary component for photosynthesis to occur?
   A. Oxygen
   B. Methane
   C. Nitrogen
   D. Carbon dioxide

3. Which of the following statements regarding the biosphere is **false**?
   A. Heat escapes into space.
   B. Greenhouse gases retain heat.
   C. All life contains carbon molecules.
   D. The albedo of the polar ice caps creates CO_2.

4. Which of the following statements about trophic levels and relative amounts of biomass in an energy pyramid is **true**?
   A. Producers have a biomass greater than all other trophic levels.
   B. Primary consumers have a biomass greater than both secondary consumers and producers.
   C. Producers have a biomass less than tertiary consumers but greater than secondary consumers.
   D. Tertiary consumers have a biomass less than quaternary consumers and greater than secondary consumers.

5. Energy in the biosphere can be perceived as a balance between photosynthesis and chemosynthesis on one side and cellular respiration on the other. Which of the following statements supports this idea?
   A. The heat energy that is released as a waste product in cellular respiration is recycled into solar energy for photosynthesis.
   B. The amount of solar energy locked into the bonds of glucose in photosynthesis equals the amount of energy released by all organisms in cellular respiration.
   C. The amount of solar energy trapped into the bonds of glucose in chemosynthesis equals the amount of energy released by all organisms in cellular respiration.
   D. The amount of ATP energy and heat released from respiring organisms equals the energy locked into glucose in photosynthesis and chemosynthesis.

6. In the nitrogen geochemical cycle, nitrogen is **not** made available for organisms through
   A. nitrogen-fixing bacteria in soil and water that convert nitrogen gas into ammonium
   B. nitrates in rainwater, which are created by lightning from atmospheric $N_{2(g)}$ and $O_{2(g)}$
   C. proteins and nucleic acids in the plants and animals that they consume for food
   D. the diffusion of atmospheric $N_{2(g)}$ directly into bodily tissues

7. The release of excess phosphate-containing compounds, such as soap, into the environment can have the same devastating effect as

   A. excess use of nitrate-containing fertilizers

   B. burning of fossil fuels, which releases excess atmospheric carbon dioxide

   C. burning of fossil fuels, which releases excess nitrogen gas into the environment

   D. clear-cutting forests, which causes an increase in atmospheric carbon dioxide

Use the following information to answer the next question.

Prior to life on Earth, very little oxygen was present in the atmosphere. Primitive life forms capable of photosynthesis first evolved in oceans, leading to an increase in the proportion of atmospheric oxygen, making evolution of terrestrial life forms possible.

8. An increased concentration of oxygen in Earth's atmosphere was **not** associated with

   A. increased cellular respiration

   B. decreased glucose production

   C. increased number of autotrophs

   D. decreased CO_2 in the atmosphere

9. Decomposers help the carbon cycle by

   A. releasing the carbon in dead plant and animal bodies back to the atmosphere

   B. combining the carbon dioxide and oxygen released from photosynthesis to produce food

   C. absorbing carbon from the animals that they decay and passing it along to their offspring

   D. absorbing the carbon dioxide and water that animals breathe out and using it to produce food

10. The transfer of food energy from plants to consumers is a food chain. The **most likely** reason that a food chain rarely has more than four trophic levels is that

    A. limiting abiotic factors act to reduce the number of organisms in each successive trophic level

    B. the number of producers in the community cannot sustain a large number of consumers

    C. third-level consumers are unable to transfer the energy of producers to fourth-level consumers

    D. most of the energy in each trophic level is lost as heat when consumed by the next level

11. Deforestation affects the hydrologic cycle in all of the following ways **except**

    A. increasing the amount of evaporation from soil

    B. increasing the amount of condensation and precipitation

    C. increasing the amount of water trapped as groundwater

    D. reducing the amount of transpirational water loss to the atmosphere

12. Which of the following properties of water contributes in a large way to the hydrologic cycle?

    A. Water is a universal solvent.

    B. Water has a high heat capacity.

    C. Water is found in all three states on Earth.

    D. Hydrogen bonding results in high cohesion of water molecules.

13. The productivity of an ecosystem is limited by the

    A. total number of organisms present

    B. availability of solar energy and the number of trophic levels

    C. cycling of physical materials and the amount of solar energy

    D. diversity of species and the number of trophic levels in the ecosystem

Use the following information to answer the next question

Scientists have discovered that oxygen in Earth's atmosphere began to rise significantly from near-zero levels billions of years ago. The fossil record shows that an abundance of photosynthetic cyanobacteria lived on Earth at this time.

14. The rise in oxygen levels in the atmosphere and the abundance of photosynthetic bacteria on ancient Earth are related in that

    A. oxygen was released during the decomposition of the abundant cyanobacteria

    B. cellular respiration by cyanobacteria released oxygen to the atmosphere as a waste product of the reaction

    C. the increase in oxygen levels increased the rate of photosynthesis because oxygen is a requirement of photosynthesis

    D. an increase in photosynthetic organisms increased oxygen levels because oxygen is a waste product of photosynthesis

Written Response

1. Give three examples of gas exchanges within the biosphere. Gas exchanges involving any of the biogeochemical cycles are acceptable.

Earth's atmosphere is largely transparent to infrared (heat) radiation emitted by the sun. Some infrared rays reaching the Earth are absorbed by the Earth's surface and some are reflected back into the atmosphere and into space. Greenhouse gases (methane, ozone, water vapour, and carbon dioxide) block infrared energy from leaving the atmosphere. This causes the temperature of the atmosphere to be higher than it would be otherwise. Without the action of greenhouse gases the Earth would be a frozen planet. Since the Industrial Revolution, the burning of fossil fuels has increased atmospheric carbon dioxide, resulting in a warmer atmosphere and warmer ocean temperatures. Scientists have predicted that between the years 1990 and 2100, Earth's temperature will increase by at least 2.5°C, affecting both terrestrial and aquatic environments and leaving no nation unaffected.

What is difficult to predict is how rising ocean temperatures will affect aquatic ecosystems, as oceans absorb more CO_2 by diffusion and evaporate more H_2O back to the atmosphere.

2. **a)** Write a brief outline of the carbon cycle and the role of cellular respiration and photosynthesis within it. Include the role of CO_2 in photosynthesis and how CO_2 is incorporated into plants and animals.

b) Describe the impact of global warming on aquatic systems and on terrestrial environments.

c) Suggest two ways that people can help reduce CO_2 emissions and reduce global warming.

ANSWERS AND SOLUTIONS—UNIT TEST

1. C	5. D	9. A	13. C
2. D	6. D	10. D	14. D
3. D	7. A	11. B	WR1. See Solution
4. A	8. B	12. C	WR2. See Solution

1. C

All processes on Earth are ultimately driven by solar energy. Plants capture light energy by photosynthesis and store the energy in the chemical bonds of carbohydrates like glucose and starch. Fossil fuels, such as coal and oil are produced from organic matter over millions of years and also have energy stored in their chemical bonds. Chemical bond energy can be derived from the sun either directly, as occurs in photosynthesis, or indirectly by converting the energy in the chemical bonds of substrate molecules, such as decaying organic matter, in a reaction into new chemical bonds. Even water stores solar energy. Water stores energy in its chemical bonds between hydrogen and oxygen and as thermal (heat) energy when a body of water is heated by the sun.

Approximately 30% of the solar energy reaching Earth is reflected back into space. Only about half of the incoming solar energy reaches the surface of the Earth.

2. D

Carbon dioxide is both a product of cellular respiration and a required component (reactant) of photosynthesis.

3. D

Heat is lost from the biosphere to outer space in order to balance the solar energy entering the system. Also, all organic life contains carbon, and carbon is an essential component of all living structures. Greenhouse gases do trap heat within the atmosphere. The only false statement given is that the albedo of the polar caps creates CO_2.

4. A

In an energy pyramid, the producers have the greatest amount of biomass. Each level has only about 10% of the energy compared to the one below it. The remaining 90% is lost as heat. Higher trophic levels do not have enough energy to attain an equal or greater biomass to the levels below them. Therefore biomass at each trophic level can be shown as producers > primary consumers > secondary consumers > tertiary consumers > quaternary consumers.

5. D

Photosynthesis and chemosynthesis take two kinds of unusable energy (sunlight and redox reactions of chemicals) and traps them into the bonds of glucose. Glucose is a usable source of energy for organisms. When organisms carry out cellular respiration in their mitochondria, the stored glucose is torn apart, releasing the energy of bonds to be used by organisms for their ATP-driven activities (growth, reproduction, movement). Unfortunately, most of the energy released in cellular respiration is not captured into ATP but is lost to the environment as heat. Decomposition is not mentioned specifically because it is just cellular respiration done by bacteria and fungi using dead sources of glucose. This model of energy balance does not include the energy that is captured into glucose in photosynthesis but is released through combustion (burning of wood and fossil fuels).

6. D

Nitrogen is not made available for organisms through the diffusion of atmospheric $N_{2(g)}$ directly into bodily tissues.

Plants and animals use nitrogen in the form of nitrates (NO_3^-) and nitrites (NO_2^-); they cannot use nitrogen gas (N_2) or ammonium (NH_4^+). Nitrates and nitrites are mainly obtained by animals in the form of proteins (and also small amounts of nucleic acid) from the plants and animals they consume. Plants and animals can also obtain NO_3^- and NO_2^- from soil and water, where some bacteria (called nitrogen-fixing bacteria) convert $N_{2(g)}$ into NH_4^+ ions. Yet other bacteria convert NH_4^+ to NO_3^- and NO_2^-. Rain also contains dissolved nitrates and nitrites from the atmosphere; NO_3^- and NO_2^- are created from $N_{2(g)}$ and $O_{2(g)}$ when electrical energy in the form of lightning creates chemical bonds.

7. A

Soil and water contain limiting quantities of both phosphates and nitrates, which are common components of fertilizers which increase plant growth. Although crops benefit from fertilizers, increasing phosphate and nitrate in soil and water can cause overgrowth of algae and plants in waterways. Nitrates are also derived from burning fossil fuels. However, most of the nitrates released into the atmosphere during combustion react chemically with moisture in the air to form nitric acid, a component of acid rain. Carbon dioxide, although used by plants for photosynthesis, is not a limiting factor for plant growth in most areas on Earth. Carbon dioxide is more limited in deep aquatic environments. Moreover, an increase in carbon dioxide has other effects on the environment, such as global warming, that are not similar to the effects of an increase in phosphorus.

8. B

An increased concentration of oxygen in Earth's atmosphere was not associated with decreased glucose production.

The first organisms to have evolved in an aquatic environment were probably similar to a form of photosynthetic bacteria present on Earth today called cyanobacteria. Recall the net chemical reaction for photosynthesis:
$$6CO_2 + 6H_2O \rightarrow C_6H_{12}O_6 + 6O_2$$

These autotrophic organisms would have produced glucose through photosynthesis and undergone cellular respiration. In the absence of light, they would also have utilized carbon dioxide, resulting in a decrease in atmospheric CO_2.

9. A

Decomposers release the carbon in dead plants and animals as they decay. Decomposer bacteria and fungi obtain their energy by using glucose and other organic molecules in dead matter to fuel the process of cellular respiration. Carbon dioxide and water are released to the atmosphere, where they can be used by photosynthesizing producers to begin a new food chain.

10. D

Only 10% of the energy from one trophic level is available to the next trophic level. This forms an energy pyramid where very little energy remains at the top level. At some point, there is not enough energy to sustain another trophic level.

11. B

Deforestation is human activity that removes trees, usually by the slash and burn method or by clear-cutting. One result is that long tree roots are no longer present to pull water from groundwater up into trees. Therefore, much of the water that percolates into the soil after it rains remains trapped as groundwater and in the water table, stopping the cycling of water from ground to air. Normally, trees lose a lot of water vapour from their leaves in the process of transpiration.

The escaping water vapour forms clouds, condenses, and results in precipitation. Thus, deforestation reduces precipitation, often resulting in desertification. Soil that is not protected by trees from sun and wind will lose its moisture much faster by evaporation, also contributing to desertification.

12. C

As water moves through the various stages of the water cycle (rivers, oceans, land, and air), it changes in state. As a liquid, it is pulled strongly by gravity, meaning condensed vapour in the atmosphere from evaporation and transpiration will fall back to the Earth as rain or snow, completing the cycle. The fact that it can be liquid also means it flows, either toward the oceans or down into groundwater. The fact that it can form gas means that it can be part of the atmosphere (water vapour and clouds).

13. C

Ecological productivity refers to both how much solar energy (sunlight) is fixed by plants into living biomass by photosynthesis and the subsequent use of that energy by consumers as it moves through the food chain. The amount of solar energy limits how much photosynthesis can occur, but the amount of minerals and other physical requirements, such as water, also limits how much photosynthesis can occur. These abiotic requirements are limited by biogeochemical cycling (carbon, water, nitrogen, and phosphorus cycles). If cycling is occurring, nutrients and water are returned to the soil and air, where they can be reused by plants in photosynthesis. If cycling is not occurring, nutrients and water are locked up and unavailable to be used in photosynthesis and other metabolic activities, reducing the productivity of the ecosystem.

The number of organisms in the ecosystem does not limit productivity but can be an indicator of how productive an ecosystem is. The more productive an ecosystem, the more energy is available to upper trophic levels, so a very productive ecosystem has more trophic levels.

14. D

Photosynthesis produces oxygen as a waste product. The abundance of photosynthesizing cyanobacteria converted Earth's atmosphere from an anoxic atmosphere to an oxygen-rich one that allowed terrestrial life forms to exist.

1. *Give three examples of gas exchanges within the biosphere.*

Some examples of gas exchanges within the biosphere include cellular respiration, which draws in gaseous oxygen and produces carbon dioxide. Photosynthesis uses gaseous carbon dioxide to produce gaseous oxygen. Decomposition can give off one of two different gases. Anaerobic decomposition produces methane, and aerobic decomposition produces carbon dioxide. Denitrification is another process that releases compounds into the atmosphere. It releases free nitrogen gas from nitrogenous compounds in the soil.

2. **a)** *Write a brief outline of the carbon cycle and the role of cellular respiration and photosynthesis within it.*

Carbon dioxide (CO_2) from the air is acquired by autotrophs (plants) through the stomata of their leaves. It combines with water and sunlight in the process of photosynthesis to produce high-energy organic molecules such as glucose ($C_6H_{12}O_6$) in the following reaction:

$$6CO_2 + 6H_2O + \text{solar energy} \rightarrow C_6H_{12}O_6 + 6O_2$$

In photosynthesis, inorganic CO_2 is fixed into organic matter as glucose. The glucose molecules produced are incorporated into the autotroph's biomass. If consumption of autotrophs by heterotrophs takes place, the organic matter is incorporated into the heterotrophs.

When the energy locked in glucose is required for metabolism and cell activities, cellular respiration uses the glucose in the body as a fuel, releasing the energy for use and the carbon dioxide as a waste product back to the atmosphere. From the atmosphere, plants will absorb CO_2 into their stomata for photosynthesis, completing the cycle. Some carbon molecules may remain part of the tissue of an organism for a long period of time until the organism dies.

Decomposer bacteria will then perform cellular respiration on the glucose locked in the dead matter, releasing CO_2 to the environment. Some plant and animal tissue may remain underground and not decay for millions of years, forming fossil fuels, such as coal, oil, or natural gas. When these fuels undergo combustion, they return carbon molecules to the cycle as CO_2, where they will be available for photosynthesis once again.

The cellular respiration reaction is as follows:
$$C_6H_{12}O_6 + 6O_2 \rightarrow 6CO_2 + 6H_2O + ATP + \text{heat energy}$$

b) *Describe the impact of global warming on aquatic systems and on terrestrial environments.*

The heating of Earth will cause the glaciers, icecaps, and icebergs to melt. These factors, plus the fact that warmer water occupies more volume, will cause sea levels to rise and will threaten low-lying coastal areas with flooding. Because most of Earth's population lives at lower elevations, this may have devastating effects. As well, organisms living in a particular ecosystem are adapted to specific abiotic conditions, including temperature. Warming would equate to a loss of suitable habitat for well-adapted organisms. Increases in water temperatures would be detrimental to a variety of aquatic wildlife because warmer water holds less oxygen. Some organisms may not tolerate the higher temperatures, leading to the extinction of some species. In terrestrial environments, increased drought and evaporation would lead to some level of desertification. A loss of vital cropland would occur, resulting in food shortages. The melting of permafrost in such biomes as the tundra would also alter the distribution and function of these ecosystems.

More extreme weather conditions would also be observed, increasing the incidence of fires, hurricanes, tornadoes, and drought—all of which alter the function and structure of an ecosystem. Consequently, while some species would be able to tolerate, adapt, or flourish with the changes brought about by global warming, others would be unable to cope and would become extinct.

c) *Suggest two ways that people can help reduce CO_2 emissions and reduce global warming.*

Any two of the following three points are considered valid and acceptable:

- Using public transportation instead of private vehicles would reduce fossil fuel combustion. Driving fuel-efficient, hybrid, or electric vehicles would have the same effect.
- Heating homes in the winter releases a great deal of CO2, which contributes to the problem. By installing proper insulation in homes and ensuring that people wear sufficient clothing, the amount of energy spent on household heating could be reduced.
- Using cleaner energy technologies (solar energy, wind energy, geothermal energy) can help to decrease CO2 emissions.

NOTES

Ecosystems and Population Change

ECOSYSTEMS AND POPULATION CHANGE

		Practice Questions	Unit Test Questions	Practice Test 1	Practice Test 2
Students will:					
B1	Explain that the biosphere is composed of ecosystems, each with distinctive biotic and abiotic characteristics.				
B1.1	define species, population, community, and ecosystem and explain the interrelationships among them	4	2, 3	1	15, NR18, 19
B1.2	explain how terrestrial and aquatic ecosystems support a diversity of organisms through a variety of habitats and niches	1, 2, 17, 18	1, 12	23	13, 14, 17
B1.3	identify biotic and abiotic characteristics and explain their influence in an aquatic and a terrestrial ecosystem in the local region	3, 7, 8	4	20, NR21, 24, 25	3, 7, 20, 49
B1.4	explain how limiting factors influence organism distribution and range	5	5, WR1	17, NR18, 19	16
B1.5	explain the fundamental principles of taxonomy and binomial nomenclature, using modes of nutrition at the kingdom level and morphological characteristics at the genus/species level	12, 19	WR2		
B2	Explain the mechanisms involved in the change of populations over time.				
B2.1	explain that variability in a species results from heritable mutations and that some mutations may have a selective advantage	6, 15	13		
B2.2	discuss the significance of sexual reproduction to individual variation in populations and to the process of evolution	9	7	26, 27	
B2.3	compare Lamarckian and Darwinian explanations of evolutionary change	13, 20, WR1	8, 14	30, 31	24
B2.4	summarize and describe lines of evidence to support the evolution of modern species from ancestral forms; i.e., the fossil record, Earth's history, biogeography, homologous and analogous structures, embryology, biochemistry	11, 16	9	28, 29	NR22, 23
B2.5	explain speciation and the conditions required for this process	10	6, 10, 15		21
B2.6	describe modern evolutionary theories; i.e., punctuated equilibrium, gradualism	14	11		

ECOSYSTEMS AND POPULATION CHANGE

B1.1   define species, population, community, and ecosystem and explain the interrelationships among them

LEVELS WITHIN ECOSYSTEMS

A **species** is a group of similar organisms that can interbreed to produce live offspring that can also reproduce with one another. All the organisms of one species living in one area form a **population**. All the species that exist in one area make up a **community**. A community has representatives of all trophic levels. A community and its physical (abiotic) environment are called an **ecosystem**. **Biomes** are climatically defined areas composed of many ecosystems.

Practice Question: 4

B1.2   explain how terrestrial and aquatic ecosystems support a diversity of organisms through a variety of habitats and niches

HABITATS AND NICHES

An ecosystem is a unique area of living things and their physical environment. It has both biotic and abiotic components. For example, within the taiga biome, there are many lakes, each of which is an ecosystem. Bogs or marshes within the taiga are also ecosystems.

The area of an ecosystem that an organism lives in is called that organism's **habitat**. It is defined by a specific set of abiotic conditions that an organism requires in order to survive.

A terrestrial biome can contain many habitats. For example, the canopy of a forest is the habitat at the top of trees. It has the highest light levels, the highest rate of photosynthesis, the highest oxygen levels, and usually the most food. The subcanopy habitat has less light, while the forest floor is much darker. Producers here are adapted to capture the most light possible. Soil habitats are dark with low oxygen levels, but they have the most nutrients because of the presence of decomposing and nitrifying bacteria or fungi.

Soil habitats can be dry or wet, basic or acidic, fertile or unproductive, and hard-packed or well-oxygenated.

Aquatic ecosystems are also made up of several habitats, depending on the depth of water. Ocean zones begin with the **littoral** or **intertidal zone**, between the high- and low-tide marks. This is a habitat of extremes in sunlight, temperature, salinity, and wind. Organisms living here must be able to live in and out of salt water. The open oceans are part of the **pelagic** zone, which can be divided into a **photic** zone, where light penetrates, and an **aphotic** zone, where it does not. All photosynthesis occurs in the photic zone, where carbon dioxide is absorbed and dissolved oxygen is released. This is the most biodiverse area, and phytoplankton and zooplankton support complete food chains in this zone. In the aphotic zone, organisms either depend on organic material that settles from above or they are part of food chains that depend on chemosynthesizers as producers. The very bottom of the aphotic zone is the **benthic** zone, which forms the ocean floor. Here, darkness, cold, and extremely high water pressure are the limiting factors. The absence of photosynthesizing plants means conditions are anaerobic, and most inhabitants are decomposers or detritivores, feeding on dead matter from above.

Lakes lack the salty conditions of oceans but are stratified into layers in much the same way as oceans. Rivers consist of moving water. Here, the levels of dissolved oxygen often limit what types of organisms can survive in this habitat. The faster and more turbulent the water, the more dissolved oxygen it contains. Colder water holds more dissolved oxygen than warmer water.

The function of an organism in its ecosystem is referred to as its **niche**. Types of niches include producers, consumers, decomposers, parasites, and scavengers. The definition of a niche includes what the organism eats and what eats it. This is true for both terrestrial and aquatic ecosystems.

Practice Questions: 1, 2, 17, 18

B1.3   identify biotic and abiotic characteristics and explain their influence in an aquatic and a terrestrial ecosystem in the local region

BIOTIC AND ABIOTIC FACTORS

Aquatic ecosystems in Alberta include freshwater lakes, ponds, wetlands, streams, and rivers. Water quality and levels of dissolved nutrients and gases are examples of abiotic factors that influence the distribution of living things in aquatic environments.

Dissolved oxygen is critical in aquatic systems because it limits the amount of cell respiration possible. Oxygen levels are higher at the surface of a water body and in cold or rapidly moving water, such as a mountain stream. Trout are examples of fish usually found in these areas because of their high oxygen requirement. Lingcod, native to the West Coast of North America, are found in deep, still, warmer water because they can tolerate low-oxygen environments.

The ability of sunlight to penetrate through water (carrying light and heat) decreases with depth, meaning producers and their dependent consumers are found mostly near the surface. Dissolved inorganic nutrients, such as nitrate and phosphate, are limiting factors to plant growth. It is common for agricultural fertilizer and sewage from livestock and human populations to run off into lakes and rivers. The phosphates and nitrates in this run-off cause massive blooms of algae referred to as **eutrophication**. The algae live for a few days and then die and fall to the bottom. Decomposer bacteria feed on the dead algae, using up all the dissolved oxygen in the water as they undergo cell respiration. This creates anoxic water conditions that often result in dramatic fish die-offs.

Terrestrial ecosystems also have numerous abiotic limiting factors. The type of bedrock on which the land sits influences the type of nutrients in the soil above it. The acidity of the soil also influences the types of plants that grow there. The existing plant species determine the types of animals that will thrive in that location. Water, temperature, and sunlight all limit the productivity of terrestrial ecosystems.

Although abiotic factors affect biotic factors, the reverse is also true. The biotic community has its own influence on the physical environment. Tall plants restrict sunlight, which can have an effect on the soil temperature and the rate of evaporation of water from the soil. Beavers build dams which cause flooding of land. Herds of herbivores influence the distribution of nutrients by grazing in one area and eliminating wastes in another. Introduction of foreign species can affect the abiotic environment and the delicate balance between the trophic levels of the food chain, often with devastating results.

It is this delicate interplay of biotic and abiotic factors that creates the features of a particular ecosystem.

Practice Questions: 3, 7, 8

B1.4   explain how limiting factors influence organism distribution and range

LIMITING FACTORS

Organisms under ideal conditions organisms within a population will distribute themselves to uniformly cover all parts of their habitat. However, the actual distribution will be limited to areas where the necessities for survival are available. If a habitat does not provide these necessities, then that organism will not be able to live there. This is the concept of a limiting factor. For example, plants require carbon dioxide, water, and sunlight. However, what limits plant growth in many habitats is the amount of soil nitrate and phosphate. In these environments nitrate and phosphate are the limiting factors.

Practice Question: 5

B1.5 *explain the fundamental principles of taxonomy and binomial nomenclature, using modes of nutrition at the kingdom level and morphological characteristics at the genus/species level*

TAXONOMY

Taxonomy is the science of classifying organisms into groups by their common characteristics. Scientists have developed different taxonomic systems as they have learned more about the different organisms that exist and the relationships between organisms. The Linnaean taxonomic system consists of five kingdoms: Plantae, Animalia, Fungi, Protista, and Monera. These are differentiated by modes of nutrition. Organisms in the kingdom Plantae are able to create their own food through photosynthesis. Animalia and Fungi are nourished by ingesting other organisms or, in the case of fungi, decaying matter. Protista and Monera are single-celled organisms and are known to use both methods of nutrition. The other six levels of the Linnaean system are based on structural characteristics. They are Phylum, Class, Order, Family, Genus, and Species. Each level is more specific than the last. For example, while the bobcat, house cat, and leopard are in the same family (Felidae), they are in different genera (*Lynx*, *Felis*, and *Panthera*, respectively).

Because naming all seven levels of classification for each organism is awkward, Linnaeus devised a shorter scientific naming system called **binomial nomenclature**. In this method, only the genus name (capitalized) and species name (uncapitalized) are given. If printed, the **scientific name** is italicized. If handwritten, it is underlined. For example, the scientific name for humans is *Homo sapiens* or <u>Homo</u> <u>sapiens</u>.

Although the Linnaean system is traditionally used in taxonomy, other classification systems exist. For example, all species can be divided into the three domains of Archaea, Bacteria, and Eukarya based on their genetic similarity.

Practice Questions: 12, 19

B2.1 *explain that variability in a species results from heritable mutations and that some mutations may have a selective advantage*

VARIATION WITHIN A SPECIES

Around 1800, Jean-Baptiste Lamarck theorized that evolution occurred due to **inheritance of acquired characteristics**. He reasoned that organisms could develop needed characteristics during their lifetimes and that these acquired characteristics could be passed on to offspring. For example, Lamarck would say that a cheetah that developed powerful muscles by running after fast-moving prey would have offspring that were also muscular. Lamarck's theory was put forward long before scientists understood the mechanisms of inheritance.

Darwin's 1859 **theory of natural selection** was based on his observations of populations. He observed that for every trait seen in organisms there is a certain amount of **variation.** For example, in any population there are variations in the trait of colour. Because the scientific study of genetics and mutation had not progressed enough, Darwin was unable to say what the source of this variation was. This is one reason his theory was not well-accepted during his lifetime.

Darwin also observed that organisms produce far more offspring than can possibly survive given the scarcity of resources (food, water, space, etc.) in ecosystems. He called this **overproduction**. As a result of these two observations, he concluded that in any population there will always be **competition** and a struggle for survival. The individuals that survive have a variation of the trait that allows the individual to thrive and to reproduce more offspring than an individual that doesn't. The term he used was **survival of the fittest**. **Fitness** refers to the reproductive success of an organism. The fittest individuals will survive, producing the most offspring, and those offspring will have the successful trait.

Each generation is changed and refined by this process as the population gradually adapts to the environmental conditions. In this way, nature selects the best-adapted (fastest, best-camouflaged, smartest, etc.) organisms to be the ones that get the resources needed for survival and reproduction. For this reason, Darwin named his theory the theory of natural selection. **Nature** refers to the specific environmental conditions that select which organisms can live and which organisms die.

Unlike Darwin, we now know that variation in the traits of a population is due to mutation of the genetic material and sexual selection. Mutations can occur randomly to any individual at any time.

When a random genetic mutation results in a trait that makes that organism more likely to survive in a particular environment, that trait is referred to as an **adaptation**. For example, a random mutation that resulted in a lighter golden coat colour would be considered an adaptation if the animal lives in a dry grass environment. The lighter color would provide camouflage from predators and prey. However, this same mutation would not be an adaptation if the animal lives in a dark wooded environment. Nature (the environmental conditions at the time) selects for survival those organisms that have suitable adaptations.

Adapted animals live longer and produce more offspring. Their offspring will inherit the adaptation, which will help them survive. For example, a zebra that survives predation by using speed and agility lives to reproduce and pass those traits on to its offspring.

Over many generations, the entire species is said to be adapting as more and more individuals inherit the adaptive trait.

An example of this gradual adaptation is the antibiotic resistance of some bacterial strains. When first developed, antibiotics killed almost all the bacteria that were exposed to them. However, because some individual variants of the bacterial population were more resistant to the antibiotics than others, some bacteria survived. The survivors produced offspring that were also resistant to the antibiotic. Continued use and overuse of antibiotics over the years has selected for bacterial strains referred to as "super bugs."

There are some antibiotics that are now almost useless because of widespread resistance in the general bacterial population. Pervasive use of antiseptics and disinfectants has a similar effect by naturally selecting for those micro-organisms most resistant to these products.

Practice Questions: 6, 15

B2.2   discuss the significance of sexual reproduction to individual variation in populations and to the process of evolution

VARIATION AND SEXUAL REPRODUCTION

In order to reproduce sexually, two individuals mate and produce offspring. The significance of sexual reproduction is in the fusion of sex cells from each parent. Each sex cell (egg or sperm) carries a unique combination of genes from one parent. When two sex cells fuse in fertilization, the offspring that result will be unique from every other offspring and every other organism in the population. A population of organisms that has more genetic variation and greater diversity of characteristics is more likely to survive if the environment changes because at least some variants should have combinations of traits that allow it to survive in the new conditions. Populations with high genetic variation are said to be more adaptive in the face of environmental change.

A population that is not experiencing selective pressure should have a great deal of variation. Populations that are under selective pressure because of changing environmental conditions will have less variation. Through this process a species can change or evolve over time.

Practice Question: 9

B2.3   compare Lamarckian and Darwinian explanations of evolutionary change

EVOLUTIONARY CHANGE

At the core of the comparison of the theories of Lamarck and Darwin is an examination of the manner in which evolutionary advantages can be passed on to future generations. Lamarck believed that an individual in a population could gradually alter its features to make it more suitable for living in its environment. These traits, once developed, could be passed on to a future generation for their benefit. Darwin, on the other hand, believed that a natural population already had variation in it, as seen in the subtle differences among organisms in a population. If the entire population were subjected to some environmental pressure, such as drought or lack of food, the individuals in the population with suitable traits would be able to reproduce to create the next generation. The next generation would have a higher proportion of individuals with that survival trait, and in that way the species would evolve.

Subsequent information about the genetics of inheritance supports Darwinian theory as an accurate representation of how evolution and speciation take place over time.

Whether or not a species survives environmental change depends on the pace of change. If the pace of environmental change is slow enough and there is enough variation in the population, there will be time for natural selection to create a population of adapted organisms.

Extinction occurs when environmental change happens too rapidly. In this case there is not enough time for the fittest variants to reproduce enough offspring to maintain the species. Extinction will also occur if there is too little genetic diversity. In this case there are no variants in the population that have suitable traits to survive in the new conditions. Presently, the rate of environmental change is so rapid that many species are not able to adapt and evolve quickly enough. The result is extinction on a massive scale.

Practice Questions: 13, 20, WR1

B2.4   summarize and describe lines of evidence to support the evolution of modern species from ancestral forms; i.e., the fossil record, Earth's history, biogeography, homologous and analogous structures, embryology, biochemistry

EVIDENCE OF EVOLUTION

The abundant **fossil record** supports the theory of evolution. **Radioactive dating** is used to determine the age of a fossil. Since radioactive isotopes decay at a regular rate, a scientist can estimate the age of the fossil by measuring how much of the isotope remains.

Homologous structures have similar functions, although they may have different physical appearances. Homologous structures occur in species that have a common ancestor. Examples of homologous structures are the fins of a whale, the hooves of a horse, and the bones in the hands of a chimpanzee or human. Scientists use these structures to trace the evolutionary path through history. **Analogous structures** are structures that have a similar structure and function even though they occur in species that are not closely related. Analogous structures show that the same design has evolved several times in the face of the same environmental pressures. Examples of analogous structures are the wings of butterflies, bats, and birds. **Biogeography** studies show that while related organisms often exist near one another, they can also be found far away due to continental drift.

In terms of **biochemical** similarities, all organisms share a certain amount of DNA. The more similar the DNA base sequences of two species, the closer their evolutionary relationship. **Embryological** similarities show that species with a common ancestry go through the same steps in their embryological development. **Vestigial organs** are those organs that no longer have functions but are still found in related species. For example, the appendix in humans is a vestigial organ.

Practice Questions: 11, 16

B2.5   explain speciation and the conditions required for this process

SPECIATION

Speciation refers to the evolution of new species over time. Although a species may change over time in response to an environmental change, it usually remains one species. In order for a new species to form, specific conditions must exist.

Geographic isolation occurs when a physical barrier, such as a canyon or rising ocean levels, separates a species into two populations that do not interact and therefore do not exchange genes. Slight differences in the environment in each area act on random variations that emerge, steering natural selection in different directions until the two populations are unable to successfully interbreed. At this point, it can be said that the two groups have become separate species.

Speciation can occur with or without geographic isolation if there is **reproductive isolation**. If for some reason two populations of one species were no longer able to interbreed due to time, location, or physical changes, then the two gene pools will eventually separate, forming new species.

Practice Question: 10

B2.6   describe modern evolutionary theories; i.e., punctuated equilibrium, gradualism

EVOLUTIONARY THEORIES

Currently, there are two popular theories that discuss the pace of evolution. The theory of **gradualism** suggests that populations are always evolving as certain variations within a population are selected for by a changing environment. Some of the fossil record supports this theory and shows species emerging in a slow, continual process. However, most of the fossil record shows long periods of stability with little change followed by brief periods of rapid change during which species disappear and others appear. This theory is known as **punctuated equilibrium**. Much of the evidence for these theories of evolution comes from fossils. However, the fossil record remains incomplete for much of the history of life on Earth. The conditions required for fossilization are relatively rare, and most organisms that have died throughout history did not become fossils. Undoubtedly, most fossils have not yet been found, and new discoveries will continue to emerge.

Practice Question: 14

PRACTICE QUESTIONS—ECOSYSTEMS AND POPULATION CHANGE

1. Which of the following terms describes a specific area within a given region that is home to a particular animal or plant?

   A. Biome

   B. Habitat

   C. Biosphere

   D. Ecosystem

2. The interdependent system of organisms and all the non-living physical and chemical factors of their environment is called

   A. a biosphere

   B. a population

   C. a community

   D. an ecosystem

Use the following information to answer the next question.

Many countries limit the amount of phosphates allowed in laundry and dish detergents to prevent the buildup of large amounts of phosphate ions in bodies of water.

3. A large amount of phosphate ions in bodies of water would **most likely** cause

   A. reduced aquatic plant growth

   B. excessive aquatic plant growth

   C. increased weathering of sedimentary rocks

   D. decreased weathering of sedimentary rocks

Use the following information to answer the next question.

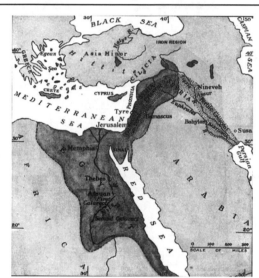

Agriculture first originated approximately 11 000 years ago in an area called the Fertile Crescent, between what are today the countries of Iran, Iraq, and Turkey. Within a few thousand years, agriculture had spread throughout Europe.

As farming became more popular and widespread, a human population explosion began. For the first time in history, humans significantly impacted the ecosystems in which they lived.

4. A biological community that includes an agricultural crop has which of the following characteristics?

   A. High species variation and relatively high biomass

   B. Low species variation and relatively high biomass

   C. High species variation and relatively low biomass

   D. Low species variation and relatively low biomass

Use the following information to answer the next question.

The increase in human population that coincided with the beginning of agriculture occurred because agriculture provided more food than hunting and gathering. Early farming practices included leaving some land fallow and ploughing organic matter and waste back into the ground for decomposition. Modern intensive farming does not follow these practices.

5. A modern farm can be characterized by

   A. high productivity levels and a high reliance on natural biogeochemical cycling

   B. high productivity levels and a low reliance on natural biogeochemical cycling

   C. low productivity levels and a high reliance on natural biogeochemical cycling

   D. low productivity levels and a low reliance on natural biogeochemical cycling

Use the following information to answer the next question.

Growing large numbers of one kind of plant close together in an area can be detrimental for plants. Each plant strives for the same resources and is susceptible to the same consumers. For example, during the Irish potato famine in 1846, a fungus attacked potato crops, destroying up to three-quarters of the harvest. As a result, many of the people who relied on potatoes as a staple of their diet faced famine and death. Present-day agriculture relies on chemicals (insecticides and fungicides) to protect crops from pests.

6. One major problem with using insecticides for agriculture is that insecticides

   A. result in the development of insecticide-resistant populations

   B. cause crops to produce more food than is natural

   C. stimulate pests to grow at a faster rate

   D. kill host plants along with harmful pests

7. Which of the following processes converts organic matter into inorganic matter?

   A. Reproduction

   B. Photosynthesis

   C. Decomposition

   D. Nitrogen fixation

8. Which of the following examples demonstrates a biotic factor affecting an abiotic factor?

   A. Female salmon use their bodies to dig an indentation in the sandy river mud in which they lay their eggs, increasing the turbidity of the water.

   B. High rates of evaporation from a river estuary increase the salinity of the water, killing many invertebrates.

   C. High competition for mates in a small goose population means that some mating pairs will not reproduce.

   D. Run-off of muddy water decreases the dissolved oxygen content of river water.

9. The **main** advantage of sexual reproduction is that it

   A. does not require more than one parent

   B. reduces the chromosome count of the offspring

   C. requires less energy than asexual reproduction

   D. leads to offspring that are genetically different from both parents

10. If a population were to undergo speciation, two possible mechanisms of speciation are

    A. competition and adaptation

    B. reproduction and natural selection

    C. survival of the fittest and migration

    D. geographic isolation and reproductive isolation

11. Which of the following structures would be considered biochemical evidence for evolution?

    A. DNA

    B. Fossils

    C. Vestigial structures

    D. Homologous structures

12. Which of the following groups is the **most narrowly** defined level used in the classification of living things?

    A. Phylum

    B. Species

    C. Order

    D. Class

13. Which of the following statements agrees with Darwin's theory of natural selection?

    A. Individual organisms can develop characteristics during their lifetimes that are not inherited by their offspring.

    B. The inheritance of an anatomical structure in offspring depends on whether the structure was used or not used in the parent.

    C. Species develop variations in response to a change in their environment.

    D. Individual organisms develop characteristics during their lifetimes that they subsequently pass on to their offspring.

14. Evidence to support the evolutionary model of punctuated equilibrium can be found in

    A. Darwin's *On the Origin of Species*

    B. Lamarck's theory of evolution

    C. Malthus' population theory

    D. the fossil record

*Use the following information to answer
the next question.*

Today, it is known that radiation and certain chemicals can alter the structure of DNA, thus mutating (or changing) genes. Genes are the ultimate instructions for the characteristics of an organism.

15. Knowing that genes can mutate would have helped Darwin explain the

A. source of variation

B. theory of natural selection

C. theory of the survival of the fittest

D. inheritance of acquired characteristics

16. Analogous organs are one type of evidence for the theory of natural selection. Body structures that are classified as analogous are

A. structurally similar

B. functionally similar

C. both structurally and functionally similar

D. neither structurally nor functionally similar

17. Which of the following pairs of characteristics would leave a group of organisms at **most** risk of being negatively impacted by global climate change?

A. Broad niche parameters and limited dispersal ability

B. Narrow niche parameters and limited dispersal ability

C. Broad niche parameters and extensive dispersal ability

D. Narrow niche parameters and extensive dispersal ability

18. The habitat of the starfish genus *Asterias* is the muddy sand of the ocean floor, where they feed on bivalves such as clams. *Asterias* is an inhabitant of which ocean zone?

A. Benthic

B. Littoral

C. Pelagic

D. Photic

19. According to the rules of binomial nomenclature, the correct scientific name of the leopard is

A. Panthera Pardus

B. panthera Pardus

C. *Panthera pardus*

D. *panthera pardus*

*Use the following information to answer
the next question.*

Scientists working in modern agriculture search for characteristics that can be improved upon. If cows with a high milk yield are desired, animal breeders select those cows that produce the largest quantity of milk. The calves of the high milk-yielding cows are then interbred. After repeating the process for a number of generations, a breed of high milk-yielding cows is produced.

20. The principle used in this case to produce high milk-yielding cows is known as

A. natural selection

B. artificial selection

C. survival of the fittest

D. inheritance of acquired characteristics

Written Response

*Use the information below to answer
the following questions.*

The monarch butterfly is the most common species of the milkweed butterflies and is found throughout the world. Each year, monarchs fly from as far as Ontario to California, Mexico, and Florida to lay their eggs on the underside of milkweed leaves. Once the eggs have been laid and the caterpillar emerges, it feeds on the milkweed and accumulates the alkaloids of the plant. The alkaloids of the milkweed contain poisonous compounds that produce strong physiological effects when consumed.
It appears that the alkaloids have no effect on the caterpillar itself, but if consumed by a predator, the caterpillar leaves a pungent taste in its predator's mouth. Another butterfly, the viceroy butterfly, is also common to North America. As an adult, it very much resembles the monarch. The two species are referred to as Müllerian mimics.

1. **a)** In terms of Darwinian evolution, explain how natural selection has favoured the monarch butterfly's association with the milkweed. Include a description of what natural selection is and a possible hypothesis of how it applies to the monarch butterfly.

b) Suggest two benefits and two costs of the trip made by the monarch butterfly.

c) Discuss why the viceroy butterfly may both benefit from and be disadvantaged by mimicking the monarch.

(12 marks)

ANSWERS AND SOLUTIONS—PRACTICE QUESTIONS

1. B	7. C	13. A	19. C
2. D	8. A	14. D	20. B
3. B	9. D	15. A	WR1. See Solution
4. D	10. D	16. C	
5. B	11. A	17. B	
6. A	12. B	18. A	

1. B

Any specific area home to a particular organism is known as its habitat. An ecosystem is made up of many habitats. A biome is made up of many ecosystems. The zone of Earth that supports living things is referred to as the biosphere.

2. D

An ecosystem is the interdependent and dynamic community of organisms and all the non-living physical and chemical factors of their environment.

All the different ecosystems together form a biosphere. A population is a group of organisms of the same species inhabiting a given area. A community is all the groups of organisms living together in the same area.

3. B

Phosphorous does not play a role in the weathering of rocks, but it is often the limiting factor in the growth of plants. This is why most fertilizers contain phosphorous. Adding phosphorous to a body of water is like adding fertilizer, and it will most likely result in eutrophication, or excessive plant growth in the lake.

4. D

A biological community that includes an agricultural crop has low species variation and relatively low biomass. Since a crop contains only the crop species, a few kinds of weeds, and some pests that eat the crop, there is not a high species variation. To have a large biomass, there would have to be trees and other large organisms in the community.

5. B

Modern crops grow quickly and yield a large harvest. The harvest is removed every year, so carbon, nitrogen, and phosphorous cycles are affected because decomposition does not occur. As a result, the soil is depleted of minerals.

To maintain current levels of food productivity, farmers must add large amounts of commercial, industrially produced fertilizer, which reduces their reliance on the natural biogeochemical cycling of nutrients. If farmers do not constantly add commercial fertilizer, the soil becomes deprived of minerals.

6. A

Insecticides are chemicals that kill insects in order to prevent them from consuming crops grown for human consumption. Insecticide use selects for insects that are insecticide-resistant, leading to an increase in the proportion of the insecticide-resistant insect population.

Insecticides will not cause crops to produce more food than is natural, and they will not kill host plants, because they are specifically formulated to target insects and not the plants.

7. C

Decomposition occurs when bacteria and fungi convert dead organic matter and organic wastes into CO_2, H_2O, and minerals (inorganic matter). This is principally the same process as cell respiration. Photosynthesis converts CO_2 and H_2O (inorganic matter) into glucose (organic matter). Nitrogen fixation involves the conversion of nitrogen (inorganic matter) to ammonia (inorganic matter). Reproduction is the process of creating new organisms from existing ones. This is an example of organic matter making more organic matter.

8. **A**

Biotic factors are living components of an ecosystem. Abiotic factors are non-living components of an ecosystem. When a biotic factor affects an abiotic factor, an organism has affected its physical environment in some way. When salmon muddy the river water, a biotic factor is affecting an abiotic factor.

When salinity (salt) kills invertebrates, an abiotic factor is affecting a biotic one. The amount of oxygen decreases in muddy water, so in this case an abiotic factor is affecting another abiotic factor. When few mates limit a goose population's reproduction, then a biotic factor is affecting another biotic factor.

9. **D**

The main advantage of sexual reproduction is that it leads to offspring that are genetically different from both parents. This leads to greater genetic diversity in a population. More diversity creates more variants in the population. If the environment were to change, the chances would be better that at least one variant would be able to survive in the new environment, preventing extinction of the species.

Sexual reproduction is more expensive in terms of energy. Finding mates requires time and resources. A single parent cannot reproduce sexually. The number of chromosomes normally does not change from generation to generation.

10. **D**

The first step in speciation is that a population of a species becomes geographically separated, possibly by a mountain, river, or island. The separated population continues to adapt to conditions that are different from the environment of other populations of the same species. Eventually, these adaptations make members of the geographically separated population so different that they cannot reproduce with members of other populations. The two steps in speciation are geographic isolation and reproductive isolation.

Competition and adaptation are constantly going on, but they themselves do not lead to a new species. The same can be said for reproduction and natural selection. Survival of the fittest and migration can provide variation, but they are not likely to lead to speciation on their own. Changing environmental conditions (biotic or abiotic) would also be required to create selective pressures for new traits.

11. **A**

DNA is the biochemical evidence for evolution. All living organisms use DNA as a template for protein manufacture. This is considered indirect evidence supporting the theory of evolution. Fossils, vestigial structures, and homologous structures do not involve chemical similarities.

12. **B**

The species level is the most specific and narrowly defined level because it describes precisely one group of organisms that are able to interbreed.

13. **A**

Darwin believed that although an organism could acquire physical characteristics during its lifetime, it did not pass them on to its offspring; only genetically inherited characteristics are passed on to offspring.

Whether or not a structure was used would not affect the inheritance of that trait. For example, in humans the appendix serves no known function but continues to persist through inheritance. Darwin did not believe that species developed variations in response to their environment, but rather that environmental stressors selected for variations that already existed in a population. Lamarck believed that individuals were able to pass acquired characteristics to their offspring.

14. **D**

The most commonly cited source of data and evidence to support the theory of punctuated equilibrium is the fossil record. The fossil record shows the development of organisms and populations over time and supports the hypothesis that evolution often occurs as an abrupt shift in the genetic characteristics, followed by long periods of stability. Rapid changes in the evolution of species indicate either extreme environmental change or isolation (reproductive or geographic) of populations.

Darwin believed that species underwent gradual change as environmental stressors selected for new traits. Malthus' population theory proposed that population growth is eventually slowed or stopped by famine, disease, and mortality. It does not specifically address evolution. Lamarck believed that an individual in a population could gradually alter its features to make it more suitable for living in its environment and pass on these characteristics to its offspring.

15. A

Darwin could not explain the source of variation, or why certain organisms would have one characteristic and others would have a different characteristic.

According to Darwin, individuals within a population have variable characteristics. Those individuals that are best-suited to survive in a particular environment will survive to produce future generations. Therefore, he could explain survival of the fittest, inheritance of acquired characteristics, and natural selection.

It is now known that differences in the outward appearance of an organism (the phenotype) and other traits, such as biochemical enzymes, are due to differences among individuals in their genetic material (DNA). These genetic differences can arise by mutation.

16. C

Analogous structures, such as the wing of a bat and an insect wing, may look similar and have a similar function but are found in organisms that do not have a similar evolutionary ancestry. They do not indicate a common ancestor. Analogous structures show that given a certain set of environmental pressures, the same design has appeared in distantly related species, often in different parts of the world.

Homologous structures have the same functions but may not look the same. Examples are the human hand, the fin of a seal, and the hoof of a horse. Homologous structures indicate that organisms have a similar embryonic and evolutionary origin, so these structures point to a common ancestry.

17. B

Organisms with limited dispersal ability are not physically able to leave their homes and migrate to similar habitats if their home habitats are threatened. Flightless birds or animals whose movement is prevented by human habitation are examples. Those organisms with narrow niche parameters have a very specific function in their ecosystem community; they can eat only certain organisms and can obtain them only in a certain manner. Two species of organisms cannot occupy the same niche. If two organisms compete for the same niche, one will not survive. A good example would be the niches of the coyote and wolf, which are very similar. When global climate change alters abiotic conditions enough to threaten habitat, those who cannot disperse elsewhere will

likely not survive. When climate change alters abiotic conditions such that there is increased competition for scarce food sources, those with a specific niche will not be able to adapt as readily and will probably not survive.

18. A

Benthic organisms live at the bottom of the ocean. The littoral zone designates the intertidal region of the shoreline between the high- and low-tide marks. The photic zone extends from the surface of the ocean to the depth where light no longer penetrates. Pelagic refers to all zones in the open ocean.

19. C

The rules of binomial nomenclature are used to determine the scientific name of an organism. A scientific name is made up of two parts: the genus name, which is capitalized and italicized, and the species name, which is italicized but not capitalized. Therefore, even if the scientific name of the panther is not known, the correct answer can be determined because only one possible answer correctly applies the rules of binomial nomenclature. The answer is *Panthera pardus*.

20. B

Scientists take advantage of natural genetic variations to improve the quality of domesticated plants and animals. They select the individuals with desired characteristics and separate them from those that do not have such characteristics. The selected individuals are then interbred. If the process is repeated for many generations, a new breed with the desired characteristics is produced. This process is called artificial selection. It differs from natural selection in that humans take the place of the environment in selecting which organisms are most successful.

The cows did not acquire their high milk-yielding characteristics during their lifetime so this is not an example of inheritance of acquired characteristics. Survival of the fittest refers to the struggle in nature to outcompete others in one's population that are competing for the same scarce resources. Those who manage to obtain the most food, water, space, etc., will reproduce more and pass on their successful traits. In artificial selection, all members of the population are given the same amounts of resources, but only some are selected for breeding.

1. **a)** *Explain how natural selection has favoured the monarch butterfly's association with the milkweed.*

Darwin observed that species produce more offspring than can survive, live to maturity, and reproduce. Therefore, there is a competition for scarce resources in which only the fittest survive. He also observed that there were variations in physical traits within species. He concluded that an organism which had physical traits that gave it an advantage in a particular environment over other similar organisms would survive and reproduce. These traits would also give a similar advantage to any offspring born with them. As organisms with this advantage became more numerous, it would make it less likely that organisms without this advantage would survive and reproduce.

A possible hypothesis of how the monarch and the milkweed became associated is that ancestors of the monarchs may have begun to lay their eggs on a variety of plants, including the milkweed. The caterpillars that consumed the milkweed leaves obtained the alkaloids and in turn were found to be distasteful to the predators; those that did not obtain the alkaloids mostly likely were eaten by the predators with no ill effect. However, predators that did eat the milkweed caterpillars experienced a distasteful experience and so learned to recognize the monarch and avoid it in future encounters. Therefore, natural selection favoured the monarchs that laid eggs on the milkweed and a permanent association became established between the milkweed and the monarch.

(Any theory similar to this, establishing in some manner that the monarch would eventually come to lay eggs on the milkweed, is sufficient.)

b) *Suggest two benefits and two costs of the trip made by the monarch butterfly.*

Any two of the following under each heading, or any other valid points, will be acceptable.

Benefits:

- Reaching the milkweed
- Obtaining the alkaloids
- Continuing the relationship with the milkweed plant

Costs:

- Not completing the trip, and dying
- Competition for sites to lay eggs may reduce offspring
- Any absence of milkweed would require further migration (more risk)

c) *Discuss why the viceroy butterfly may both benefit from and be disadvantaged by mimicking the monarch.*

Because of its similar markings and appearance to the monarch butterfly, the viceroy butterfly benefits from the predators' avoidance of the monarch. Once a predator has had an experience with the monarch butterfly, it learns to recognize its appearance and to avoid it during future encounters. The viceroy is then also avoided because of its close resemblance to the monarch, even though it is safe to eat. Thus, it is spared from predators.

If the viceroy caterpillar were to emerge prior to the monarch, the results may be harmful to the viceroy. The best time for a viceroy adult to emerge from a cocoon is after the emergence of the adult monarch butterfly. This gives enough time for predators to be exposed to the monarch butterfly and experience its effects and be able to make a correlation between the butterfly and what occurs when it is eaten. Thus, predators that avoid monarchs will also avoid viceroys.

(Any other appropriate advantage or disadvantage may also be accepted.)

UNIT TEST—ECOSYSTEMS AND POPULATION CHANGE

Use the following information to answer the next question.

Prior to modern discoveries, people thought that the only life forms present at the cold depths of the open ocean were occasional scavengers living off dead matter that drifted  downward from the ocean surface. In general, this is true. However, beginning in 1977, a number of concentrated communities have been discovered around deep sea vents. The vents discharge hydrogen sulfide and hot water. Bacteria around the vent convert the hydrogen sulfide to organic matter. Clams, crabs, tube worms, spaghetti worms, and other assorted animals feed on the bacteria.

1. This ocean bed community provides evidence that

   A. decomposers can also be autotrophs

   B. wherever there is warmth, life is possible

   C. producers are not always needed in a community

   D. life can exist without energy derived from the sun

Use the following information to answer the next two questions.

On a weekend hike through the woods in Jasper National Park, Jorge slipped and tripped over a rotting log. The log cracked open, revealing a variety of fungi, insects, and worms. Using a small light microscope, Jorge discovered that numerous micro-organisms also lived in the log.

2. The various organisms of the rotting log compose many

   A. ecosystems

   B. food pyramids

   C. detritus food chains

   D. isolated communities

CHALLENGER QUESTION

3. Had Jorge left the log open, he would have altered the log's community by

   A. allowing decomposers to enter

   B. altering its abiotic characteristics

   C. making it accessible to predators

   D. allowing its inhabitants to escape

Use the following information to answer the next question.

For experimental purposes, a lake was divided in half by an impermeable plastic curtain. Carbon, nitrogen, and phosphorus were added to the north side of the lake. On the south side, only carbon and nitrogen were added.

CHALLENGER QUESTION

4. An algal bloom soon covered the north side of the lake, but not the south side. This appears to indicate that

   A. algae growth is limited by a lack of phosphorus

   B. carbon and nitrogen are plant growth stimulants

   C. phosphorus is needed to activate carbon and nitrogen

   D. algae grow better at the cooler temperatures of the north side of the lake

Use the following information to answer the next question.

A kangaroo rat produces dry, crumbly feces and urine that is composed of roughly 23% toxic urea. In comparison, human urine contains about 2% urea diluted with 95% water.

5. These characteristics of the kangaroo rat are adaptations for life in which of the following habitats?

   A. Desert

   B. Tundra

   C. Burrows

   D. Rain forest

6. Pouched marsupials, such as the kangaroo and koala, are found only in Australia. The uniqueness of these Australian animals can be attributed to

   A. competition between organisms

   B. Australia's unique environment

   C. the geographical isolation of the Australian continent

   D. **the** limited human impact on the Australian environment

7. Which of the following statements about sexual reproduction is **false**?

   A. It leads to genetic variations.

   B. It involves the fusion of two gametes.

   C. It eventually leads to the process of speciation.

   D. It involves a single organism that produces offspring.

Use the following information to answer the next question.

I. Cheetahs frequently run in pursuit of a meal, leading to muscle development. Offspring of these cheetahs inherit their parents' developed muscles.

II. Sparrows exist in a range of colours. The best camouflaged sparrows are most likely to avoid predators and produce similarly coloured offspring.

CHALLENGER QUESTION

8. Which theorist does each statement support?

   A. Statement I—Lamarck
      Statement II—Darwin

   B. Statement I—Darwin
      Statement II—Lamarck

   C. Statement I—Lamarck
      Statement II—Lamarck

   D. Statement I—Darwin
      Statement II—Darwin

Use the following information to answer the next question.

This fossil record reveals changes in the bone structure of camels dating back to 65 million years ago.

9. This fossil record of camels indicates that

    A. camel embryos have changed, but adults have not

    B. camels have increased in size morphologically

    C. camels express gradual mutation through asexual reproduction

    D. camels used to have more teeth when they lived in benthic environments

10. Which of the following statements provides the **best** support for the existence of macroevolution?

    A. Every organism is made up of many unique characteristics.

    B. Species today are more complex than in prehistoric times.

    C. Many insects have become resistant to pesticides.

    D. A large and diverse number of organisms exist.

11. Which of the following factors is **most likely** to increase the rate of evolutionary change in a population?

    A. Geographic isolation

    B. Reproductive rate

    C. Trophic level

    D. Morphology

12. One of the impacts of global climate change is rising sea levels, which will lead to coastal flooding. The effect that coastal flooding will **most likely** have on terrestrial coastal communities is

    A. habitat loss, resulting in a decrease in biodiversity

    B. habitat loss, resulting in an increase in biodiversity

    C. habitat expansion, resulting in a decrease in biodiversity

    D. habitat expansion, resulting in an increase in biodiversity

Use the following information to answer the next question.

The fathead minnow, a small fish common in Alberta waters, is used as a food source by many different predators. When injured, some minnows secrete a chemical called *Schreckstoff* that both attracts predators and causes other minnows to huddle in large groups. Approaching predators tend to be distracted by the mass of minnows and by one another. Often, injured minnows can escape.

13. In the future, the frequency of the gene that causes the production of *Schreckstoff* by minnows will **most likely**

    A. increase in the population

    B. decrease in the population

    C. stay the same in the population because natural selection is occurring

    D. stay the same in the gene pool of the population because natural selection is not occurring

14. Despite Darwin's methodical approach, his theories were met with storms of protest. A critic may rightfully have doubted Darwin's theories when they were first published because of Darwin's inability to explain

   A. why peppered moths were becoming darker in industrialized England

   B. how one kind of organism becomes another kind

   C. why there is a struggle for existence

   D. how variations in a trait originate

15. The punctuated equilibrium model of evolution suggests that new species appear

   A. suddenly

   B. gradually

   C. randomly

   D. continuously

Use the following information to answer the next question.

Rainbow trout are a favourite catch for many North American fishermen. To maintain a healthy rainbow trout population, optimal levels of temperature, pH, oxygen, and light must be present, as well as an adequate food supply. At temperatures between 10 and 18°C, trout will grow rapidly and remain active. Temperatures below 10°C will impede growth rates and cause slower activity. For optimal survival, pH levels must be between 6.7 and 9.0. Conditions that are either too alkaline or too acidic upset the electrolyte balance of the trout. Oxygen levels must remain in the range of 8 and 12 mg/L. Fish suffocate at oxygen levels below 8 mg/L.

Horseshoe Lake Conditions, Winter

Depth (m)	Oxygen levels (mg/L)	Temperature (°C)
0.00	2.34	0.35
0.50	1.52	0.55
1.00	0.49	1.60
1.50	0.31	2.20
2.00	0.22	2.70
2.50	0.19	3.30

pH = 7.63

Written Response

1. a) Draw and label line graphs of the following:

   i) Depth versus oxygen

   ii) Depth versus temperature

   b) Determine if it is likely that rainbow trout could survive a winter in Horseshoe Lake. Explain why or why not.

c) Oxygen levels appear to decrease at lower depths in Horseshoe Lake. Why might this occur?

d) What are the abiotic factors involved in the study of rainbow trout?

e) What ecological factors would change if a biological competitor to the rainbow trout were introduced in Horseshoe Lake?

(12 marks)

Use the following information to answer the next question.

Living organisms are categorized and named according to a Latin scientific naming system that uses two classification levels—genus and species—to designate each type of organism. This is known as binomial nomenclature.

2. **a)** Identify the person who developed the system of binomial nomenclature.

b) List two benefits of using this system.

(6 marks)

ANSWERS AND SOLUTIONS—UNIT TEST

1. D	6. C	11. B	WR1. See Solution
2. C	7. D	12. A	WR2. See Solution
3. B	8. A	13. A	
4. A	9. B	14. D	
5. A	10. D	15. A	

1. D

Since it is dark at the bottom of the ocean and the producers of the deep sea vent communities gain their energy from hydrogen sulfide by undergoing chemosynthesis, life can exist without energy from the sun. The bacteria that convert the hydrogen sulfide into organic matter are producers.

Although the water around these vents is warm, it does not follow that life is possible anywhere there is warmth. There may be warm places with no life. There is no evidence that the autotrophic bacteria of the deep sea vents also act as decomposers.

2. C

A detritus food chain is one that begins with a decomposer. Since the source of energy for the food chains in this case is the decomposing wood in the rotting log, it is a detritus food chain.

All the populations living in the log can be thought of as one community, and members of the log community interact with organisms outside of the log. An ecosystem is made up of many communities. The log would be considered an ecosystem containing a community of organisms. Only one food pyramid would be present in the log community.

3. B

Leaving the log open would expose the inside to greater evaporation, more airflow, and perhaps different temperatures. These factors are abiotic.

Most predators would be able to make their way into the rotting log. The inhabitants of the log do not want to escape. The major decomposers of a log are bacteria and fungi, which are already present in the log.

4. A

Algae are floating micro-organisms that must absorb mineral nutrients from water. The only difference between the north and south sides of the lake would appear to be the levels of phosphorous in the water (manipulated variable). Since there was an algae bloom on the north side where there was an addition of phosphorous, a lack of phosphorus would limit algae growth.

This experiment does not reveal any interaction between phosphorous, carbon, and nitrogen, and there is no reason to assume that the north side of the lake is cooler. The exact mechanism by which phosphorus stimulated an algal bloom is not known.

5. A

Dry feces and urine composed of relatively less water suggest an adaptation to reduce water loss, a useful adaptation for dry desert environments.

Reduced water loss is not an adaptation that would help life in a burrow or rain forest. The tundra is very cold, so evaporation rates are low; moisture is not in short supply.

6. C

Being separated geographically from other organisms has given Australian organisms the first step to speciation and, hence, their unique characteristics.

Australia is a dry, flat land, but there are other dry, flat lands in the world and they do not have the same types of organisms that Australia has. Humans have been in Australia for a very long time. There is no evidence given to suggest that there is more or less competition between organisms in Australia than there is anywhere else.

7. D

Sexual reproduction is the fusion of two gametes to form a zygote, which develops into a new organism. The act of fusion is called fertilization. During fertilization, the nuclei of the gametes fuse and bring together two sets of chromosomes, one set from each parent. Therefore, offspring are produced from two parents. Sexual reproduction leads to genetic variations and eventually to the process of speciation.

8. A

Lamarck believed that animals adapt to their environment during their lifetimes and that the adapted traits can be passed on to their offspring. For example, giraffes have long necks in order to reach high up into trees for leaves that they consume for food. A giraffe would develop a longer neck during its lifetime in order to reach the leaves. The offspring of that giraffe would therefore be born with the long neck that the parent developed.

Darwin believed that organisms are born with certain traits that are variable within a population. Of those organisms, the ones best-suited for their environment will survive to produce future generations. For example, giraffes born with long necks will be able to survive more often (because they can reach the tree leaves) and reach reproductive age to produce offspring. The next generation will inherit the characteristic of the long neck from their parents.

Statement I fits with Lamarck's ideas (the cheetahs pass on the muscles they develop to their offspring).

Statement II fits with Darwin's ideas (only the best-camouflaged sparrows survive to produce offspring).

9. B

The fossil record can be used to indicate a great number of things, but the interpretation of the available information must be carefully made. The only valid conclusion that can be reached from the information given is that camels have generally increased in size over time. Both the skull and the vertebra of the camels have become larger, which are strong indicators that the overall pattern of body size has increased over time.

Neither of the fossils presented is in an embryonic state, since both have adult teeth. Camels have never lived in benthic environments, and they are mammals that reproduce sexually.

10. D

It has been suggested that the fossil record shows a very low biodiversity throughout the approximately 600 million years it represents. Conservative estimates put the number of species represented in the fossil record at around 250 000. Considering that the number of species living on Earth at the present time is at least 3.5 million and could be as high as 30 million, it seems likely that there are more species now than at any one other time period in Earth's history. There has been a gradual increase in the number of species over time. Only macroevolution, evolution involving the formation of new species, could explain this.

There is no reason to suggest that species today are more complex. Regardless, this is evidence for evolution from one species to another.
The fact that organisms have unique characteristics does not mean there has been macroevolution. Becoming resistant to pesticides is a change within one type of organism, or microevolution.

11. B

As the rate of reproduction of a population increases, so too does the opportunity for more genetic variation and mutation. For this reason, many geneticists study population diversity and evolution by using the fruit fly *Drosophila melanogaster*. The rapid reproduction of new generations demonstrates natural selection as successful new characteristics are adopted and reproduced. An increased rate of reproduction will increase the rate of evolutionary change.

12. A

Rising sea levels on a terrestrial coastal community will decrease the amount of suitable habitat for organisms that normally make their homes there. Increased competition for dwindling resources such as food and space would reduce the number of variants that could survive there. Less variation means reduced biodiversity, so there would be a decrease in biodiversity.

13. A

Schreckstoff appears to provide minnows with a survival advantage, but only some minnows are able to secrete it. Therefore, the minnows with the gene for *Schreckstoff* are more likely to survive long enough to reproduce. Those without the gene are less likely to live long enough to produce offspring. Thus, the frequency of the *Schreckstoff* gene is likely to increase in the population. Individuals that do not have the gene are not as likely to survive.

14. D

Because the study of genetics had not yet revealed how genes can mutate, Darwin was unable to explain how variations in a trait originate. Darwin provided a strong outline of how speciation could occur. Darwin's observation of the large number of offspring produced illustrates that most organisms that are born will not be able to survive. As a result, there is a struggle for existence. The peppered moths were adapting to a changing environment, and this was explained by Darwin's theory of natural selection.

15. A

The punctuated equilibrium model of evolution suggests that new species appear so suddenly that intermediate forms between the new and the old do not exist. According to this model, species remain unchanged for long periods of time before giving rise to new species in comparatively short periods of time.

1. **a)** **i)** *Draw and label a line graph of depth versus oxygen.*

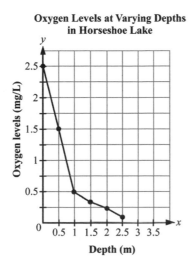

Oxygen Levels at Varying Depths in Horseshoe Lake

ii) *Draw and label a line graph of depth versus temperature.*

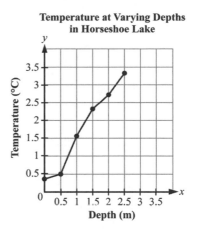

Temperature at Varying Depths in Horseshoe Lake

Label the *x*-axes as *depth* and the *y*-axes as either *oxygen levels* or *temperature*. The graphs show that as depth increases, oxygen levels decrease; therefore, an inverse relationship exists between depth and oxygen levels. As depth increases, temperature also increases. Therefore, a positive relationship exists between depth and temperature.

b) *Determine if it is likely that rainbow trout could survive a winter in Horseshoe Lake.*

Comparing the data collected to the information provided, it may be concluded that the trout will not survive over winter in this lake. Oxygen levels are too low to maintain a population of trout. The highest oxygen levels, found near the surface of the lake, are below 5.0 mg/L. As the depth increases, the O_2 concentration decreases, making survival at any depth of the lake impossible. Because the O_2 levels are insufficient at any level, rainbow trout would not survive in Horseshoe Lake.

The temperature, although low, would allow for a substantial amount of growth, but the trout would be small and their metabolic rate would be slow. The pH of 7.63 falls within the normal range of tolerance for the rainbow trout and would, therefore, pose no real threat to their survival.

c) *Oxygen levels appear to decrease at lower depths in Horseshoe Lake. Why might this occur?*

At lower depths of the lake, less sunlight penetrates the water. Lacking sufficient sunlight, green plants are unable to carry out photosynthesis. Because only a small amount of photosynthesis occurs under low-light conditions, very little O_2 will be returned to the water.

The maximum amount of oxygen that can be dissolved in warm water is less than the amount of oxygen that can be dissolved in cold water. Therefore, as the water temperature increases toward the bottom of the lake, the amount of oxygen that will dissolve decreases.

d) *What are the abiotic factors involved in the study of rainbow trout?*

Abiotic factors are the non-living components of a biological environment. In this study, temperature, light, oxygen, and pH are all abiotic factors.

e) *What ecological factors would change if a biological competitor to the rainbow trout were introduced in Horseshoe Lake?*

Any factor that is dependent upon other organisms is a biotic factor. In this case, food supply may be reduced and predation may result from introducing a competitor to the lake. The reduced supply of nutrients required by the trout will be exhausted by other organisms and not by factors such as light, pH, or temperature, which are abiotic factors. Thus, by introducing a competitor, biotic factors will be altered.

2. **a)** *Identify the person who developed the system of binomial nomenclature.*

Carl Linnaeus, known as the father of modern taxonomy, developed the system of binomial nomenclature.

b) *List two benefits of using this system.*

Some benefits of using the binomial nomenclature system are given below:

- Promotes consistency and stability in naming
- Standardizes the naming process
- Provides the same name regardless of the native language of the researchers
- Decreases the probability of misnomers
- Eliminates confusion associated with common names

Photosynthesis and Cellular Respiration

PHOTOSYNTHESIS AND CELLULAR RESPIRATION

Table of Correlations				
Specific Expectation	**Practice Questions**	**Unit Test Questions**	**Practice Test 1**	**Practice Test 2**
Students will:				
C1 *Relate photosynthesis to storage of energy in organic compounds.*				
C1.1 *explain, in general terms, how energy is absorbed by pigments, transferred through the reduction of nicotinamide adenine dinucleotide phosphate (NADP) to NADPH, and then transferred as chemical potential energy to ATP by chemiosmosis; and describe where in the chloroplast these processes occur*	1, 5, 19, WR1	1, 10, WR1	4, 5, 6, 7, 8	3, 4, 5, 6, 7
C1.2 *explain, in general terms, how the products of the light-dependent reactions, NADPH and ATP, are used to reduce carbon in the light-independent reactions for the production of glucose; and describe where in the chloroplast these processes occur*	7, 8, 9, 10	2, 3, 9, 13	9, 10, 11	2, 7, NR2, 11
C2 *Explain the role of cellular respiration in releasing potential energy from organic compounds.*				
C2.1 *explain, in general terms, how glucose is oxidized during glycolysis and the Krebs cycle to produce reducing power in NADH and FADH; and describe where in the cell these processes occur*	11, 12, 15, 16, 17	4, 5	15	9, 10, 12
C2.2 *explain, in general terms, how chemiosmosis converts the reducing power of NADH and FADH to store chemical potential energy as ATP; and describe where in the mitochondrion these processes occur*	4, 6, 13, 14, 18, NR1, NR2, NR3	6	12, NR1	
C2.3 *distinguish, in general terms, between aerobic and anaerobic respiration and fermentation in plants, animals and yeast*	3, 20	7, 11, 12	16	
C2.4 *summarize and explain the role of ATP in cellular metabolism*	2	8		

PHOTOSYNTHESIS AND CELLULAR RESPIRATION

C1.1   explain, in general terms, how energy is absorbed by pigments, transferred through the reduction of nicotinamide adenine dinucleotide phosphate (NADP) to NADPH, and then transferred as chemical potential energy to ATP by chemiosmosis; and describe where in the chloroplast these processes occur

CONVERTING LIGHT ENERGY INTO CHEMICAL ENERGY

Photosynthesis is an endergonic reaction occurring in the leaves of green plants and algae. It captures the energy of sunlight in the bonds of glucose.

Chloroplast

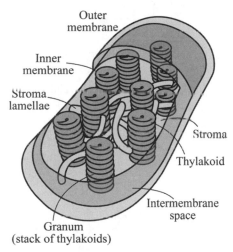

Outer membrane
Inner membrane
Stroma lamellae
Stroma
Thylakoid
Intermembrane space
Granum (stack of thylakoids)

Photosynthesis consists of a series of light-dependent reactions followed by a series of light-independent reactions. The light-dependent reactions of photosynthesis occur in the green **thylakoids** within the **chloroplasts**. The thylakoids contain two **photosystems**, each of which uses the green photosynthetic pigment **chlorophyll** to absorb solar energy. An **electron transport chain is then used** to convert the absorbed light energy into ATP through the process of chemiosmosis.

Chlorophyll is a photosynthetic **pigment** that absorbs most of the frequencies of white light, particularly red and blue wavelengths. Because chlorophyll reflects the wavelengths of green light it appears green.

The Overall Equation for Photosynthesis

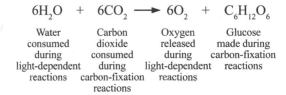

$$6H_2O + 6CO_2 \longrightarrow 6O_2 + C_6H_{12}O_6$$

| Water consumed during light-dependent reactions | Carbon dioxide consumed during carbon-fixation reactions | Oxygen released during light-dependent reactions | Glucose made during carbon-fixation reactions |

The **light-dependent reaction** begins when light splits water molecules in the process of **photolysis**. This process releases H^+ ions and electrons, and it releases oxygen as a waste. The oxygen is released into the atmosphere, becoming part of the air organisms breathe.

Two photosystems (II followed by I) are embedded in the thylakoid membrane. Each photosystem is made of chlorophyll molecules that gather the energy of sunlight and an electron transport chain made of protein carrier molecules that extract energy from excited chlorophyll electrons to make ATP. ATP is needed for photosynthesis because the reduction of carbon (addition of H to CO_2) to form glucose is **endergonic** and requires energy to occur.

The path through the photosystems begins with chlorophyll. When chlorophyll molecules are exposed to sunlight, excited chlorophyll electrons are passed from one protein carrier of the electron transport chain to another. Each carrier extracts a little bit of energy from the excited electrons and uses it to actively transport a few H^+ ions from the stroma into the thylakoid space, or lumen. The point of this activity is to build up a huge electrochemical potential energy gradient between the high concentration of H^+ inside the thylakoid and the low concentration of H^+ outside the thylakoid in the stroma.

At the end of each photosystem is a very large enzyme molecule called **ATP synthase**. When the difference in the concentration gradient between the inside and the outside of the thylakoid becomes great enough, H^+ ions flow from the inside of the thylakoid through the ATP synthase molecule to the outside stroma, releasing the energy of the electrochemical gradient. The released energy is captured into the high-energy bond that attaches ADP to P, forming ATP. Indirectly then, it is the energy of sunlight that forms the high-energy bond of ATP. The process of capturing the power of an energy gradient across a membrane using ATP synthase is called **chemiosmosis.**

Once the high-energy electrons that move through the electron transport chain reach the end of the photosystem, they are depleted of energy and are used to reduce $NADP^+$ to NADPH, which is known as a hydrogen carrier or **hydrogen acceptor.**

The two useful products of the light-dependent reactions (ATP and NADPH) move from the thylakoid to the stroma, where the light-independent reactions occur. The electrons that are lost from chlorophyll when it is excited by sunlight are replaced by the hydrogen electrons that are a product of the photolysis of water.

Note that even though photosynthesis produces ATP in the light-dependent reactions, it only produces enough ATP to drive the reduction of carbon in the light-independent reactions. Cell respiration produces very large amounts of ATP by comparison.

Practice Questions: 1, 5, 19, WR1

C1.2   explain, in general terms, how the products of the light-dependent reactions, NADPH and ATP, are used to reduce carbon in the light-independent reactions for the production of glucose; and describe where in the chloroplast these processes occur

THE LIGHT-INDEPENDENT REACTIONS (THE CALVIN-BENSON CYCLE)

The light-independent reactions take place in the **stroma** of the chloroplast. Their name derives from the fact that light is not necessary for these reactions to occur. The goal of the light-independent reactions is to convert the glucose precursor 5-carbon RuBP (ribulose biphosphate) into 6-carbon glucose. RuBP is not a true carbohydrate because it is missing carbon, and hydrogen. The missing carbon is provided by CO_2 that enters the leaf through the stomata. The missing hydrogen is provided by NADPH coming from the light-dependent reaction. The donation of hydrogen by NADPH is called a reduction. ATP from the light-dependent reactions is needed for this reaction because the reduction, of carbon is very endergonic. This means it will not occur without the addition of significant energy.

The Calvin cycle begins when 5-carbon RuBP already in the stroma combines with CO_2 from the plant's stomata to form a 6-carbon precursor molecule with a structure that is closer to being a true carbohydrate. This incorporation of inorganic carbon dioxide into an organic molecule is referred to as carbon fixation. The precursor molecule is reduced when NADPH donates its hydrogen. This reduction will not occur without the addition of significant amounts of energy. The energy needed to power the reduction is provided by the splitting of ATP into ADP, P, and energy. The result is a 6-carbon true carbohydrate that splits into two 3-carbon PGAL (G3P) molecules. There are three possible fates of the PGAL molecules. They can join to reform 6-carbon glucose again and be used in cellular respiration, be stored as starch or cellulose, or be used to make more RuBP to keep the Calvin cycle going. NADP, ADP, and P are returned to the thylakoid to take part in the light reactions again.

The Calvin Cycle

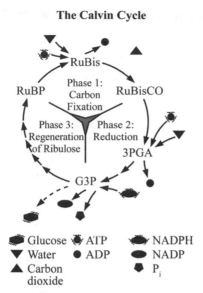

Glucose ATP NADPH
Water ADP NADP
Carbon dioxide P_i

The following table shows the substances used and produced in the light-dependent and light-independent reactions.

	Substances Used	Substances Produced
Light-dependent reaction	Water Sunlight	ATP NADPH O_2
Light-independent reaction	CO_2 from stomata ATP from light reaction NADPH from light reaction	Glucose (2 PGAL) ADP/P (reused in light reaction) NADP (reused in light reaction)

Practice Questions: 7, 8, 9, 10

C2.1 explain, in general terms, how glucose is oxidized during glycolysis and the Krebs cycle to produce reducing power in NADH and FADH; and describe where in the cell these processes occur

CELLULAR RESPIRATION

Once a plant has undergone photosynthesis and transformed the sun's energy into glucose, it stores this potential chemical energy in its fruit, stem, or roots as small sugars, starch, or cellulose. At some point, the demands of growth, reproduction, and metabolism require that the plant spend its stored energy. Unfortunately, the stored energy of glucose is of no value to the organism unless the energy locked in its bonds is released and captured into the bond between adenosine diphosphate (ADP) and phosphate (P) to form adenosine triphosphate (ATP).

The same is true of an animal that eats a plant, incorporating the plant's glucose into its bloodstream. The need for ATP energy to power muscle contraction, nerve conduction, growth, and reproduction means that the energy in glucose molecules must be released.

Cellular respiration is the process that releases the potential energy of glucose into ATP. Since cell respiration releases rather than absorbs energy, the reaction is **exergonic**.

The Overall Equation for Cellular Respiration

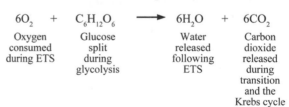

$$6O_2 + C_6H_{12}O_6 \longrightarrow 6H_2O + 6CO_2$$

Oxygen consumed during ETS | Glucose split during glycolysis | Water released following ETS | Carbon dioxide released during transition and the Krebs cycle

Respiration involves the oxidation of glucose, that is, the removal of the hydrogen electrons and their transfer to oxygen to form waste H_2O. Glucose stripped of its hydrogen forms CO_2 molecules. Both CO_2 and H_2O are released as waste products back into the environment.

The breaking of bonds that occurs as hydrogen is transferred from glucose to oxygen releases abundant energy. This energy is trapped in the high-energy bonds between ADP and P, forming ATP. ATP can be used by a cell to do work at any time. The process of capturing energy into ATP is termed **oxidative phosphorylation.**

Cell respiration is a complex process with many steps, the pace of which is controlled by enzymes. If all the hydrogen were transferred from glucose to oxygen at once (as occurs when wood is burned), then a dangerous amount of energy would be released as heat. During cell respiration, a glucose molecule is broken down progressively, releasing small amounts of energy that are captured into ATP. To accomplish this oxidation, glucose is progressively stripped of its high energy hydrogen pairs which are fed to the electron transport chain where ATP is produced through the process of chemiosmosis.

Cell respiration occurs in the cytoplasm and mitochondria of cells. Like all transfers of energy, cell respiration reactions are not very efficient. **Efficiency** is measured by how much ATP is liberated compared with how much energy is lost as heat for each molecule of glucose oxidized. The percentage efficiency is calculated with the following equation:

$$\text{Efficiency} = \frac{\text{Useful energy output}}{\text{Total energy output}}$$

The more efficient cell respiration is, the more ATP is gathered and the less heat is produced. In aerobic conditions (when oxygen is present), cell respiration is about 40% efficient, with 60% of the energy of glucose lost to heat. In anaerobic conditions (when there is no oxygen present), cell respiration is only 2% efficient. Although the amount of ATP it produces is very small, anaerobic respiration allows certain organisms to survive without oxygen.

Cell respiration can be divided into three parts: **glycolysis** (in the cell's cytoplasm), the **Krebs cycle** (in the mitochondrial matrix), and the **electron transport chain** (on the folded inner membranes of the mitochondria called **cristae**).

GLYCOLYSIS AND THE KREBS (CITRIC ACID) CYCLE

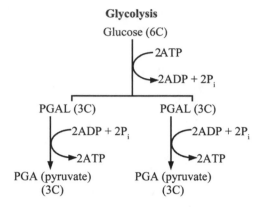

Glycolysis begins the progressive breakdown of glucose and occurs in the cell cytoplasm. The word *glycolysis* means the splitting of glucose. First, glucose is activated by the expenditure of 2 ATP. It is then split into two 3C molecules, each of which is oxidized (loses a hydrogen pair), releasing 2 ATP and leaving 3C pyruvate (PGA). This completes glycolysis. In glycolysis then, glucose is split in two, and a net total of only two ATP are produced for each glucose molecule metabolized.

Glycolysis requires no oxygen to produce ATP. Yeast cells or muscle cells starved of oxygen can use glycolysis to meet their energy needs. This is referred to as anaerobic respiration.

Glycolysis is followed by a transition phase where pyruvate loses a hydrogen pair to the acceptor molecule NAD^+ to become $NADH + H^+$ which move to the electron transport chain. Pyruvate also loses a CO_2 molecule, and combines with coenzyme A to become 2C acetyl Co-A (active acetate). Acetyl Co-A then leaves the cytoplasm and enters the Krebs cycle in the matrix of the mitochondrion.

The purpose of the Krebs cycle is to progressively strip off more high-energy hydrogen pairs from glucose fuel fragments and send them to NAD^+ and the electron transport chain where they will be used to make ATP. The Krebs cycle begins when incoming 2C acetyl co-A joins with a 4C fuel fragment that is finishing the cycle, to form 6C citric acid. This molecule is rich in high-energy hydrogen pairs. The rest of the cycle will be devoted to progressive oxidation as hydrogen pairs are stripped off of the fuel fragments and accepted by NAD+ to become $NADH + H^+$ which will move to the electron transport chain. CO_2 molecules are also removed during the Krebs cycle, leaving behind 5C and then 4C fuel fragments. The removed CO_2 is released as a waste product by diffusion and exhalation. At the end of the Krebs cycle, the remaining 4-carbon fragment joins with another incoming 2-carbon acetyl co-A, reforming 6-carbon citric acid. The cycle continues as long as there is an adequate amount of glucose undergoing glycolysis.

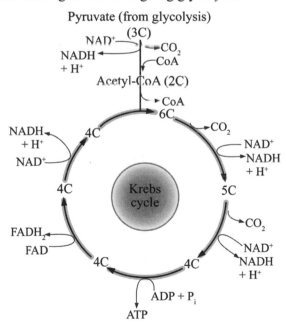

THE ELECTRON TRANSPORT CHAIN

At this point in cell respiration, very little ATP has been produced. Many high-energy hydrogen pairs have been stripped off glucose fuel fragments in the Krebs cycle and sent to NAD^+ and the electron transport chain. The components of the chain are protein pumps and carriers embedded in the inner mitochondrial membrane.

A Mitochrondrion

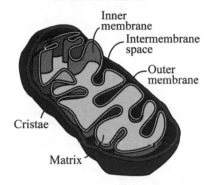

For the most part, electron transport chains in the mitochondria are the same as the chloroplast electron transport chains that produce ATP in photosynthesis.

The protein carriers that make up the complexes of the electron transport chain are slightly different, but they function in the same way.

High-energy NADH molecules have been produced in glycolysis, transition, and the Krebs cycle when NAD^+ is reduced by hydrogen atoms. In the final step of aerobic cellular respiration, NADH releases an H^+ ion into the mitochondrial matrix and two high-energy electrons enter the electron transport chain. Each chain is made up of four complexes that lie embedded in the inner mitochondrial membrane. When $NADH + H^+$ molecules enter the first complex, protons (H^+) and high-energy electrons (e^-) are split away, leaving NAD^+. The high-energy electrons are passed down the chain from one complex to the next. Each complex extracts a bit of the energy from these high-energy electrons and uses it to power the active transport of H^+ from the matrix of the mitochondrion into the intermembranal space. The accumulation of H^+ in this space sets up an electrochemical gradient between the intermembranal space and the mitochondrial matrix. The potential energy in this gradient will be used to drive the production of ATP during chemiosmosis.

When two electrons emerge from the last complex in the ET chain depleted of energy, they join two H^+ ions that will be released from ATP synthase after chemiosmosis. Oxygen, a reactant for cell respiration, combines with the spent electrons and H^+ ions, forming H_2O as a waste product.

Surprisingly, the only function of oxygen in cell respiration is to act as this final hydrogen and electron acceptor at the end of the ET chain, where it combines to form water. However, without oxygen present to carry out this function, chemiosmosis and ATP production stop. The water produced in chemiosmosis is eliminated from the body by breath, perspiration, evaporation, or osmosis.

Cycling of Matter in Photosynthesis and Cellular Respiration

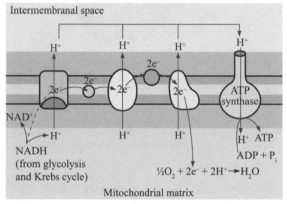

Practice Questions: 11, 12, 15, 16, 17

C2.2 *explain, in general terms, how chemiosmosis converts the reducing power of NADH and FADH to store chemical potential energy as ATP; and describe where in the mitochondrion these processes occur*

CHEMIOSMOSIS

Chemiosmosis is the process of releasing the potential energy of an electrochemical gradient and using that energy to create ATP. It is also known as oxidative phosphorylation.

To this point in cellular respiration, NADH and FADH have gathered hydrogen from fuel fragments in glycolysis, transition, and the Kreb's cycle. NADH and FADH have donated their high energy electrons to the protein complexes making up the ET chain. The protein complexes have harnessed the energy of the high energy electrons and used it to actively transport H^+ ions into the intermembranal space creating an electrochemical gradient between the intermembranal space and the mitochondrial matrix. The ATP synthase molecule sitting at the end of the ET chain now comes into play carrying out chemiosmosis. When the accumulated H^+ in the intermembranal space forms a great enough gradient, H^+ shoots through the ATP synthase molecule into the matrix, releasing the potential energy of the gradient. ADP and P capture this released energy into a high-energy bond, forming ATP.

The rate of ATP production depends on a number of factors. The more hydrogen pairs that are stripped from glucose fuel fragments in glycolysis, transition, and the Kreb's cycle, the more NADH there is available to donate high energy electrons to the ET chain. The more electrons that pass through the ET chain the greater the electrochemical gradient created and the greater the amount of ATP produced in chemiosmosis. Although glucose is the fuel of choice for cellular respiration, fat (lipid) is much richer in hydrogen and produces over twice as much ATP energy as glucose per gram. Fats must be broken down to 2- and 3-carbon segments before entering the respiration pathway as pyruvate or acetyl Co-A.

Practice Questions: 4, 6, 13, 14, 18, NR1, NR2, NR3

C2.3   distinguish, in general terms, between aerobic and anaerobic respiration and fermentation in plants, animals and yeast

AEROBIC AND ANAEROBIC RESPIRATION

Aerobic respiration occurs in the presence of oxygen. It involves the full respiratory pathway of glycolysis, the Krebs cycle, the ET chain, and chemiosmosis. Oxygen acts as the final hydrogen and electron acceptor at the end of the ET chain. CO_2, H_2O, and heat are waste products. The net production of ATP per each molecule of glucose oxidized is 36. The process is 40% efficient at capturing the energy of glucose into ATP molecules. 60% of the potential energy of glucose is lost as heat.

Anaerobic respiration occurs when no oxygen is available. It is also referred to as fermentation. Only a few organisms (yeast, anaerobic bacteria, and muscle cells) are capable of it. The reactions are simply a modified form of glycolysis. The net production of ATP is only 2 ATP per glucose molecule oxidized. The rest of the respiratory pathway cannot be accessed because the remaining steps of respiration require the presence of oxygen.

The waste products of anaerobic respiration are different than those produced in aerobic respiration. A yeast cell denied oxygen goes through the steps of glycolysis producing 2 ATP. The hydrogen pair removed from PGAL is used to reduce pyruvate to the waste products ethyl alcohol and CO_2. This is the fermentation process that is used to produce commercial alcohol and other fermented products. If an oxygen-starved muscle cell goes through glycolysis, 2 ATP are produced, but the waste products are slightly different than those seen with yeast. The hydrogen pair removed from PGAL reduces pyruvate to the waste products lactic acid and CO_2. In both yeast and muscle cells, the final hydrogen acceptor is pyruvate.

The waste products lactic acid and alcohol both become toxic in high enough concentrations. For this reason anaerobic respiration is not sustainable indefinitely. Yeast cells will eventually be killed by the alcohol they produce. Similarly, muscle cells can only undergo anaerobic respiration for short periods of time because the accumulated lactic acid creates a burning sensation and paralyzes the muscle tissue.

By taking advantage of the part of the respiratory pathway that does not require oxygen, organisms in anaerobic conditions can still produce 2 ATP for every glucose molecule burned. If the entire aerobic respiratory pathway were accessed, the ATP production would be 36 ATP per glucose. Anaerobic respiration is 2% efficient at releasing the potential energy in glucose while aerobic respiration is 40% efficient. Although very inefficient, anaerobic respiration is still an effective survival strategy.

Practice Questions: 3, 20

C2.4   summarize and explain the role of ATP in cellular metabolism

THE ROLE OF ATP IN METABOLISM

The chemical activity of a cell is referred to as metabolism. This chemical activity requires energy. Cells produce usable energy in the form of ATP during cellular respiration that takes place in mitochondria.

When cells require energy to do work, ATP is split to form ADP, phosphate, and energy. The process of splitting ATP is termed **dephosphorylation.**

Several examples of the role of ATP in cell metabolism are described in the following sections.

ACTIVE TRANSPORT

There are times when cells need to accumulate high concentrations of molecules or ions inside their cytoplasm. Because the process of diffusion will always equalize concentrations across a membrane, it is not useful in these situations. Similarly, there are occasions in which a cell needs to completely remove all of a particular substance, such as a waste or poison. Again, the equilibrium that results from diffusion will not be sufficient. Active transport is the process of using proteins in the cell membrane to pump chemicals against a concentration gradient. This requires a large amount of energy which is provided by the splitting (dephosphorylation) of ATP molecules.

CYTOPLASMIC STREAMING

Cytoplasmic streaming is the movement of the cytoplasm within the cell. There are several scenarios in which cells benefit from the movement of cytoplasm. The first and most obvious reason is to mix cell contents. If a substance diffuses across the membrane, the movement of cytoplasm can help to distribute the substance. Single-celled organisms like amoebas direct cytoplasm to move, creating extensions of the cell membrane called pseudopods. All animal cells that undergo cell division must divide the cytoplasm into the two newly formed daughter cells. Cytoplasmic streaming is required to help move the cytoplasm.

In all these instances, ATP provides the energy that causes cytoplasmic streaming.

PHAGOCYTOSIS

Many molecules are too large to pass through a cell membrane. Cells can undergo a process called phagocytosis that makes it possible for cells to engulf large molecules. During phagocytosis, the cell membrane invaginates and forms a vacuole around the molecule.

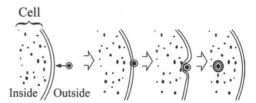

This complex receptor-mediated cellular process requires an input of energy in the form of ATP.

BIOCHEMICAL SYNTHESIS

Generally speaking, any biochemical process that breaks chemical bonds in a molecule will release energy. If a cell is going to assemble a molecule (for example, combining amino acids to form protein), new bonds need to be formed. This is referred to as biochemical synthesis. In this process a larger molecule is formed from two or more smaller molecules. ATP supplies the energy needed to perform synthesis reactions.

MUSCLE CONTRACTION

Muscles contract when protein filaments within the muscle slide past each other. The mechanism requires that actin and myosin proteins pull against each other. This motion requires the expenditure of energy. Muscle activity, therefore, requires energy in the form of ATP.

HEAT PRODUCTION

Warm-blooded animals maintain body temperatures that are higher than their surroundings. Because of its inefficiency, cell respiration releases most of the energy of glucose as waste heat. This heat serves the purpose of maintaining body temperature. If the surroundings are cold and the body is relatively inactive, not enough heat energy will be created to maintain body temperature. Involuntary shivering of muscle tissue is often the result of the body burning ATP to stay warm.

Practice Question: 2

PRACTICE QUESTIONS—PHOTOSYNTHESIS AND CELLULAR RESPIRATION

Use the following diagram to answer the next question.

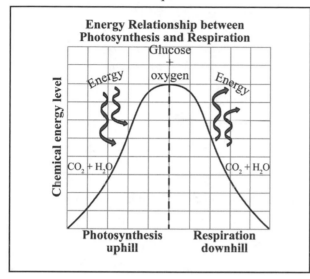

Energy Relationship between Photosynthesis and Respiration

Glucose + oxygen

Energy

Energy

Chemical energy level

$CO_2 + H_2O$

$CO_2 + H_2O$

Photosynthesis uphill

Respiration downhill

CHALLENGER QUESTION

1. According to the given diagram, photosynthesis is analogous to moving uphill, and respiration is analogous to moving downhill because photosynthesis
   A. occurs first and respiration occurs later
   B. stores energy and respiration releases it
   C. consumes CO_2 and respiration releases CO_2
   D. occurs in plants and respiration occurs in all life forms

---

2. During respiration, energy is released in the form of
   A. CO_2 and H_2O
   B. ATP and heat
   C. glucose and O_2
   D. $FADH_2$ and NADH

3. More energy is produced by aerobic respiration than by anaerobic respiration because during anaerobic respiration,
   A. alcohol is produced
   B. oxygen is not required
   C. food is incompletely oxidized
   D. very few enzymes are involved

4. Which of the following statements comparing photosynthesis and respiration is **false**?
   A. Photosynthesis is endergonic, whereas respiration is exergonic.
   B. Respiration results in a net production of ATP, whereas photosynthesis does not.
   C. Photosynthesis involves oxidation of carbon, whereas respiration involves reduction of carbon.
   D. Only autotrophs carry out photosynthesis, whereas all organisms carry out respiration.

5. Electron transport is linked to ATP synthesis in the inner mitochondrial membrane by which of the following mechanisms?
   A. Oxidation
   B. Glycolysis
   C. Fermentation
   D. Chemiosmosis

6. When hydrogen is carried to the electron transport chain it
   A. becomes ADP
   B. forms methane
   C. ends up in water
   D. is recycled in glycolysis

7. Light-independent reactions produce

A. $NADP^+$, ATP, and oxygen

B. NADPH and ATP

C. water and H^+

D. glucose

Use the following diagram to answer the next three questions.

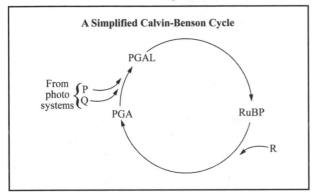

A Simplified Calvin-Benson Cycle

CHALLENGER QUESTION

8. The labels *P* and *Q* represent

A. H_2O and CO_2

B. NADPH and ATP

C. light and chemical energy

D. two thylakoid membranes

---

9. A comparison of PGAL and PGA on the given diagram shows that

A. there is more PGAL than PGA

B. glucose can be formed from PGA or PGAL

C. PGAL contains more chemical energy than PGA

D. PGA and PGAL are made in the photosystems

10. Operation of the Calvin-Benson cycle requires a constant supply of

A. light

B. glucose

C. CO_2 and H_2O

D. C, H, O, and energy

Use the following information to answer the next question.

Two reaction equations are given.

$$NAD^+ + H^+ + 2e^- \rightarrow NADH$$
$$NADH \rightarrow NAD^+ + H^+ + 2e^-$$

11. The given reactions, respectively, show

A. reduction and oxidation

B. oxidation and oxidation

C. reduction and reduction

D. oxidation and reduction

Use the following diagram to answer the next seven questions.

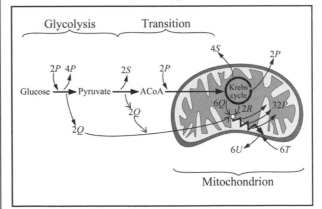

12. During cellular respiration, glucose is broken down step by step to release high-energy electrons. All the steps require the assistance of

A. ATP

B. oxygen

C. pyruvate

D. enzymes

Use the following additional information to answer the next question.

Energy derived from the high-energy electrons of glucose is used to form ATP. ATP is a readily useable form of chemical energy that is used to power metabolic activities.

CHALLENGER QUESTION

13. In the diagram, the letter that represents ATP is
   A. *P*
   B. *Q*
   C. *R*
   D. *S*

14. The diagram indicates that most of the ATP is generated
   A. during glycolysis
   B. before the Krebs cycle
   C. during the transition reaction
   D. in the electron transport system

Use the following additional information to answer the next question.

Once the high-energy electrons are removed from glucose, they are loaded onto the electron carriers NADH and FADH$_2$.

CHALLENGER QUESTION

15. In the diagram, NADH and FADH, respectively, are labelled
   A. *T* and *P*
   B. *P* and *S*
   C. *Q* and *R*
   D. *R* and *T*

Use the following additional information to answer the next question.

The byproduct carbon dioxide (CO_2) is what remains of the glucose after the hydrogen ions (and associated electrons) are removed.

16. In the diagram, CO_2 is labelled
   A. *Q*
   B. *T*
   C. *U*
   D. *S*

Use the following additional information to answer the next question.

Usually, a person's supply of glucose is metabolized overnight. If breakfast is skipped, the body may begin to metabolize fats. The fats are broken down to small fragments. Then, they enter the chemical reactions of cellular respiration as active acetate (acetyl coenzyme A).

CHALLENGER QUESTION

17. Which stage of cellular respiration is skipped entirely in the metabolism of fats?
   A. Glycolysis
   B. Krebs cycle
   C. Transition reaction
   D. Electron transport system

Use the following additional information to answer the next question.

The energy within high-energy electrons is used to assemble ATP. Once the ATP is assembled, the electrons are converted to a lower energy state. The low-energy electrons are picked up along with hydrogen ions (H^+, protons) by T, the final electron acceptor.

CHALLENGER QUESTION

18. The final electron acceptor, represented by the letter T, is
    A. CO_2
    B. NAD^+
    C. oxygen
    D. glucose

Use the following information to answer the next three questions.

One glucose molecule contains 680 kcal of energy. During anaerobic respiration, there is a net gain of 2 ATP. During aerobic respiration, there is a net gain of 36 ATP. Each ATP is equivalent to 8 kcal of energy. One kilocalorie of energy contains 4 180 J of energy.

CHALLENGER QUESTION

1. What is the percentage efficiency of anaerobic respiration? _____% (Record your answer rounded to **one** decimal place.)

2. What is the percentage efficiency of aerobic respiration? _____% (Record your answer rounded to **one** decimal place.)

3. What percentage of the energy of the glucose molecule is lost during aerobic respiration? _____% (Record your answer rounded to **one** decimal place.)

Use the following information to answer the next question.

The electron transport chain embedded in the membrane of the thylakoid passes electrons from carrier to carrier. In this process, energy is released and is used to pump particles from the stroma to the thylakoid lumen.

19. Which of the following particles move to the thylakoid lumen during this process?
    A. H^+ ions
    B. Oxygen
    C. Glucose
    D. Electrons

20. Aerobic respiration has an advantage over anaerobic respiration in that it
    A. results in the splitting of glucose
    B. leads to the production of alcohol
    C. leads to the complete oxidation of food
    D. requires very few steps for its completion

Written Response

Use the following information to answer the next question.

The graph illustrates the rate of photosynthesis against different wavelengths of visible light in a particular plant.

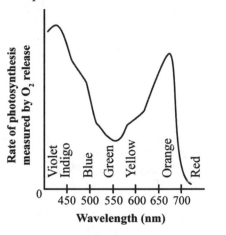

1. **a)** At approximately what wavelength of light is the rate of photosynthesis the highest?

(1 mark)

b) What colour of the spectrum is found between 520 nm and 565 nm?

(1 mark)

c) Explain the relationship between the colour of the light and the rate of photosynthesis.

(2 marks)

d) Propose a hypothesis to explain why the rate of photosynthesis differs drastically from one end of the visible light spectrum to the other.

(4 marks)

ANSWERS AND SOLUTIONS—PRACTICE QUESTIONS

1. B	6. C	11. A	16. D	NR3. 57.6
2. B	7. D	12. D	17. A	19. A
3. C	8. B	13. A	18. C	20. C
4. C	9. C	14. D	NR1. 2.4	WR1. See Solution
5. D	10. D	15. C	NR2. 42.4	

1. B

According to the graph, the reactants for photosynthesis ($6CO_2$ and $6H_2O$) have low chemical energy. These molecules are small, have few bonds, and therefore have little bond energy. In photosynthesis, the atoms in CO_2 and H_2O are rearranged to form glucose ($C_6H_{12}O_6$), a larger and more complex molecule with many bonds. The energy needed to create these bonds comes from sunlight. Photosynthesis captures the energy of sunlight in the bonds of glucose. Because bonds store energy, glucose with its many bonds is said to have much more potential energy than its reactants. In the graph, photosynthesis is depicted as an uphill climb because low energy reactants, CO_2 and H_2O, must draw energy from the sun to complete the formation of high-energy glucose. In cellular respiration, glucose is slowly torn apart, bonds are broken, and the potential energy in these bonds is released and captured into a molecule of ATP, which is used to do cellular work. What remains as products of respiration are CO_2 and H_2O, the small, low-energy molecules that were the reactants for photosynthesis. On the graph, cellular respiration is depicted as a downhill process because high-energy glucose is converted into low-energy waste products of H_2O and CO_2.

2. B

The following equation shows the reaction for cellular respiration:

$$6C_6H_{12}O_6 + 6O_2 \rightarrow 6H_2O + 6CO_2 + ATP$$
$$\text{(glucose)} \quad \text{(oxygen)} \quad \text{(water)} \quad \text{(carbon dioxide)}$$

The reaction converts glucose into readily useable energy. Some energy is lost as heat during this reaction.

3. C

Anaerobic respiration is modified glycolysis, the first stage in respiration. In this stage glucose is split into two 3C fragments referred to as PGAL. Each PGAL is oxidized when a hydrogen pair is removed resulting in two PGA or pyruvate molecules. After this point no more oxidation occurs. In aerobic respiration the pathway would continue from pyruvate through transition and the Krebs cycle. In each process more hydrogen pairs would be stripped off, progressively oxidizing the fuel fragments more and more. The more hydrogen pairs removed, the more ATP energy produced. Therefore, anaerobic respiration produces less energy than complete aerobic respiration because the food fragment is incompletely oxidized.

4. C

Oxidation involves losing electrons; reduction involves gaining electrons. In photosynthesis, the carbon molecule (CO_2) is reduced to become $C_6H_{12}O_6$. In respiration, the carbon molecule ($C_6H_{12}O_6$) is oxidized to produce H_2O and CO_2.

Endergonic reactions absorb energy; exergonic reactions release energy. In photosynthesis, light energy is absorbed and used to make glucose. In respiration, glucose is broken down, releasing useable energy in the form of ATP. ATP is produced during photosynthesis, but only enough to generate glucose during carbon fixation.

The purpose of cellular respiration is to convert the energy stored in sugars to ATP, a form readily useable by the cell. Thus, cellular respiration results in net ATP production, whereas photosynthesis does not.

Autotrophs are the only organisms that can obtain energy from the sun. All other organisms are heterotrophs and are either directly or indirectly dependent on autotrophs for energy.

5. D

Chemiosmosis is the mechanism that links the energy released by the flow of electrons in the electron transport chain to ATP synthesis. Electron flow creates proton movement across the inner mitochondrial membrane, ultimately leading to proton movement through ATP synthase. ATP synthase is a protein complex embedded in the inner mitochondrial membrane that converts ADP to ATP.

6. C

Oxygen plays the final role in the electron transport chain by combining with the two energy-depleted hydrogen electrons that emerge from the ET chain, and the $2H^+$ that were released from ATP synthase. Together, the $2H^+$, $2e^-$ and $\frac{1}{2} O_2$ form water. The production of water keeps the hydrogen ion concentrations low in the matrix compared to H^+ ion concentrations in the intermembranal space. This, combined with the pumping of H^+ ions into the intermembranal space from the mitochondrial matrix, helps to maintain the electrochemical potential of the H^+ ion gradient. This concentration of H^+ on the outside of the inner mitochondrial membrane is the source of energy that is used to generate ATP through chemiosmosis.

7. D

Sugars in the form of glucose and related conversions of glucose into sucrose, starch, and cellulose are the major products of light-independent reactions. This is the Calvin cycle. NADPH and ATP are products of the light-dependent reactions along with oxygen, which is not mentioned. $NADP^+$ is a product of the Calvin cycle, but ATP and oxygen are products of light-dependent reactions. In the light-independent reactions, water is not a product. Water is not consumed in the Calvin cycle, only in the light-dependant stage (i.e., during photolysis).

8. B

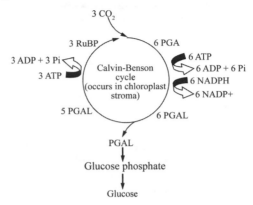

The given Calvin-Benson cycle diagram shows that the required inputs for the production of PGAL from PGA are ATP and NADPH. NADPH donates the hydrogen needed to reduce PGA to PGAL. ATP donates the energy needed to drive the endergonic reduction. Water is required during the light-dependent reactions; CO_2 is required one step before the conversion of PGA to PGAL. Although chemical energy (in the form of ATP and NADPH) is required, light energy is not directly needed by the Calvin-Benson cycle. Thylakoid membranes are the site in the chloroplast where the light-dependent reactions occur. So while the thylakoid membranes provide NADPH and ATP for the Calvin-Benson cycle, the membranes themselves do not enter the Calvin-Benson cycle.

9. C

The diagram indicates that the numbers of PGAL and PGAL molecules are the same. PGAL occurs later in the cycle than PGA. PGA is converted chemically to PGAL by the addition of energy and hydrogen atoms donated by ATP (*P*) and NADPH (*Q*). Thus, PGAL contains more chemical energy than PGA. PGAL and PGAL are not part of or products of the photosystems of the light-dependent reactions. In photosynthesis, two 3C PGAL molecules can be joined chemically to produce glucose, a 6C sugar. 3C PGA cannot be used directly to generate glucose.

10. D

The Calvin-Benson cycle results in carbon fixation: the incorporation of carbon atoms from carbon dioxide into glucose. Glucose ($C_6H_{12}O_6$) is a product of Calvin-Benson cycle reactions. Light is not directly required for operation of the Calvin-Benson cycle because energy is stored chemically as ATP.

C and O are provided to the carbon cycle by CO_2 and RuBP. H is provided to the cycle by RuBP and NADPH. Energy is provided to the cycle by both ATP and the chemical bond energy of intermediates in the cycle. C, O, and H atoms and energy are all necessary for the carbon cycle. Water is not used during the Calvin-Benson cycle. H_2O is required during photosystem II to replace chlorophyll electrons lost in excitation.

11. A

Oxidation involves a loss of electrons, and reduction involves a gain of electrons. During the processes of photosynthesis and respiration, hydrogen atoms lose and gain electrons. Apply this knowledge to the reactions shown.

$NAD^+ + H^+ + 2e^- \rightarrow NADH$
Gain of elections (reduction

$NADH \rightarrow NAD^+ + H^2 + 2e^-$
Loss of electrons (oxidation)

12. D

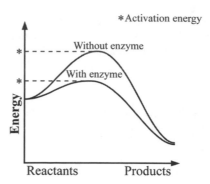

Cellular respiration is a series of chemical reactions that ultimately result in the breakdown of glucose to release energy in the form of ATP (and waste heat energy). Many reactions do not occur spontaneously because the reactants require some activation energy to convert them to products. Often, this activation energy is more than can be provided by the surrounding environment. Most reactions require enzymes to bind to the reactants and lower the activation energy required to start the reaction (see diagram). The enzymes are catalysts. Enzymes are required at each step of cellular respiration, and each step of respiration requires a different enzyme. The diagram in the preamble shows that pyruvate is required at one step early in the pathway.

Similarly, ATP and oxygen, although required for cellular respiration, are not required at all steps of the process.

13. A

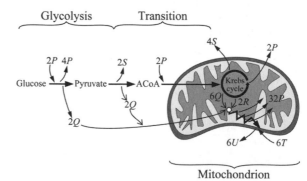

The solution is given by the following key:

P = ATP   Q = NADH
R = FADH   S = CO_2

14. D

The letter P in the diagram represents ATP. Notice that most of the ATP (32 molecules) are generated after the Krebs cycle within the membrane of the mitochondrion in the electron transport system. In the electron transport system, NADH and FADH transfer their electrons to the protein complexes that make up the electron transport chain. At each transfer, one ATP is generated. One NADH generates three ATP molecules, whereas one FADH generates two ATP molecules. Glycolysis is the reaction between glucose and pyruvate, during which only four ATP are released. The transition reaction between pyruvate and Acetyl-coA consumes two ATP. Only two ATP are produced from the Krebs cycle.

15. C

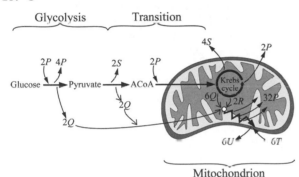

The solution is given by the following key:
P = ATP Q = NADH
R = FADH S = CO_2
T = O_2

16. D

The solution is given by the following key:

P = ATP Q = NADH
R = FADH S = CO_2
T = O_2

17. A

Active acetate is a 2-carbon molecule. Glycolysis takes 6-carbon glucose and splits it into two 3-carbon molecules. Therefore, a fat fuel fragment entering the pathway as active acetate would have completely bypassed glycolysis.

18. C

After passing through the electron transport system, the electrons and protons (H^+), which together make up hydrogen atoms, join oxygen to form water. Therefore oxygen is the final electron acceptor. Water is a final product of respiration, but it is not a final electron acceptor. NAD^+ accepts electrons (as NADH) but only transfers them along the ET chain. CO_2 is released during the Krebs cycle as a waste product after high-energy electrons are removed from the remnants of glucose. CO_2 is not an electron acceptor. Glucose is broken down during respiration. It serves as the initial electron donor.

NR 1   2.4

Use the given information to calculate the percentage efficiency.

$$\text{Efficiency} = \frac{\text{Useful energy output}}{\text{Total energy output}}$$

$$\text{Efficiency} = \frac{2\,\text{ATP} \times 8\,\text{kcal/ATP}}{680\,\text{kcal}}$$

$$= \frac{16\,\text{kcal}}{680\,\text{kcal}}$$

$$= 2.4\%$$

NR 2   42.4

Use the given information to calculate the percentage efficiency.

$$\text{Efficiency} = \frac{\text{Useful energy output}}{\text{Total energy output}}$$

$$\text{Efficiency} = \frac{36\,\text{ATP} \times 8\,\text{kcal/ATP}}{680\,\text{kcal}}$$

$$= \frac{288\,\text{kcal}}{680\,\text{kcal}}$$

$$= 42.4\%$$

NR 3   57.6

If 42.4% of the energy is converted into ATP, the remainder, 57.6%, is lost.

19. A

The electron transport system in the membrane of the thylakoid uses the energy of energized electrons to pump protons from the stroma to the thylakoid lumen. A proton with no electron is a hydrogen ion.

20. C

During aerobic respiration, glucose is completely oxidized to produce 36 ATP per glucose molecule. Anaerobic respiration is incomplete and produces only two ATP per glucose molecule.
Both processes begin with the splitting of glucose. Only anaerobic respiration by yeast can produce alcohol. Aerobic respiration has many steps because of the slow oxidation of glucose.
This prevents an excessive amount of heat energy from being released at once.

1.

a) *At approximately what wavelength of light is the rate of photosynthesis the highest?*

The highest *y*-value of the line as graphed lies at approximately 430 nm.

b) *What colour of the spectrum is found between 520 nm and 565 nm?*

Wavelengths between 520 nm and 565 nm fall in the middle of the color spectrum which corresponds to green color.

c) *Explain the relationship between the colour of the light and the relative rate of photosynthesis.*

The graph indicates that photosynthesis occurs mostly in the presence of blue and red light. Very little photosynthesis occurs in the presence of green light. This observation can be verified by observing that chlorophyll pigment which is essential to photosynthesis, is green, meaning it reflects green wavelengths and does not absorb them.

d) *Propose a hypothesis to explain why the relative rate of photosynthesis differs drastically from one end of the visible light spectrum to the other.*

Although there is a range of effects between the extreme ends of the visible spectrum of light, the line of the graph is very high at the far left and very low at the far right. Shorter wavelengths outside of the visible spectrum seem to produce a much higher rate of photosynthetic activity in the plant being measured than longer wavelengths.

The shortest wavelengths outside of the visible spectrum are ultraviolet (UV) radiation. The longest wavelengths outside of the visible spectrum are infrared (IR) radiation.

Because shorter wavelengths tend to cause more photosynthetic activity, it is safe to hypothesize that radiation with a shorter wavelength contains more energy. Therefore, plants will grow and produce more effectively in ultraviolet radiation than in infrared radiation.

UNIT TEST—PHOTOSYNTHESIS AND CELLULAR RESPIRATION

1. During photosynthesis, energy is taken in as
   A. heat
   B. ATP
   C. light
   D. glucose

   Use the following information to answer the next question.

   > In the eighteenth century, Jan Ingenhousz performed a series of experiments in which he compared plants grown in light to plants kept in the dark.

2. With these experiments, Ingenhousz correctly discovered that plants in the light
   A. consume a lot of CO_2, and plants in the dark consume nothing
   B. produce a lot of O_2, and plants in the dark produce a bit of CO_2
   C. produce a lot of O_2, and plants in the dark produce nothing
   D. consume a lot of CO_2, as do plants in the dark

3. Where does the Calvin-Benson cycle occur?
   A. Stroma
   B. Thylakoid space
   C. Outside chloroplast
   D. Thylakoid membrane

4. Which stage of cellular respiration requires the input of energy as ATP?
   A. Glycolysis
   B. Krebs cycle
   C. Chemiosmosis
   D. Electron transport chain

   Use the following information to answer the next two questions.

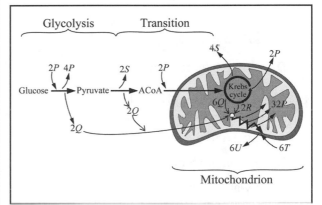

5. Which stage of cellular respiration occurs entirely outside the mitochondrion?
   A. Glycolysis
   B. Krebs cycle
   C. Transition reaction
   D. Electron transport system

6. Once the electrons and protons are picked up by the final electron acceptor, they are carried away as the waste product *U*, which is
   A. ATP
   B. water
   C. oxygen
   D. carbon dioxide

7. Which of the following statements about aerobic and anaerobic respiration is **true**?

A. Anaerobic respiration is less efficient than aerobic respiration.

B. Aerobic respiration is less efficient than anaerobic respiration.

C. Aerobic respiration requires less oxygen than anaerobic respiration.

D. Anaerobic respiration produces more energy than aerobic respiration.

8. Which of the following processes does **not** require ATP?

A. Osmosis

B. Phagocytosis

C. Active transport

D. Muscle contraction

9. The photosystems are made of proteins embedded in the

A. thylakoid membrane

B. stroma of chloroplasts

C. thylakoid lumen or space

D. space between the inner and outer mitochondrial membranes

10. Respiration is related to energy liberation, while photosynthesis is related to the process of energy

A. expulsion

B. absorption

C. dissipation

D. conduction

11. Which pathway is common to both aerobic and anaerobic respiration?

A. Glycolysis

B. Krebs cycle

C. Fermentation

D. Electron transport chain

12. Cardiac muscle produces very little lactic acid, so it can be assumed that cardiac muscle

A. uses little oxygen

B. lacks mitochondria

C. functions mainly aerobically

D. uses small amounts of glucose

13. The product of the light-dependent reaction needed to reduce carbon in the light-independent reaction is

A. CO_2

B. ATP

C. NAD

D. NADPH

Written Response

Use the following diagram to answer the next question.

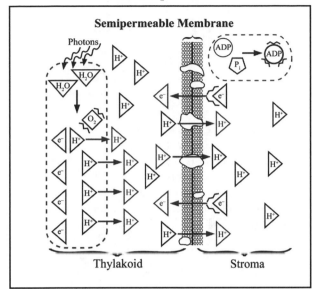

Semipermeable Membrane

Photons

Thylakoid   Stroma

1. **a)** Describe the processes that occur in the thylakoid and stroma during photosynthesis and how they relate to one another.

(2 marks)

b) What substance makes up the semipermeable membrane in the given diagram, and what properties does it have in relation to the transfer of energy in photosynthetic activity?

(2 marks)

c) Explain where a reduction of carbon is found in the photosynthetic process.

(2 marks)

ANSWERS AND SOLUTIONS—UNIT TEST

1. C	5. A	9. A	13. D
2. B	6. B	10. B	WR1. See solution
3. A	7. A	11. A	
4. A	8. A	12. C	

1. C

The following equation shows the photosynthesis reaction:

$$6CO_2 + 6H_2O + \text{solar energy}$$
(carbon dioxide)   (water)

$$\rightarrow C_6H_{12}O_6 + 6O_2$$
(glucose)   (oxygen)

Energy is required for photosynthesis to occur in chloroplasts. The energy is derived from sunlight. Glucose is a product of photosynthesis and is the form in which plants store energy. During cellular respiration, glucose is broken down into readily useable energy in the form of ATP. Heat is not used to fuel photosynthesis, although it is a form of energy. Heat energy is usually lost as a byproduct of energy conversions.

2. B

Photosynthesis consumes carbon dioxide and releases oxygen. Cell respiration consumes oxygen and releases carbon dioxide. Cell respiration occurs 24 hours a day. Photosynthesis (at least photolysis which releases oxygen) occurs only in the light. However, during the day, photosynthesis produces much more oxygen than cell respiration releases carbon dioxide. Plants in the dark consume oxygen and do not consume carbon dioxide.

3. A

The Calvin-Benson cycle occurs within the stroma. Structures associated with PS II, PS I, and the electron transport chains are located within the thylakoid membrane. Photolysis occurs within the thylakoid space.

4. A

All of the stages of cellular respiration release energy in the form of ATP. Glycolysis, however, requires the expenditure of two ATP per glucose molecule to accomplish the initial splitting of the glucose molecule. The resulting energy release provides 4ATP and 2NADH, which is a net energy gain overall.

5. A

From the diagram, it is obvious that the Krebs cycle and the electron transport chain occur within the mitochondrion. Glycolysis is the first set of reactions of cellular respiration. It occurs in the cytoplasm of a cell. During the transition reaction, pyruvate (the product of glycolysis) is transported across the mitochondrial membrane into the mitochondrion where it is converted into Acetyl-coA by the addition of coenzyme A.

6. B

After passing through the electron transport system, electrons and protons join oxygen to form water. Carbon dioxide is a waste product of the Krebs cycle and is not an electron acceptor. ATP is produced by respiration but could not be thought of as a waste product. Oxygen is consumed during respiration.

7. A

Aerobic respiration requires oxygen to produce energy, whereas anaerobic respiration does not. Because aerobic respiration produces more ATP molecules than anaerobic respiration, it is more efficient than anaerobic respiration.

8. A

ATP is required when a cell does work.
ATP is needed to move a molecule across a cell membrane by active transport or to move materials through the cell membrane by exocytosis. Muscle contraction requires large amounts of ATP energy.

Osmosis is the process in which water moves across a membrane from a region of high concentration to a region of lower concentration. Osmosis is an example of passive transport. It does not require energy in the form of ATP.

9. A

The photosystem proteins are found embedded in the thylakoid membrane.

10. B

Respiration is the process of energy liberation, while photosynthesis is the process of energy absorption. During photosynthesis, solar energy is absorbed and converted to the chemical energy of food. In cell respiration, the chemical energy of food is released as ATP and heat.

11. A

Glycolysis is the initial activation of glucose by ATP and its splitting into two PGAL molecules that are then converted to two PGA (pyruvate) molecules. This pathway is common to both aerobic and anaerobic respiration, although it is somewhat modified in anaerobic respiration. If oxygen is available, the respiratory pathway continues through the Krebs cycle and the electron transport chain. Fermentation occurs when no oxygen is available.

12. C

Lactic acid is produced when cells respire anaerobically. If little lactic acid is being produced, the cells must be respiring mainly aerobically. This means they must use significant amounts of oxygen. Most of aerobic respiration takes place in mitochondria.

13. D

The products of the light-dependent reaction are oxygen, NADPH, and ATP. While ATP energy is needed in the light-independent reaction, it does not carry out the reduction. It provides energy to drive the reduction, which is endergonic. The hydrogen for the reduction of carbon is provided by NADPH, which donates its hydrogen during the Calvin cycle. CO_2 is not the answer because even though it is required in the Calvin cycle, it does not provide reducing power, just missing carbon.

1. **a)** *Describe the processes that occur in the thylakoid and stroma during photosynthesis and how they relate to one another.*

The light-dependent reactions occur in the thylakoid. Here, the energy of sunlight is transferred to chloroplasts, electrons, and the other components of the photosystems, and it is captured into molecules of ATP. NADP is also reduced to NADPH in the thylakoid. The products of the light reaction, ATP and NADPH, leave the thylakoid and enter the stroma, where the light-independent reactions occur. Here, the Calvin-Benson cycle carries out carbon fixation. In this process, 5C RuBP, CO_2 from the stomata, hydrogen from oxidized NADPH, and energy from the splitting of ATP act together to create true carbohydrates (two 3C PGAL), which can form glucose.

b) *What substance makes up the semipermeable membrane in the given diagram, and what properties does it have in relation to the transfer of energy in photosynthetic activity?*

Semipermeable Membrane

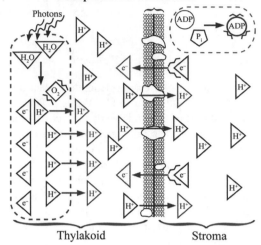

Thylakoid   Stroma

Two photosystems are embedded in the thylakoid membrane, which is the semipermeable membrane in the given diagram. Each photosystem contains chlorophyll molecules, which capture the energy of sunlight and use it to excite electrons. The photosystems also contain an electron transport chain made of protein carriers, such as NAD and FAD. The job of the ET chain is to extract energy from excited chlorophyll electrons and make ATP.

When chlorophyll molecules are hit with sunlight, excited electrons are passed from one ET chain protein carrier to the next. Each carrier extracts a little bit of energy from the excited electrons and uses it to actively transport a few H^+ ions into the thylakoid space. The point of this is to build up a large electrochemical gradient between the high concentration of H^+ inside the thylakoid lumen and the low H^+ outside the thylakoid . Sitting at the end of a photosystem is an enzyme called ATP synthase. When the concentration gradient between inside and outside becomes great, H^+ ions shoot through ATP synthase, which captures this energy into the high-energy bond that attaches ADP to P, forming ATP. This process of extracting energy from excited chlorophyll electrons and using it to make ATP is called chemiosmosis.

The nearly exhausted electrons are then taken up by $NADP^+$ to form NADPH. The two useful products of the light-dependent reactions (ATP and NADPH) move from the thylakoid to the stroma, where the light-independent reactions occur. NADPH provides hydrogen to reduce precursors to carbohydrates in the Calvin cycle. ATP provides energy to drive the reduction which will not occur without the application of significant energy.

The proteins that span the bilayer of the thylakoid membrane and make up the electron transport chain pump H^+ ions into the thylakoid. The ion gradient between the inside and the outside of the thylakoid is the source of energy that is used to make ATP when the H^+ ions flow through the ATP synthase complex during chemiosmosis.

c) *Explain where a reduction of carbon is found in the photosynthetic process.*

Reduction is the gain of electrons—in this case, hydrogen electrons. NADP is reduced to NADPH during the light-dependent reaction that occurs in the membrane of the thylakoids of chloroplasts. NADPH then enters the stroma of the chloroplast to take part in the light-independent reaction. Here, the Calvin cycle has already brought together 5C RuDP and 1C CO2 from the stomata to form a 6C molecule that splits to two 3C PGA molecules. These molecules are almost true carbohydrates but lack some hydrogen. At this point, NADPH enters the cycle and, powered by the splitting of ATP, donates its H to PGA, reducing PGA to PGAL—a true carbohydrate. NADP returns to the thylakoid where it will again be reduced to NADPH. Two 3C PGAL molecules will eventually join to form the final product, 6C glucose, which can be metabolized for energy in cell respiration, stored as starch, or converted to cellulose.

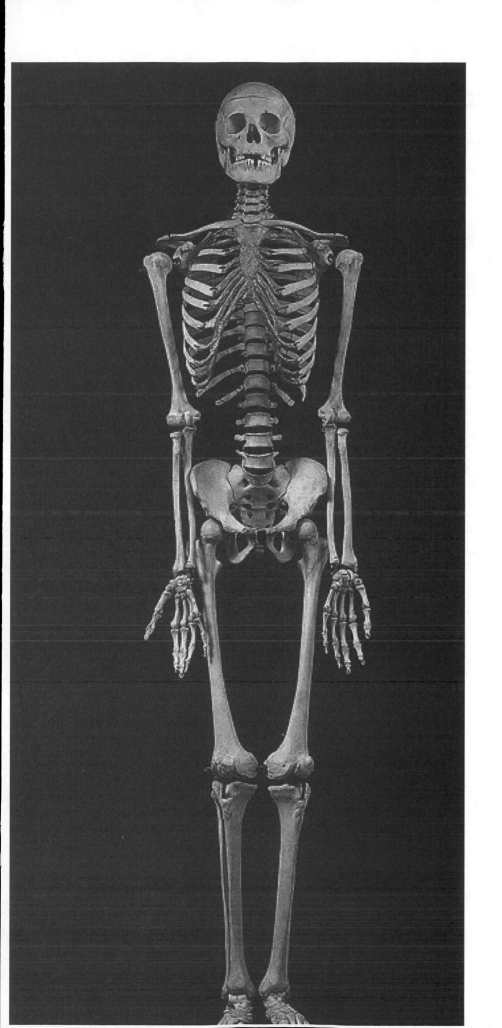

HUMAN SYSTEMS

Table of Correlations				
Specific Expectation	**Practice Questions**	**Unit Test Questions**	**Practice Test 1**	**Practice Test 2**
Students will:				
D1 *Explain how the human digestive and respiratory systems exchange energy and matter with the environment.*				
D1.1 identify the principal structures of the digestive and respiratory systems	5, 6, 7, 8, 13, 41	1	33	29, NR41
D1.2 describe the chemical nature of carbohydrates, lipids and proteins and their enzymes	9, 10, 11, 12, 14, 15, 16	2	36	46
D1.3 explain enzyme action and factors influencing their action	4, 22, WR2	3	32, 34, 35	25, 26, 27, 30
D1.4 describe the chemical and physical processing of matter through the digestive system into the circulatory system	1, 2, 3, 20, 21, NR1, 23, 24, 25	4	37, 38, 39	28, 31
D1.5 explain the exchange of matter and the transfer of thermal energy between the body and the environment, using the mechanism of breathing in gas exchange, removal of foreign material and heat loss	NR2, 27, 28, NR3, 46		NR47, NR48	
D2 *Explain the role of the circulatory and defence systems in maintaining an internal equilibrium.*				
D2.1 identify the principal structures of the heart and associated blood vessels; i.e., atria, ventricles, septa, valves, aorta, venae cavae, pulmonary arteries and veins, sinoatrial node, atrioventricular node, Purkinje fibres	30, 39	5, 10, 13	46	NR50
D2.2 describe the action of the heart, blood pressure and the general circulation of blood through coronary, pulmonary and systemic pathways	17, 26, 29, 33, WR1	6, 7	41, 44	36, 37, NR38, 39, 40
D2.3 describe the structure and function of blood vessels; i.e., arteries, veins and capillaries	31	8		32, 33, 34
D2.4 describe the main components of blood and their role in transport, clotting and resisting the influence of pathogens; i.e., plasma, erythrocytes, platelets, leucocytes	36, 37	9		45
D2.5 explain the role of the circulatory system at the capillary level in aiding the digestive, excretory, respiratory and motor systems' exchange of energy and matter with the environment	35, 40, 43, 44, 45	11, 12	13, 42, NR43, 45, 54	
D2.6 explain the role of blood in regulating body temperature	18			
D2.7 describe and explain, in general terms, the function of the lymphatic system	47		40	35
D2.8 list the main cellular and noncellular components of the human defence system and describe their role; i.e., skin, macrophage, helper T cell, B cell, killer T cell, suppressor T cell, memory T cell	32, 42, 48	20		43, 44, WR2
D2.9 describe the ABO and Rh blood groups on the basis of antigens and antibodies	34, 38		55	

D3	Explain the role of the excretory system in maintaining an internal equilibrium in humans through the exchange of energy and matter with the environment.				
D3.1	identify the principal structures in the excretory system; i.e., kidneys, ureters, urinary bladder, urethra	49	14		
D3.2	identify the major and associated structures of the nephron, including the glomerulus, Bowman's capsule, tubules, loop of Henle, collecting duct, afferent and efferent arterioles, and capillary net, and explain their function in maintaining plasma compositions	50, 51	15, 19	WR2 a, b	42, 48
D3.3	describe the function of the kidney in excreting metabolic wastes and expelling them into the environment	19, 53		49, 50, 51, WR2 c, d	
D3.4	identify the role of antidiuretic hormone (ADH) and aldosterone in water and sodium ion reabsorption, excretion and blood pressure regulation	52	18		
D4	Explain the role of the motor system in the function of other body systems.				
D4.1	explain how the motor system supports body functions (i.e., digestive, circulatory, respiratory, excretory and locomotory), referencing smooth, cardiac and striated muscle	54, 55	16	52, 53	47, WR1
D4.2	describe, in general, the action of actin and myosin in muscle contraction and heat production	56	17		

HUMAN SYSTEMS

D1.1   identify the principal structures of the digestive and respiratory systems

DIGESTION

The digestive tract is a very long tube adapted to provide the time and surface area for maximum extraction of nutrients. In the mouth, food is masticated (chewed) to increase its surface area and combined with saliva from **salivary glands**. Chewed food is moved through the **esophagus** by **peristalsis**, the rhythmic contraction of the smooth muscles around the digestive tube.

Digestive System

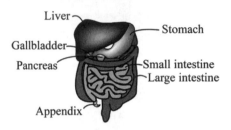

In the stomach, food is churned through muscular action. The chewing and churning of food to increase surface area is called **mechanical digestion**. While the food is being churned in the stomach and combined with digestive enzymes, the **cardiac sphincter**, at the top of the stomach, and the **pyloric sphincter**, at the bottom, remain closed. A **sphincter** is a valve that can be closed or opened to allow matter to pass through. Eventually, the pyloric sphincter opens to allow food to pass to the 7-metre long **small intestine**, where most **chemical digestion** occurs and absorption of digestive end products into the bloodstream occurs. The **liver** is outside of the gut. It secretes **bile**, which is stored in the **gallbladder** before being released through the common bile duct into the small intestine.

The **pancreas** releases pancreatic juice into the small intestine through the common bile duct. The wall of the small intestine also produces enzymes that combine with the food from the stomach, the secretions of the pancreas, and the bile from the liver. Once digestion is completed in the small intestine, the digestive end products are absorbed into the **villi**-lined walls of the small intestine and then into the bloodstream.

Indigestible cellulose (fibre) and water continue to the **large intestine** (large bowel, colon). The **appendix** is a vestigial pouch off the large intestine that sometimes becomes inflamed and can even burst. The large intestine is where water is absorbed into the bloodstream, certain vitamins are synthesized, and waste is prepared for egestion through the **rectum** and **anus**.

BREATHING

Pulmonary respiration is the exchange of O_2 and CO_2 between the body and the environment. It is not the same as cellular respiration, which is the burning of glucose with oxygen in the mitochondria of cells to produce ATP. The mechanism of **breathing** (inspiration and expiration) allows air to be brought into the lungs and then removed.

Nostrils are adapted for air passage by having sticky mucus, debris-trapping hairs, a scroll-like turbinate bone that warms incoming air, and an olfactory epithelium that senses the smell of airborne molecules. At the back of the throat, the **pharynx** leads to the trachea, which is covered by a flap-like **epiglottis** that prevents food from entering the air passages. The **trachea** leads to the **bronchi**, **bronchioles**, and eventually the grapelike clusters of **alveoli**. The trachea and bronchi are lined with smooth muscle that can dilate or constrict and are supported by rings of cartilage. The entire air passage is lined with mucus-secreting ciliated epithelium that traps debris and transports it upward to the throat.

Wanted: Designers Creators Inventors Thinkers Dreamers

Lead and succeed as part of a team

Bring new ideas to life

Build healthier, happier, safer communities

Solve challenging problems

Develop clean, sustainable energy sources

Fight poverty by developing affordable technology

Become an engineer.
Visit www.engineering.ualberta.ca

 UNIVERSITY OF ALBERTA

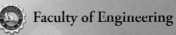 Faculty of Engineering

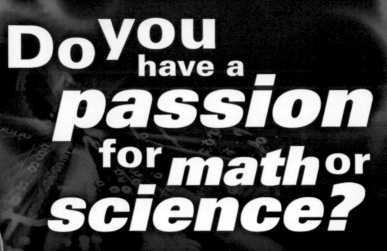

Do you have a passion for math or science?

PLAN A GREAT CAREER PATH IN TECHNOLOGY

What are the requirements? Visit:
www.aset.ab.ca/careers

ASET
The Association of Science and Engineering Technology Professionals of Alberta

Phone: 780.425.0626 Toll free within Alberta: 1.800.272.5619
or visit www.aset.ab.ca

The mechanism of breathing involves the creation of a vacuum in the lungs. Air is sucked into the lungs, not pushed in by positive pressure. Inspiration occurs when the medulla stimulates the external **intercostal muscles** to pull outward and the **diaphragm** to drop downward. Because the lungs are attached by pleural membranes to both these structures, the lungs are pulled downward and outward. The increase in the volume of the thoracic cavity creates a vacuum or negative pressure zone in the lungs. This causes air to be sucked into the trachea, filling the lungs. Expiration occurs passively as the diaphragm relaxes upward and the intercostal muscles relax inward.

The respiratory rate is normally between 14 and 20 breaths per minute. Increasing blood acidity (lowered pH) stimulates carotid and aortic chemoreceptors to signal the medulla to increase the breathing rate and increase the depth of breathing. Exercise lowers blood pH as CO_2 combines with water to form carbonic acid (H_2CO_3).

The volume of the lungs varies with gender, size, and fitness level. An average total lung capacity of 5 L gives the following values:

- The tidal volume (which is exchanged with each normal inhalation and exhalation) is about 0.5 L.

- The tidal volume (0.5 L) plus the inspiratory reserve volume (2.5 L) plus the expiratory reserve volume (1 L) equals the individual's vital capacity (4 L).

- The residual volume is the remaining 1.0 L of air that remains in the breathing passages after maximal expiration.

Gas exchange occurs in two places: in the lungs and in the tissues. In the lungs, branches of the bronchioles lead to clusters of thin-walled, grapelike alveoli where gas exchange occurs. Oxygen diffuses across the moist alveolar membrane into the blood, along its concentration gradient. There, the neutral pH, relatively cool temperature, high pO_2 and low pCO_2 produce the conditions in which hemoglobin in the red blood cells binds to oxygen, forming oxyhemoglobin ($HgbO_2$).

At the same time, the concentration and pressure gradient for carbon dioxide cause it to diffuse from the blood into the alveoli.

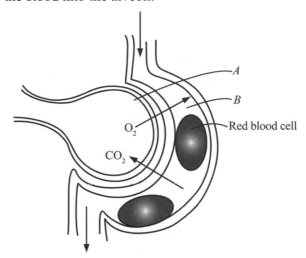

Oxygenated blood passes into the pulmonary veins, through the left side of the heart, then out the aorta to the arteries, arterioles, and finally the capillaries.

When blood reaches the capillaries, the second gas exchange occurs. The higher temperatures, low pH, low pO_2, and high pCO_2 of the tissues create the conditions that cause oxyhemoglobin to dissociate, releasing oxygen to the plasma. A combination of the pressure of the blood in the capillaries and the leakiness of the walls of the capillaries cause oxygen-rich plasma to flow into the tissues. The low oxygen concentrations in the tissues allow oxygen to then diffuse into the waiting respiring cells. The high CO_2 concentrations created by the rapidly respiring tissues cause the diffusion of CO_2 into the surrounding interstitial fluid. The waste-rich interstitial fluid will be returned to the capillaries by the osmotic pull of plasma proteins.

Returning CO_2 to the lungs through the venous system is problematic because CO_2 combines with water to produce carbonic acid, potentially causing a dangerous drop in the pH of the blood. For this reason, only 5% of the returning CO_2 is carried in solution in the plasma. Much of the CO_2 that needs to return to the lungs combines with haemoglobin to form carbaminohemoglobin ($HgbCO_2$), and is carried through the venous system in this way

The most common method CO_2 is returned to the lungs is as bicarbonate ion (HCO_3^-). In this method CO_2 and H_2O released from the tissues into the capillaries combine to form carbonic acid (H_2CO_3) which is split by the enzyme carbonic anhydrase into H^+ and HCO_3^-. These ions enter red blood cells. Here, the potentially dangerous H^+ is buffered by hemoglobin in the red blood cell cytoplasm, and the HCO_3^- (which contains the CO_2 molecule) is harmlessly dissolved in the red blood cell cytoplasm. In this way large amounts of CO_2 can be transported back to the lungs without dropping the pH of the blood. When the red blood cell reaches the lungs the process is reversed. H^+ and HCO_3^- recombine to form H_2CO_3 which splits into H_2O and CO_2. These waste products diffuse into the alveoli and are exhaled from the body.

Practice Questions: 5, 6, 7, 8, 13, 41

D1.2   describe the chemical nature of carbohydrates, lipids and proteins and their enzymes

KEY COMPOUNDS IN THE HUMAN BODY

All organic compounds are derived from glucose that was formed in photosynthesis. Most organic macromolecules that make up organisms are **polymers** made up of repeating subunits or **monomers**. The macromolecules of interest are carbohydrates, lipids, and proteins.

Carbohydrates are composed of carbon, hydrogen, and oxygen with a 2:1 ratio of hydrogen to oxygen. The monomer of carbohydrates is a **monosaccharide**. Large carbohydrate polymers are made of strings of monosaccharides. The monosaccharides are fructose, galactose, and glucose. Small carbohydrates (mono-, di-, and trisaccharides) are called sugars. The common disaccharides are sucrose, maltose, and lactose. Complex carbohydrates, or **polysaccharides**, include plant starch, cellulose, and animal glycogen.

Lipids (fats) are also made of carbon, hydrogen, and oxygen. Lipids are not polymers made of monomers. A **triglyceride** molecule consists of three **fatty acids** attached to a single glycerol molecule. The fewer double bonds there are in the fatty acids of a triglyceride, the more saturated the fat is. Saturated fats tend to be animal fats, while unsaturated fats are plant fats. Monounsaturated fats such as canola and olive oil have only one unsaturated bond and are recommended for health reasons. Phospholipids, which make up cell membranes, consist of two fatty acids attached to a glycerol and a phosphate group. Lipids have a very high hydrogen-to-carbon ratio, so they release large amounts of ATP energy when respired. Steroids are a group of lipids that are made of four carbon rings. They are the basis of cholesterol, all sex hormones, and hormones associated with the adrenal cortex.

Proteins are composed of nitrogen, carbon, hydrogen, and oxygen. Proteins are large, complex polymers made of monomers called **amino acids**. There are 20 different amino acids. The bond that holds one amino acid to another is called a **peptide bond**. A chain of amino acids is a **polypeptide**. Rearranging the sequence of amino acids in a polypeptide chain provides a nearly infinite variety of proteins. Once a polypeptide chain has been formed, it twists into a sequence-specific three-dimensional shape. It is this shape that determines the function that the protein performs.

Practice Questions: 9, 10, 11, 12, 14, 15, 16

D1.3   explain enzyme action and factors influencing their action

ENZYMES

Biological reactions rarely occur quickly. Each reaction has an **activation energy** that must be overcome before the reactants will combine to form products. Enzymes are three-dimensional proteins that are needed to speed up or **catalyze** chemical reactions in the body.

Structurally, every enzyme has a specific three-dimensional **binding site** that allows it to combine with the molecule it acts on, called its **substrate**. Because the substrate has a shape that is **complementary** to the enzyme, they fit together like a lock and key. When the two combine to form an **enzyme-substrate complex**, the activation energy of the reaction is lowered, and the reaction occurs immediately, releasing the products. The enzyme is released unchanged and can be used over and over.

One method of naming enzymes is to name the substrate and then add the suffix -*ase*. For example, lipase is a digestive enzyme that catalyzes the breakdown of a lipid into its components of three fatty acids and one glycerol. The combining of a lipase molecule and lipid molecule forms an enzyme-substrate complex that lowers the activation energy of the reaction. The products (three fatty acids and one glycerol) are formed immediately.

Extreme conditions (low or high pH, high temperature, salinity, heavy metals, electricity) can change the shape of an enzyme's binding site such that it can no longer combine with its substrate. This change in shape is called **denaturation**. For this reason, enzymes are very fragile and must be kept at conditions that are optimal. For example, the enzyme pepsin is a stomach protease that requires a pH of 1 to 3 and a temperature around 37°C. The enzyme trypsin is a protease in the small intestine that requires the same temperature but will only work at a basic pH of 8 to 9.

Substances can plug up the active site of an enzyme and prevent it from combining with its substrate, in turn preventing the reaction from occurring. Some of these **competitive inhibitors** are poisons, such as cyanide and heavy metals, but some are therapeutic drugs used to prevent a harmful enzyme from functioning.

Digestive enzymes are needed to catalyze the breakdown or **hydrolysis** of large macromolecules (proteins, lipids, carbohydrates, and nucleic acids) into their monomers. To accomplish hydrolysis, an enzyme must insert a water molecule into the bonds between the monomers. For example, a protease enzyme will physically combine with a polypeptide and insert a water molecule into the peptide bonds, breaking the polypeptide into individual amino acids, which can then be absorbed from the gut into the bloodstream. The enzyme molecule can be reused indefinitely, going on to combine with another protein molecule. Digestion of all foods then requires water and hydrolytic enzymes to occur.

Dehydration synthesis is the reverse and occurs when two smaller subunits are brought together to form a larger one. Dehydration refers to the removal of a water molecule from the connecting bond. Therefore, water is a product of all dehydration reactions.

Digestive enzymes fall into four categories: carbohydrases, lipases, proteases, and nucleases.

Carbohydrases digest polysaccharides into monosaccharides by introducing a water molecule into the bond between two monosaccharide units. Salivary amylase is secreted in the mouth and hydrolyzes starch to maltose at pH 7. Pancreatic amylase does the same job in the small intestine but requires a pH of 8 to 9.

Lipases hydrolyze triglyceride molecules by introducing a water molecule into each of the bonds between the glycerol molecule and the three fatty acid chains of a triglyceride. Lipases are secreted from the pancreas into the small intestine and require a basic pH of 8 to 9.

Proteases hydrolyze proteins by inserting a water molecule into the peptide bond between amino acids. Proteases are secreted in the stomach (pH 2) and in the small intestine (pH 8 to 9).

Nucleases hydrolyze DNA and RNA into their component nucleotides. This process is similar to protein hydrolysis.

Practice Questions: 4, 22, WR2

D1.4   describe the chemical and physical processing of matter through the digestive system into the circulatory system

DIGESTION AND ABSORPTION

Digestion is divided into a mechanical and chemical component. **Mechanical digestion** increases the surface area available for enzyme action. It includes chewing and the mixing actions of the gut that are powered by the ripple-like smooth muscle contractions of **peristalsis**. **Chemical digestion** refers to enzyme-catalyzed hydrolysis of macromolecules into monomers that are small enough to be absorbed into the bloodstream.

In the mouth, food is chewed to increase its surface area and combined with saliva from **salivary glands**. The enzyme salivary amylase acts in the neutral pH environment of the mouth to convert starch to the disaccharide maltose. Chewed food is moved by peristalsis through the **esophagus** to the bag-like stomach. Gastric juice, which is secreted from the gastric glands of the stomach, contains HCl, pepsinogen, and mucus. The acidity of HCl (pH 1 to 3) sterilizes food, denatures proteins, and activates inactive pepsinogen into the active protein-digesting enzyme pepsin.

Mucus prevents the digestion of the stomach walls. While the food is being churned in the stomach, the **cardiac sphincter** (at the top of the stomach) and the **pyloric sphincter** (at the bottom) remain closed. A **sphincter** is a smooth muscle valve that can be closed or opened to allow matter to pass through. After about three hours, protein is in peptide form, and the pyloric sphincter opens to allow food to pass to the **small intestine**.

Most **chemical digestion** and all absorption of digestive end products into the bloodstream occur in the small intestine. The partially digested food from the stomach and the secretions from the walls of the small intestine, the liver, and the pancreas all meet in the small intestine.

The walls of the intestine secrete disaccharidases and proteases. The **liver** secretes **bile**, which is stored in the **gallbladder** before being released into the small intestine through the common bile duct. Bile is not an enzyme—it emulsifies fat, increasing its surface area for lipase action. The **pancreas** releases pancreatic juice into the small intestine through the common bile duct. **Pancreatic juice** consists of an amylase, a lipase, several proteases, and sodium bicarbonate, which provides the small intestine with the basic pH (8 to 9) needed for its enzymes to function. Near the end of the small intestine, digestion is complete.

Absorption occurs when the digestive end products (monosaccharides, amino acids, fatty acids, and glycerol) cross by diffusion through the walls of the small intestine into the bloodstream. The small intestine is lined with projections called **villi** that resemble brush bristles and serve to increase the surface area for absorption. Each villus is covered with microvilli, which increase the surface area for absorption even further. Villi are supplied with blood and lymph vessels that carry absorbed digestive end products to the body's cells.

Indigestible cellulose (fibre) and water continue into the large intestine. Here, water is finally absorbed into the bloodstream, and vitamins are synthesized by *E. coli* and other bacterial flora. The indigestible cellulose is propelled through the muscular rectum for **egestion** out the anus.

Control of digestion is both nervous and hormonal. The sight, smell, and anticipation of food cause the brain to send impulses to the stomach that cause the release of gastric juice. In addition, the presence of protein in the stomach causes cells in the stomach lining to secrete the hormone **gastrin** into the bloodstream. Gastrin causes the gastric glands to secrete gastric juice.

Practice Questions: 1, 2, 3, 20, 21, NR1, 23, 24, 25

D1.5 explain the exchange of matter and the transfer of thermal energy between the body and the environment, using the mechanisms of breathing in gas exchange, removal of foreign material, and heat loss

MATTER EXCHANGE AND THE HUMAN BODY

The human body is constantly interacting with its environment to supply the basic needs of life. Most matter is brought into the body by the digestive system in the form of food. There is a difference between food **ingestion** and nutrition, however, in that nutrients represent the portion of food material that the human body is able to absorb and use in cell metabolism. For a **nutrient** to be usable, it must first be able to pass through the wall of the digestive tract and enter the bloodstream. Digestive enzymes assist in the hydrolysis of large macromolecules into monomers that are small enough to be absorbed. The absorbed nutrients can either be used as an immediate **catabolic** energy source for cell respiration or be used for **anabolism**, the process of building large molecules such as muscle or bone. Some material will remain undigested or unabsorbed and will simply pass through the digestive system and be eliminated as feces in **egestion**.

The kidney eliminates soluble wastes and toxins that would otherwise collect in the bloodstream. When excess amino acids accumulate, the liver **deaminates** them, creating the toxic waste **urea**. The filtering processes of the kidneys remove urea from the blood and excrete it in the urine.

Breathing permits the transfer of oxygen from the environment into the bloodstream and the transfer of carbon dioxide in the reverse direction. Significant amounts of water and heat are also lost through exhalation.

Heat is produced in the mitochondria of each cell when glucose is burned in cell respiration. Blood flow distributes heat from the hotter core to the cooler extremities and skin. A drop in blood temperature drastically lowers the rate of all metabolic reactions and the functioning of enzymes. Heat is lost through radiation, conduction, and convection acting on the skin.

If body temperature falls, voluntary muscle contraction (exercise) can be used to produce heat. Involuntary muscle contraction (shivering) is a homeostatic heat-producing response. Shunting of blood from the skin to the core helps retain heat. Heat loss is further reduced by insulating fat layers and hair or fur. A rise in blood temperature puts enzymes in danger of denaturation, potentially stopping metabolic reactions. Involuntary homeostatic mechanisms such as shunting of blood from the core to the skin will allow more heat to be dissipated. Perspiration moves water and dissolved salts from the blood onto the surface of the skin. Because water has a high heat capacity, a great deal of heat from the skin is used to evaporate the water, leaving the skin cooler. Unfortunately, perspiration can dehydrate the blood and rob it of salts that contribute to the osmotic balance of the blood.

Practice Questions: NR2, 27, 28, NR3, 46

D2.1 identify the principal structures of the heart and associated blood vessels; i.e., atria, ventricles, septa, valves, aorta, venae cavae, pulmonary arteries and veins, sinoatrial node, atrioventricular node, Purkinje fibres

D2.2 describe the action of the heart, blood pressure and the general circulation of blood through coronary, pulmonary and systemic pathways

CIRCULATION

The right side of the heart collects **deoxygenated** blood from the body and pumps it to the lungs. The left side of the heart collects **oxygenated** blood from the lungs and pumps it to the body's organs.

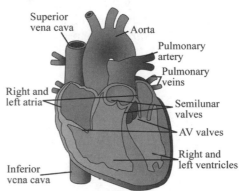

Each side of the heart has two chambers: a stretchy **atrium** that gathers blood into the heart and a thick-walled **ventricle** that pumps blood out of the heart. Separating the two sides is the **septum**. Blood travels the following pathway through the heart: right atrium, tricuspid valve, right ventricle, pulmonary semilunar valve, pulmonary artery, lungs, pulmonary veins, left atrium, bicuspid valve, left ventricle, aortic semilunar valve, and aorta.

First, deoxygenated blood from the tissues enters the **right atrium** from the superior and inferior vena cava. The atrial walls contract and move the blood through the one-way right **atrioventricular valve (tricuspid valve)** into the right ventricle.

The muscular wall of the right ventricle contracts, which pushes blood up against the flaps of the tricuspid valve. This prevents blood from reentering the right atrium. Blood is pushed through the **pulmonary semilunar valve** to the **pulmonary artery**, which transports the deoxygenated blood to the lungs. When the ventricle relaxes, blood in the pulmonary artery tends to fall back into the ventricle. This is prevented by the cups of the semilunar pulmonary valve that snap open to prevent backflow from occurring.

After oxygenation in the lungs, blood returns to the left side of the heart through the **pulmonary veins** to the **left atrium**. The left atrium contracts, pushing blood through the left atrioventricular valve (bicuspid or mitral valve) and into the **left ventricle**. The ventricle then contracts, pushing blood up against the flaps of the bicuspid valve and preventing backflow into the atrium. Blood flows through the **aortic pulmonary valve** into the **aorta** and out of the heart into the systemic system. Backflow from the aorta into the left atrium is captured by the opening of the cups of the aortic valve. Note that both atria contract together, and both ventricles contract together.

Heart sounds (lubb-dubb … pause … lubb-dubb … pause …) heard through a stethoscope are the sounds of the heart valves. *Lubb* is the sound of the cusps of the atrioventricular (AV) valves snapping closed when the ventricles contract. *Dubb* is the sound of the pulmonary and aortic semilunar valves snapping open when blood attempts to backflow into the heart after ventricular contraction.

The passage of an electrical impulse through the heart allows it to contract. The heart structures that make this possible are the **sinoatrial node** (SA node), the **atrioventricular node** (AV node), and the Purkinje fibres.

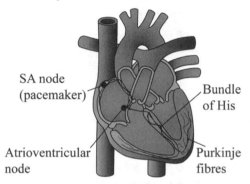

The SA node is often called the **pacemaker** of the heart, since it is independently able to generate nervous signals to get the heart to contract without any other nervous connection. It is located in the wall of the right atrium, and when it fires, it causes the muscles of the atria to contract and squeeze blood into each ventricle through the atrioventricular valves.

The SA signal reaches the **atrioventricular node** (AV node) located in the septum. It passes down the septum and up the sides of the ventricle through the **Purkinje** fibres. The ventricles now contract, starting from the bottom and squeezing the blood upward and out the semilunar valves. This sequence occurs on average 72 times per minute. The passage of an electrical impulse through the heart can be visualized using an electrocardiogram (ECG).

Heart rate is controlled by chemoreceptors and baroreceptors in the aorta, carotid artery, and medulla. When blood CO_2 increases and pH falls, these chemoreceptors cause the heart rate to rise. Baroreceptors sense extremely high blood pressures and cause a drop in heart rate.

Blood pressure is the pressure the blood exerts on the walls of a blood vessel. It is measured with a **sphygmomanometer** and recorded in millimetres of mercury (mmHg). Two measurements are taken when blood pressure is recorded: systolic blood pressure and diastolic blood pressure. **Systolic** blood pressure represents the maximum pressure within an artery. It is produced when the heart is in systole, or ventricular contraction. Systolic blood pressure is typically 120 mmHg. **Diastolic** blood pressure is the pressure in the artery during diastole, when the ventricles are at rest. Diastolic blood pressure is typically 80 mmHg. Blood pressure is reported as a ratio of systolic blood pressure over diastolic blood pressure—normal being 120/80. Continuous high blood pressure (over 140/90) is called **hypertension** and can be caused by partial blockage of arteries (atherosclerosis), stress, stimulant drugs, and obesity. Hypertension is a risk factor for heart attack and stroke.

The circulatory system can be divided into three different systems or circuits. The **pulmonary circulatory system** includes the pulmonary arteries that bring deoxygenated blood from the heart to the lungs, the capillaries that carry out gas exchange between the blood and lungs, and the pulmonary veins that return oxygenated blood back to the heart.

The **coronary circulatory system** consists of the blood vessels that supply the heart muscle itself. Coronary arteries branch off the aorta and spread over the surface of the heart, subdividing into many smaller coronary vessels. Each provides oxygen and nutrients particularly to the ventricles, allowing them to continue contracting without rest. The coronary vein recycles deoxygenated blood from the heart muscle to the right atrium.

A blockage in a branch of the coronary arteries due to atherosclerosis interrupts the flow of oxygen and nutrients to the heart muscle. The result is a **heart attack** or myocardial infarction. The portion of the heart deprived of oxygen and nutrients stops contracting and dies.

The **systemic circulatory system** supplies the tissues of the body. The pathway of the systemic circuit runs from the aorta to the arteries, arterioles, capillaries, venules, veins, superior and inferior vena cavae, and back to the right ventricle.

Practice Questions: 17, 26, 29, 33, WR1

D2.3   describe the structure and function of blood vessels; i.e., arteries, veins, and capillaries

BLOOD VESSELS

The circulatory system is a network of blood vessels, including arteries, veins, capillaries, and lymph vessels.

Arteries have thick, flexible, very muscular walls and carry blood away from the heart. All arteries except the pulmonary artery carry oxygenated blood. Vasoconstriction and vasodilation of arteries allow blood to be sent to various body parts depending on the priority at the moment.

Veins have thin walls and one-way semilunar valves to ensure that blood only flows back toward the heart. Most venous flow is against gravity, so blood moves through veins primarily because of skeletal muscles squeezing on the veins.

Capillaries are very tiny, porous vessels forming a web among tissue cells. This high surface area is necessary, since this is the site of exchange of nutrients and gases between blood and the tissues. The diameter of a capillary is slightly wider than one red blood cell. This serves to slow the flow of blood and enhance the diffusion of oxygen and nutrients out of the bloodstream and the return of carbon dioxide and wastes back to the bloodstream. Once wastes are returned to the capillaries, the venous system returns the deoxygenated blood back to the heart and lungs.

By opening and closing pre-capillary sphincters, blood can be shunted from one capillary bed to the other depending on need. Opening all capillary beds simultaneously drops blood pressure drastically and leads to shock.

Practice Question: 31

D2.4   describe the main components of blood and their role in transport, clotting and resisting the influence of pathogens; i.e., plasma, erythrocytes, platelets, leukocytes

THE BLOOD

Blood volume is approximately 4 to 5 L. Blood is mostly composed of straw-coloured **plasma**, made of water, dissolved ions (electrolytes), urea, and plasma proteins such as clotting proteins, antibodies, and albumin. Suspended in the plasma are three kinds of blood cells: erythrocytes, thrombocytes, and leukocytes. They are all formed in the bone marrow.

Erythrocytes (red blood cells) are by far the most numerous and appear as biconcave discs. They contain the protein **hemoglobin**, which transports oxygen to the tissues and carbon dioxide to the lungs. Red blood cell production is stimulated by the hormone **erythropoietin**, which is secreted by the kidney when blood oxygen is low, as in anemia or exposure to high altitudes.

Thrombocytes (platelets) are thin-walled cell fragments that initiate blood clotting. When a blood vessel is cut, platelets rupture on the rough edges of the vessel. This releases an enzyme that starts a cascade of chemical reactions, leading to the formation of a clot. The soluble blood protein **fibrinogen** is converted to the insoluble protein **fibrin**. Fibrin forms as sticky threads that cling to the cut vessel edges, forming a clot that blocks the flow of blood. The clotting sequence is dependent on the presence of calcium ions (Ca^{2+}) in the blood.

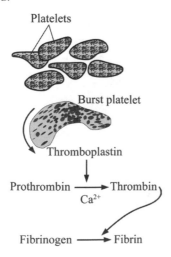

Leukocytes (white blood cells) have large nuclei and form the body's immune system, protecting the body from disease.

Practice Questions: 36, 37

D2.5   explain the role of the circulatory system at the capillary level in aiding the digestive, excretory, respiratory and motor systems' exchange of energy and matter with the environment

FLUID EXCHANGE IN CAPILLARIES

Capillaries branch out into the tissues in a fine network where no cell is more than two cells away from a capillary. The fluid around the cells is called **interstitial fluid**. Nutrients and oxygen must diffuse from the blood into the interstitial fluid and then into the waiting cells. CO_2 must do the reverse.

The mechanism for fluid exchange at the capillary is complex and depends on the osmotic gradient created by plasma proteins in the blood. At the beginning (arteriolar end) of a capillary bed, blood pressure is higher than the pressure of the fluids in the tissues. Blood plasma (minus the large plasma proteins) leaks out of the porous capillaries and bathes the cells in the surrounding tissues with oxygen and other nutrients. When the plasma leaks out, it is now referred to as interstitial fluid. The interstitial fluid is also able to accept CO_2 and waste products diffusing from the cells. Interstitial fluid containing these wastes is pulled back into the venous end of the capillary by the osmotic pull created by plasma proteins in the blood. Without adequate plasma proteins in the blood (as in starvation), wastes and fluid cannot be returned to the bloodstream, and fluid accumulates in the tissues, causing swelling. If any interstitial fluid does build up in the tissues, it is returned to the bloodstream through lymph vessels.

Practice Questions: 35, 40, 43, 44, 45

D2.6   explain the role of blood in regulating body temperature

THE ROLE OF BLOOD IN TEMPERATURE REGULATION

Human tissues and organs function at an internal temperature between 36.1 and 37.5°C. This temperature range is crucial for the functioning of enzymes. While a drop in body temperature seems to be less problematic, a significant rise in body temperature (as seen in fever) can denature proteins and result in death.

Blood flow is necessary for the distribution of heat throughout the body. Those parts of the body that are rapidly respiring (such as muscles and organs) produce heat. Those parts of the body that are not actively respiring (such as skin, hands, and feet) rely on blood flow from the muscles and organs to bring heat to them.

When environmental temperatures rise or fall, the body uses a system of priority **shunting** to minimize the loss of heat in cold temperatures and to maximize the loss of heat in hot temperatures. In cold conditions, the blood vessels of the periphery (skin and body surface) constrict, and those of the core dilate, preventing heat loss by radiation and convection. In hot conditions, the reverse occurs as the body attempts to rid itself of extra heat. The blood vessels of the core constrict, and vessels in the periphery dilate, increasing blood flow to the surface. This turns the skin red and increases heat loss to the environment by radiation and convection.

Practice Question: 18

D2.7   describe and explain, in general terms, the function of the lymphatic system

THE LYMPHATIC SYSTEM

Excess interstitial fluid could build up in all tissues causing swelling or edema if it were not for the actions of the **lymphatic system**. Lymph vessels lie parallel to blood vessels and serve as the body's drainage ditches by picking up dead cells, bacteria, and fluid that have accumulated in tissue spaces. The fluid is screened by lymph nodes and returned to the bloodstream through major veins.

Lymphoid tissue in lymph nodes removes pathogens from the bloodstream. Lymphoid tissue elsewhere in the body contributes to the formation of immune cells known as lymphocytes and is involved in the formation of antibodies.

Practice Question: 47

D2.8   list the main cellular and non-cellular components of the human defence system and describe their role; i.e., skin, macrophage, helper T cell, B cell, killer T cell, suppressor T cell, memory T cell

THE IMMUNE SYSTEM

The human immune system is complex, but all white blood cells (leukocytes) have a role to play. Non-cellular defences prevent pathogens from gaining access to the body. The unbroken barrier of skin has the biggest role in preventing entry of pathogens. The sticky mucus lining of the breathing passages traps pathogens to protect the lungs. Hydrochloric acid in the stomach protects the gastrointestinal tract from infection.

When bacteria or viruses that cause disease do enter the body, various kinds of white blood cells respond. White blood cells called **macrophages** phagocytose some invaders and destroy them. **Killer T cells** destroy any of the body's own cells that have been taken over by viruses. **Helper T cells** detect the antigen (recognizable part of the invader) and instruct **B cells** to make **antibodies** (proteins that destroy invaders with that antigen). When the battle against the pathogen has been won, **suppressor T cells** shut down the immune response. **Memory T cells** retain a record of the antigen for future reference.

A second exposure to the same pathogen will result in a much faster and much stronger production of antibodies, such that the person may be unaware of the attack.

Practice Questions: 32, 42, 48

D2.9 describe the ABO and Rh blood groups on the basis of antigens and antibodies

BLOOD TYPES

Red blood cell membranes have marker proteins called **antigens** embedded in the membrane surface. In terms of ABO antigens, an individual can have A, B, both, or neither antigen.

- If A antigens are present, then the blood is type A.
- If B antigens are present, then the blood is type B.
- If both A and B antigens are present, then the blood is type AB.
- If no antigens are present, then the blood is type O.

If foreign antigens are introduced into the body in the form of an incompatible blood transfusion, the body's defence mechanisms are mobilized. Antibodies attach to the foreign antigen, inactivating it. This antigen-antibody reaction causes the blood to clump (agglutinate). If agglutination occurs on a large scale, blood will stop flowing and death can occur. For this reason it is important for the donor's and recipient's blood to be matched prior to a transfusion

A person with type A blood has A antigens but also has antibodies against B (anti-B antibodies). If type B blood were to be transfused into the bloodstream, the anti-B antibodies would attack the foreign B antigens causing clumping. Those with blood type B have B antigens and anti-A antibodies. Those with O blood are called universal donors because they have no antigens that can cause trouble in a recipient. Those with AB blood are universal recipients. They have both antigens but do not have any antibodies. Because they have no antibodies, any antigens can be transfused into them without fear of an antigen-antibody reaction.

The Rh (Rhesus) factor is another blood antigen present on the red blood cells of some people. Those with the Rhesus antigen are Rh^+; those without it are Rh^-. If an individual with Rh^- blood were to receive a transfusion from an Rh^+ donor, their anti-Rh antibodies would agglutinate the blood. Transfusing with Rh^- blood is therefore safe.

Practice Questions: 34, 38

D3.1 identify the principal structures in the excretory system; i.e., kidneys, ureters, urinary bladder, urethra

EXCRETORY SYSTEM

Excretion is the process of the elimination of wastes produced by **cellular metabolism**. **Lungs** are excretory organs because they excrete carbon dioxide. The **sweat glands** in the skin excrete a variety of salts and water. The main excretory organ is the kidney. Each kidney receives a continuous supply of blood through a renal artery and excretes the wastes as urine. The most toxic waste in urine is the yellow **urea** produced when excess amino acids in the diet are deaminated by the liver. If urea is not removed from the blood, death will occur.

The kidney itself is made of millions of functional units called **nephrons** whose main purpose is to remove urea while balancing the amount of electrolytes (ions) and water remaining in the blood.

Urine empties from the collecting duct of each nephron into the renal pelvis of each kidney. From there, urine enters the ureters, which drain into the bladder. Sphincters at the base of the bladder control when urine is released out of the urethra into the external environment.

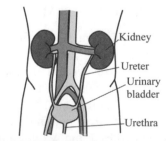

Practice Question: 49

Class Focus 100 Castle Rock Research

D3.2   identify the major and associated structures of the nephron, including the glomerulus, Bowman's capsule, tubules, loop of Henle, collecting duct, afferent and efferent arterioles, and capillary net, and explain their function in maintaining plasma compositions

THE NEPHRON

Urine follows this path through the nephron: Bowman's capsule, proximal tubule, loop of Henle, distal tubule, and collecting duct.

Each nephron is supplied with a blood vessel known as the **afferent arteriole** that contains blood that must be cleaned of toxic urea and excess substances.

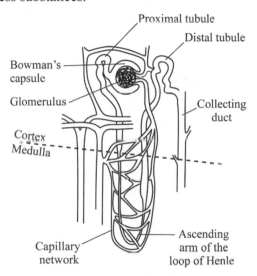

Formation of urine involves three steps: filtration, reabsorption, and secretion. In **filtration**, the urea-rich afferent arteriole curls into a **glomerulus** that sits like a nest in the sieve-like cup of the nephron's **Bowman's capsule**. The capsule allows water-soluble substances from the glomerulus, such as water, urea, nutrients, and ions, to pass through into the **proximal tubule** of the nephron, but it does not allow blood cells or large proteins to pass. These large substances remain in the **efferent arteriole** that leads out of the glomerulus and continues as a **capillary net** that wraps around the nephron tubules. The proximity of the capillary net to the nephron tubules will allow substances to be reabsorbed from the tubules back into the blood if necessary.

After filtration, the urine found in the proximal tubule contains urea and other substances that should be excreted. It also contains small molecules such as nutrients (amino acids, glucose, and so on), ions, and large volumes of water that are all far too valuable to be excreted in the urine. Because of this, the proximal tubule and the loop of Henle are involved in the second job of the nephron, which is reabsorption.

In **reabsorption**, nutrients are actively transported from the proximal tubule back into the efferent arteriole, making the arteriole very hypertonic. This creates an osmotic gradient that draws water from the proximal tubule back into the bloodstream by osmosis. Even more water is absorbed back into the bloodstream as urine moves through the descending **loop of Henle**. The salty tissue around the loop acts osmotically to pull more water out of the nephron, reabsorbing it back into the bloodstream. Sodium is actively transported from the ascending loop back out to the tissues to keep it salty. As the urine passes through the distal tubule and collecting duct nephron, it continues to become more and more concentrated as more water is reabsorbed from the urine into the bloodstream.

The third job of the nephron is **tubular secretion**, in which the efferent arteriole has a last opportunity to actively secrete into the urine any wastes, urea, and drugs that did not get filtered out in the Bowman's capsule. Once past the collecting the urine flows into the renal pelvis, ureter, bladder, and urethra.

Practice Questions: 50, 51

D3.3   describe the function of the kidney in excreting metabolic wastes and expelling them into the environment

THE ROLE OF THE KIDNEYS

The kidney is responsible for controlling the composition of the blood. Urea, the yellow, nitrogenous waste product produced by deamination of excess amino acids is removed from the blood. The kidney also maintains homeostatic levels of water, pH, and ions, as well as excreting hormones and drug metabolites. It controls blood volume and thus blood pressure, as well as sensing and controlling the production of red blood cells in the bone marrow. The pair of kidneys in a human body can process as much as 25% of its blood supply in one hour.

When kidneys fail, the technology of dialysis is employed to clean the blood. Blood from a patient with kidney failure is passed through a semipermeable tube surrounded by dialyzing fluid. The dialyzing fluid contains low concentrations of those substances that should be removed from the blood. As the blood passes through the semipermeable tubing, diffusion removes those substances that are harmful. Because the process of diffusion is slow and concentration gradients of the dialyzing fluid must be continually modified, the process of dialysis is long and must be repeated a few times a week.

Practice Questions: 19, 53

D3.4   identify the role of antidiuretic hormone (ADH) and aldosterone in water and sodium ion reabsorption, excretion and blood pressure regulation

THE ROLE OF HORMONES IN HYDRATION AND BLOOD PRESSURE REGULATION

The water concentration of blood is regulated by the antidiuretic hormone (ADH), which is produced by the **hypothalamus** of the brain and secreted from the posterior pituitary gland. If blood is too concentrated, perhaps due to excessive perspiration, thirst, vomiting, or diarrhea, ADH is released, causing the collecting ducts to become more permeable to water. As a

result, more water is reabsorbed into the blood from the collecting ducts, making the blood more dilute. If the volume of blood or blood pressure is too low (perhaps due to hemorrhage, extreme dehydration, or lack of salt), the hormone **aldosterone** is released from the adrenal gland. Aldosterone stimulates the nephron to actively transport more salt (Na^+) back to the blood from the proximal tubule. As a result, the osmosis of water from the distal tubule to the blood increases. This increases blood volume and thus blood pressure without altering blood concentration.

Practice Question: 52

D4.1   explain how the motor system supports body functions (i.e., digestive, circulatory, respiratory, excretory and locomotory), referencing smooth, cardiac, and striated muscle

MUSCLE SYSTEMS

There are three types of muscles in the human body: cardiac, smooth, and striated.

Cardiac muscle makes up the heart and is involuntary muscle.

Smooth (circular) muscles surround tubular organs but are not under voluntary control. The smooth muscle of the digestive tract contracts in waves, resulting in peristalsis. Sphincters that regulate the flow of food through the gut are also made of smooth muscle. The smooth muscle that lines arteries and arterioles allows vasoconstriction and vasodilation to occur. The trachea, bronchi, and bronchioles are lined with smooth muscle that can constrict or relax in response to the need for oxygen. The smooth muscle that lines the bladder and forms the sphincters of the urethra controls the release of urine through the urethra.

Striated (skeletal) muscle accomplishes locomotion. Typically, skeletal muscles attach across joints and, under voluntary control, are able to move the skeleton. Skeletal muscle cells are called **muscle fibres**. Each muscle fibre extends the length of a muscle and contains hundreds of nuclei and many mitochondria for ATP production. Each muscle fibre is made up of a bundle of straw-like parallel filaments called **myofibrils**.

Practice Questions: 54, 55

D4.2   describe, in general, the action of actin and myosin in muscle contraction and heat production

ACTIN AND MYOSIN

Myofibrils are broken up into repeating units called sarcomeres. Each sarcomere contains two types of protein filaments—**myosin** (thick filaments) and **actin** (thin filaments). When a muscle fibre is stimulated by a nerve, calcium ions flood into the cell and cause the actin and myosin to slide past each other, thereby shortening or contracting the myofibril. Paddle-like heads on myosin filaments form cross-bridges with actin, keeping the sarcomere contracted. The overlapping of actin and myosin filaments creates the striped or striated appearance of skeletal muscle.

The process of muscle contraction consumes ATP and produces carbon dioxide, water, and heat as long as oxygen is available for aerobic cell respiration. If oxygen cannot be supplied by the lungs and heart rapidly enough, alternate methods of producing energy are used. Creatine phosphate is a molecule similar to ATP. When ATP production is too slow, creatine phosphate splits, releasing the energy from its high-energy bond. When creatine phosphate is exhausted, anaerobic respiration begins. Under anaerobic conditions, little ATP is produced, and lactic acid and heat are produced as waste products.

Anaerobic respiration can only be sustained for short periods because the acidity of lactic acid fatigues the muscle. At this point, contraction stops. Any toxic lactic acid accumulated must be converted to glycogen—a process that requires significant ATP. Therefore, after strenuous exercise, an individual will continue to breathe rapidly in order to produce enough ATP for the conversion. This is referred to as making up the **oxygen debt**.

Each motor nerve innervates a certain number of myofibrils. The nerve and the myofibrils it innervates make up a **motor unit**. The greater the number of motor units that fire, the greater the strength of muscle contraction. Muscles capable of fine movement have small motor units.

Contracted myofibril

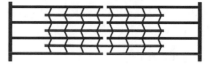

Relaxed myofibril

Actin   Myosin

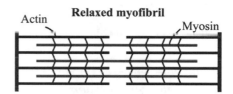

Practice Question: 56

PRACTICE QUESTIONS—HUMAN SYSTEMS

1. Prior to absorption, true fats are emulsified in the digestive tract by
   A. bile
   B. renin
   C. lipases
   D. hydrochloric acid

Use the following reaction to answer the next question.

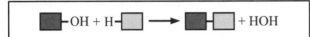

2. The illustrated reaction depicts the process of
   A. hydrolysis
   B. neutralization
   C. catalyst formation
   D. dehydration synthesis

Use the following graphic to answer the next question.

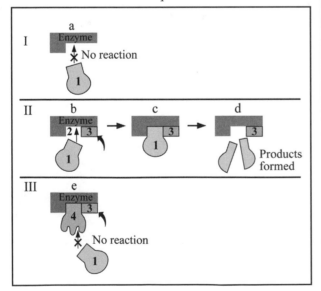

3. The process illustrated in sequence II could be
   A. an anabolic reaction
   B. the emulsification of a fat
   C. the hydrolysis of a disaccharide
   D. the dehydration synthesis of a dipeptide

Use the following diagram to answer the next question.

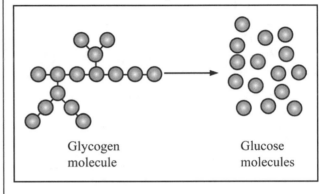

4. Two terms that describe the process shown in the diagram are
   A. hydrolysis and anabolism
   B. hydrolysis and catabolism
   C. dehydration synthesis and anabolism
   D. dehydration synthesis and catabolism

Use the following information to answer the next question.

All vertebrates possess similar digestive systems. The vertebrate digestive system can be described as having a tube-within-a-tube structure.

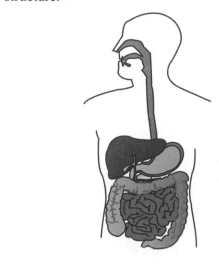

5. The outer tube of the tube-within-a-tube structure is the
   A. body
   B. digestive tract
   C. esophageal canal
   D. inner lining of the digestive tube

CHALLENGER QUESTION

6. Fluid leaking into the body cavity from a burst appendix would
   A. contain insulin
   B. contain enzymes from the stomach
   C. have an acidic pH due to the presence of hydrochloric acid
   D. have a neutral pH due to the presence of alkaline pancreatic juice

Use the following information to answer the next question.

The passage of food from the stomach to the small intestine is tightly controlled by a circular muscle at the junction point between these two organs. This muscle is very strong because it plays a crucial role in preventing food from passing from the stomach to the small intestine unchecked, and it participates in the contraction of the stomach muscles during the mechanical breakdown of food.

7. The circular muscle located at the junction between the stomach and the small intestine is the
   A. tricuspid valve
   B. ileocecal valve
   C. cardiac sphincter
   D. pyloric sphincter

8. Normally, the gag reflex prevents food from entering the respiratory system. The structure at the back of the throat that normally closes off the trachea during swallowing is the
   A. uvula   B. tongue
   C. pharynx   D. epiglottis

Use the following information to answer the next question.

Proteins are composed of many amino acids. Individual amino acids are linked to form a chain, or polypeptide. A protein is composed of one or more polypeptides.

9. Which type of chemical bond exists between individual amino acids of a protein?
   A. Ionic bond
   B. Peptide bond
   C. Hydrogen bond
   D. Phosphodiester bond

Use the following diagram to answer the next question.

I   II   I   II

H—N—▨—C—OH   H—N—▢—C—OH
    | ‖ | ‖
    H   O   H   O

Amino acid   Amino acid

10. In the given diagram, the structures labelled I and II refer to

A. an amino group and an acid group

B. a nitrate group and a carbon group

C. a protein end and a carbohydrate end

D. a single-bond end and a double-bond end

11. Which of the following statements regarding proteins is **false**?

A. Proteins are two-dimensional.

B. Proteins can serve as enzymes.

C. Proteins are made of amino acids.

D. Many hormones are made of proteins.

12. Which of the following events occurs when two amino acids join to form a dipeptide?

A. H joins N, and H_2 is released.

B. H joins N, and CO_2 is released.

C. C joins C, and water is released.

D. C joins N, and water is released.

Use the following information to answer the next question.

The jaws and teeth of vertebrates are well adapted to their diet. An archaeologist uncovered a fossilized jaw bone with the following characteristics: blade-like incisors, pointed canines small enough to allow for jaw rotation, flat premolars, and molars with small ridges on the distal surface.

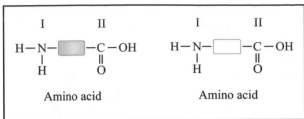

CHALLENGER QUESTION

13. The jaw described is **most likely** specialized for which of the following types of diet?

A. A carnivorous diet

B. An omnivorous diet

C. A diet made up exclusively of vegetation

D. A diet made up of tough plant material like branches and twigs

Use the following information to answer the next two questions.

The occurrence of cell-cell interactions, such as viral cells attaching to and invading human body cells, is often determined by the carbohydrate-protein structures (glycoproteins) that are present on the surface of each cell. Glycoproteins are a unique set of molecules that combine specific carbohydrate molecules with proteins. Recently, chemists at the University of Alberta have helped characterize a glycoprotein on the parasite *Trichinella spiralis*, which is responsible for contamination of pork. This research led to the development of a test to detect the parasite in both hogs and humans.

14. This glycoprotein must have a specific shape in order to function properly. Which of the following environmental factors would **not** denature this protein and inhibit its function?

A. Low pH

B. High pH

C. Low temperature

D. High temperature

15. The carbohydrate component of the glycoprotein is typical of other types of carbohydrates. The ratio of hydrogen to oxygen in all carbohydrates is

A. 3:1   **B.** 2:1

C. 1:2   **D.** 1:1

A college graduate is working in a laboratory and categorizing different kinds of sugars into a research database.

16. The terms *monosaccharide*, *disaccharide*, and *polysaccharide* are correctly categorized in which of the following rows?

	Monosaccharide	Disaccharide	Polysaccharide
A.	Glucose	Maltose	Starch
B.	Sucrose	Lactose	Cellulose
C.	Fructose	Glycogen	Starch
D.	Fructose	Glucose	Glycogen

17. Which of the following sequences shows the correct flow of blood through the cardiopulmonary system as it returns to the heart from the body?

A. vena cava → right atrium
   → right ventricle → pulmonary artery
   → pulmonary vein → left atrium
   → left ventricle → aorta

B. vena cava → right atrium
   → right ventricle → pulmonary vein
   → pulmonary artery → left atrium
   → left ventricle → aorta

C. aorta → left ventricle → left atrium
   → pulmonary vein → pulmonary artery
   → right ventricle → right atrium
   → vena cava

D. vena cava → right atrium → left atrium
   → pulmonary artery → pulmonary vein
   → right ventricle → left ventricle → aorta

18. When bare skin is exposed to cold air, body heat is initially conserved by which of the following responses?

A. Increased heart rate

B. Decreased heart rate

C. Arteriolar vasodilation near the skin

D. Arteriolar vasoconstriction near the skin

19. Which of the following statements **best** explains reabsorption from the proximal tubule to the efferent arteriole?

A. Nutrients diffuse from the proximal tubule into the blood.

B. Nutrients are actively transported out, and water follows by osmosis.

C. Water is actively transported out, and nutrients follow by diffusion.

D. Nutrients are actively transported out, while water remains in the proximal tubule.

Use the following information to answer the next two questions.

Cystic fibrosis (CF) is a serious genetic disease that affects roughly one in 2 000 children in Canada. The disease is characterized by the production of an excess amount of thick, sticky mucus in the respiratory and digestive systems.

20. CF could impair functioning of the digestive tract by preventing

A. fat absorption from the stomach

B. pancreatic juices from reaching the intestine

C. gastric juices from reaching the large intestine

D. digested food from being absorbed by the stomach lining

21. CF sufferers are less likely to develop ulcers than those who do not have CF. A reasonable explanation for this is that

   A. the thick mucus protects the stomach lining from acid

   B. CF sufferers maintain a carefully controlled diet

   C. a person with CF has frequent medical checkups

   D. CF sufferers lead relatively stress-free lives

CHALLENGER QUESTION

22. On which of the following substrates do the pancreatic enzymes trypsin, lipase, and amylase act upon, respectively?

   A. Protein, fat, starch

   B. Vitamin, fat, starch

   C. Protein, lipid, cellulose

   D. Polypeptides, lipid, vitamin

Use the following information to answer the next question.

The stretching of the stomach wall and the presence of partially digested protein in the stomach stimulate the cells lining the stomach to secrete the hormone gastrin into the blood. When gastrin makes its way to the upper stomach via the bloodstream, it stimulates the gastric glands to secrete gastric juice.

The following flow chart symbolizes this series of events.

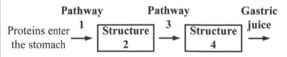

CHALLENGER QUESTION

Numerical Response

1. At what point on the flow chart would gastrin be in the blood? _____
(Insert the number of the appropriate pathway or structure.)

23. One surgical treatment of colon cancer involves the removal of a section of large intestine. An outcome of this surgery is that the person would experience

   A. less water reabsorption, resulting in watery feces

   B. more water reabsorption, resulting in watery feces

   C. less water reabsorption, resulting in dry feces

   D. more water reabsorption, resulting in dry feces

24. Surface area in the small intestine is **not** increased by

   A. the length of the small intestine

   B. the numerous branches of the small intestine

   C. projections called villi inside the small intestine

   D. microvilli in the membranes of cells lining the small intestine

Use the following information to answer the next question.

While on holiday in Toronto, Jorge and Ruby splurged on lunch. Each ate a lean 300 g steak (assume that it is pure protein) served with garlic toast (20 g piece of bread with 1 g of butter). Feeling very full after the meal, Ruby decided to combine sightseeing with exercise by climbing the stairs of the CN tower. Jorge went back to the hotel and relaxed by lying on the sofa.

The following two tables show the amount of energy per gram of nutrient and the rate of energy usage, respectively.

Table I: Energy Release

Nutrient	Energy (J)
Carbohydrate	17.2
Fat	38.9
Protein	17.2

Table II: Rate of Energy Use for Various Activities

Activity	Energy Used (kJ/h)
At rest	418
Jogging	2 385
Swimming	2 092
Dressing and undressing	494
Walking up stairs	4 602

CHALLENGER QUESTION

Numerical Response

2. Calculate the difference in time it will take Jorge and Ruby to work off the energy consumed at lunch if they maintain their current activities. _____ h
(Correct to **one** decimal place.)

Use the following information to answer the next question.

The fact that cigarette smoke is harmful to a fetus is well documented. Babies born to mothers who smoke are smaller, have many more health problems, and are more likely to die at a younger age. Nicotine, one of the components of cigarette smoke, stimulates arteries in the brain and skeletal muscles to dilate and other arteries to constrict.

CHALLENGER QUESTION

25. Given this information, which of the following conclusions about the fetuses of smoking mothers is reasonable?
   A. They are surrounded by a smaller placenta than the fetuses of non-smoking mothers.
   B. They are exposed to increased nutrient flow from dilated blood vessels.
   C. They have smaller brains than fetuses of non-smoking mothers.
   D. They are deprived of nutrients and oxygen.

26. While smoking a cigarette, a smoker's complexion will become somewhat paler than usual. This is because the act of smoking will temporarily cause

A. anemia in the smoker

B. a decrease in the smoker's heart rate

C. dilation of the blood vessels in the smoker's skin

D. constriction of the blood vessels in the smoker's skin

27. Blood moves through veins due to the

A. force of gravity

B. squeezing of venous valves

C. contraction of heart ventricles

D. contraction of skeletal muscles

Use the following graph to answer the next question.

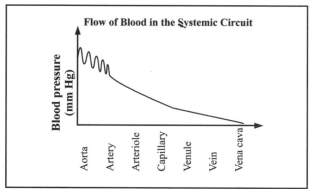

28. From the information in the graph, it can be inferred that hypertension would be **most problematic** in a person's

A. heart

B. blood vessels

C. aorta and arteries

D. veins and vena cava

Use the following information to answer the next question.

Although high blood cholesterol is associated with negative health risks, cholesterol biochemistry is complex. Since cholesterol is not readily soluble in blood plasma, it must be attached to a special carrier molecule for transport through the bloodstream.

Two such carrier molecules are low-density lipoproteins (LDLs) and high-density lipoproteins (HDLs). HDLs are considered to be good cholesterol. They transport cholesterol from the blood back to the liver. The LDLs are commonly called bad cholesterol because they transport cholesterol from the liver into the bloodstream. There, cholesterol-LDL complexes stick to artery walls, where they attract white blood cells. The white blood cells consume the cholesterol-LDL complexes, but these cells ultimately burst, leaving behind fatty streaks on the artery wall that then leads to the formation of plaque. Enough plaque can block blood flow through arteries. When people have their cholesterol checked, the total amount of cholesterol in the bloodstream is reported, as well as the levels of HDLs and LDLs.

29. Which of the following statements regarding cholesterol is likely **true**?

A. A high HDL blood level is associated with stroke.

B. A low LDL blood level is associated with heart disease.

C. Low LDL and high HDL levels are associated with good health.

D. High LDL and high HDL levels are associated with good health.

30. Which of the following components of blood is **not** a leukocyte?

A. Platelets

B. Macrophages

C. T cells

D. B cells

31. Diastolic arterial blood pressure is the pressure in the arteries at the time of cardiac diastole. Another way of saying this is that diastolic blood pressure is the

   A. minimum pressure present in the arteries

   B. maximum pressure present in the arteries

   C. pressure in the arteries when the ventricles contract

   D. pressure in the arteries during ventricular contraction over the pressure in the arteries during ventricular relaxation

32. Which of the following transfusions would result in agglutination of the blood?

   A. Type O donor + type B recipient

   B. Type B donor + type O recipient

   C. Type A donor + type AB recipient

   D. Type AB donor + type AB recipient

Use the following information to answer the next question.

Some types of artificial blood contain PFCs (perfluorocarbons)— chemicals that can absorb large quantities of oxygen. In 1960, L. Clark showed that a mouse immersed in PFC liquid was able to breathe almost normally. The challenge in creating artificial blood is discovering a substance that absorbs oxygen in the environment of the lungs and releases oxygen at the capillary beds.

33. A substance that binds oxygen in the lungs and releases oxygen in the capillary beds would mimic

   A. plasma

   B. hemoglobin

   C. carbon dioxide

   D. carbonic anhydrase

34. Platelets start a clotting reaction that ultimately produces a clot composed of fibrin, which is a form of

   A. antibody

   B. protein thread

   C. dead blood cell

   D. white blood cell

35. A dietary mineral required for the clotting reaction is

   A. iron

   B. iodine

   C. sodium

   D. calcium

Use the following information to answer the next question.

To perform a standard test for blood type, three drops of blood are placed on a microscope slide. To these drops are added anti-A antibodies, anti-B antibodies, and anti-Rh antibodies. If agglutination (clumping) of a blood drop occurs, the antibodies have reacted with antigens. The results of four blood tests are shown in the diagram.

	Anti A	Anti B	Anti Rh^+
Individual			
1			
2			
3			
4			

36. Which individual has blood type B^+?

   A. 1

   B. 2

   C. 3

   D. 4

Use the following information to answer the next question.

The heart of a fetus has an opening (called the foramen ovale) that directly connects the right and left atria.

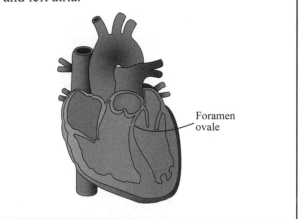

Foramen ovale

37. The benefit that the foramen ovale provides to the developing fetus is that it enables blood to

A. be pumped

B. bypass the lungs

C. be held in large volumes in the heart

D. be pumped effectively by the left ventricle

Use the following information to answer the next question.

Hemoglobin is an amazing molecule in that it is able to release more oxygen in the tissues if more oxygen is needed. For example, when tissues are actively respiring, they produce more CO_2, which combines with water to form carbonic acid. The more acidic the tissue, the more oxygen is released from hemoglobin.

38. In the muscle cells of a sprinter during a race, one could predict that there would be

A. low pH and a high oxygen release from hemoglobin

B. high pH and a high oxygen release from hemoglobin

C. low pH and a low oxygen release from hemoglobin

D. high pH and a low oxygen release from hemoglobin

39. The function of the cilia lining breathing passages is to

A. absorb water and gases

B. circulate gases in the lungs

C. increase surface area for gas exchange

D. sweep mucus and debris out of the lungs

Use the following table to answer the next three questions.

Typical Partial Pressures of Gas in Blood (mmHg) in the Lungs (at Sea Level)				
	Gas Atmosphere	Alveoli	Blood Entering	Blood Leaving
Oxygen	158	100	40	95
Carbon dioxide	0.3	40	45	40

CHALLENGER QUESTION

Numerical Response

3. The change in the partial pressure of oxygen in blood as it moves through the lungs is _____ mmHg.

40. At a very high altitude, one could expect the partial pressure of oxygen in the alveoli to be

A. 40 mmHg

B. 100 mmHg

C. 118 mmHg

D. 158 mmHg

41. The change in the partial pressure of carbon dioxide between blood entering the lungs and blood leaving the lungs is accompanied by which of the following changes in blood pH?

    A. Slight increase

    B. Large increase

    C. Large decrease

    D. Slight decrease

Use the following information to answer the next question.

People affected with cystic fibrosis (CF) suffer from an accumulation of thick mucus inside breathing passages. The thick mucus cannot easily be expelled. In fact, children with CF must be regularly pounded on the back to loosen the mucus so that it can be coughed up.

42. Besides reducing the rate of gas exchange, mucus buildup would

    A. raise the pH of the blood

    B. eventually result in a collapsed lung

    C. make the removal of infectious agents more difficult

    D. make the affected person more prone to asthma attacks

43. Chemicals in cigarette smoke paralyze the cilia of cells lining the trachea and bronchi. As a result, cigarette smokers often experience

    A. low stamina

    B. pale complexions

    C. frequent coughing

    D. premature wrinkling of skin

Use the following information to answer the next question.

Groups of lymph nodes are situated on the courses of lymphatic vessels and are composed of lymphatic tissue enclosed within a fibrous capsule. The lymphoid tissue in the nodes performs various functions.

44. Which of the following functions is **not** carried out by lymphoid tissue?

    A. Formation of lymphocytes

    B. Development of erythrocytes

    C. Formation of antibodies and antitoxins

    D. Filtration of particulate matter for breakdown

45. Which of the following types of cells takes part in the formation of antibodies to an attacking antigen?

    A. B cells

    B. Macrophages

    C. Cytotoxic T cells

    D. Natural killer cells

46. The ureter serves as a connective link between the

    A. bladder and urethra

    B. kidney and bladder

    C. liver and urethra

    D. kidney and liver

Use the following diagram to answer the next three questions.

A Simplified Diagram of a Nephron

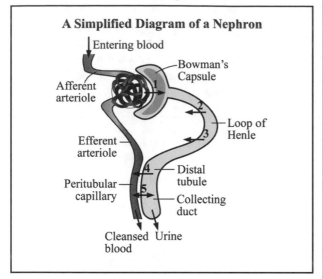

49. ADH and aldosterone initially stimulate processes

A. 3 and 4, respectively

B. 1 and 3, respectively

C. 5 and 4, respectively

D. 1 and 2, respectively

50. When the nephron is working properly, blood samples taken from the renal artery and the renal vein will show that the

A. amount of urea in the renal vein is less than in the renal artery, and the amount of glucose is the same

B. amount of urea in the renal vein is the same as in the renal artery, and the amount of glucose is less

C. amounts of both urea and glucose in the renal vein are the same as in the renal artery

D. amounts of both urea and glucose in the renal vein are less than in the renal artery

CHALLENGER QUESTION

47. When comparing blood in the efferent arteriole to blood in the afferent arteriole of the kidney, blood in the efferent arteriole has a higher concentration of

A. cells and protein

B. water and H^+ ions

C. ADH and aldosterone

D. salt and carbon dioxide

48. The process labelled 1 is due to

A. osmosis

B. diffusion

C. filtration

D. active transport

**Some Characteristics of Smooth and
Skeletal Muscles**

I.   The muscle is in the form of long fibres.

II.   The fibres show striations.

III.   The fibres do not show striations.

IV.   The muscle is under involuntary control.

V.   The muscle is under voluntary control.

VI.   Individual cells are not distinguishable.

VII.   Cells are arranged in sheets.

VIII. Individual cells are easily seen.

51. The **main** features of skeletal muscle are
described by statements

  A. I, II, V, and VI

  B. I, II, VI, and VII

  C. I, V, VII, and VIII

  D. III, IV, VII, and VIII

52. Intentional movement of bones is
accomplished by

  A. smooth muscles

  B. skeletal muscles

  C. involuntary muscles

  D. non-striated muscles

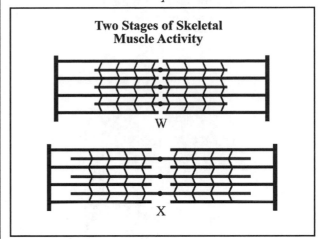

**Two Stages of Skeletal
Muscle Activity**

53. Diagram W represents a

  A. relaxed myosin fibre

  B. relaxed myofibril unit

  C. contracted myosin fibre

  D. contracted myofibril unit

Written Response

Use the following information to answer the next question.

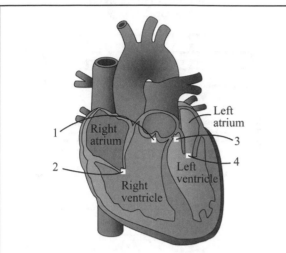

In July 1997, the Mayo Clinic in Rochester, Minnesota, reported that 24 women with no previous history of heart abnormalities were found to be suffering from valvular disease and hypertension. All 24 women were currently taking, or had taken in the past, the weight loss drug fen-phen.

The following symptoms were identified in the 24 women:

• Abnormally functioning, weak heart valves that caused mixing of blood between the atria and the ventricles

• Thickening and narrowing of the heart valves

• In a few cases, high blood pressure in the vessels carrying blood from the heart to the lungs

The Mayo Clinic report does not define a clear cause-effect relationship between fen-phen use and heart abnormalities; however, the report does state that there is an association between fen-phen use and heart problems.

1. **a)** Identify the four valves shown in the diagram that may have been affected in the 24 women in the study.

(2 marks)

b) One reported result was mitral stenosis, where the left atrioventricular valve narrows and thickens. Predict two ways that blood flow or blood pressure in the heart or lungs might be affected. Justify your response.

(2 marks)

c) Define the term hypertension.

(1 mark)

Use the following additional information to answer the next two parts.

In a few of the women taking weight-loss drugs such as fen-phen, the primary pulmonary hypertension (PPH) observed ranged from moderate to severe. In all types of hypertension, both the systolic and diastolic pressures are elevated.

The following table lists blood pressure readings in mild to very severe cases of hypertension.

Category	Systolic (mmHg*)	Diastolic (mmHg*)
Normal**	< 130	< 85
High normal	130–139	85–89
Hypertension		
Stage 1 (Mild)	140–159	90–99
Stage 2 (Moderate)	160–179	100–109
Stage 3 (Severe)	180–209	110–119
Stage 4 (Very severe)	> 209	> 119

* Measured in millimetres of mercury.
** Optimal blood pressure is less than 120/80 mmHg. Unusually low readings should be evaluated by a physician.

Classification of blood pressure levels are for adults 18 years and older. Systolic pressure, the higher number of a blood pressure reading, is the pressure as the heart pumps; diastolic pressure is the pressure when the heart relaxes between beats.

Source: Joint National Committee on Detection. Evaluation and Treatment of High Blood Pressure National Institute of Health.

d) Blood pressure is given as a ratio between two factors. Identify and describe each of the factors.

(4 marks)

e) What are the lowest and highest possible blood pressures that may be observed in women taking fen-phen?

(2 marks)

Use the following information to answer the next question.

On average, a person metabolizes 100 mg of alcohol per kilogram of body weight per hour. First, alcohol is broken down to less toxic acetaldehyde, which is then broken down into acetic acid, an even less toxic substance. The first reaction is assisted by alcohol dehydrogenase (ADH). The second reaction is assisted by acetaldehyde dehydrogrenase (ALDH).

Note: The letters ADH in this case do not refer to antidiuretic hormone.

Alcohol $\xrightarrow{\text{ADH}}$ Acetaldehyde
$\xrightarrow{\text{ALDH}}$ Acetic acid

2. a) What type of molecule is ADH?

(2 marks)

b) The term *induced fit* refers to the mechanism by which ADH works on its substrate. Why is this term used?

(2 marks)

Use the following additional diagram to answer the next part.

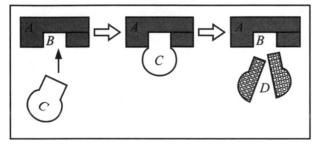

c) If ALDH is labelled *A*, what structures or substances are represented by the labels *B*, *C*, and *D*, respectively?

(2 marks)

Use this additional information to answer the next two parts.

Once acetaldehyde is in the blood, it must quickly be converted to a less toxic metabolite by acetaldehyde dehydrogenase (ALDH). ALDH converts CH_3CHO into CH_3COOH (acetic acid), which may be further broken down.

d) How might the absence of ALDH be detected in a person?

(2 marks)

e) A number of antagonistic drugs exist that cause the inhibition of ALDH. These inhibitors are used to help control excess alcohol consumption. The drugs also cause nausea, flushing, and perspiration. Give one mechanism by which these drugs could inhibit ALDH.

(2 marks)

ANSWERS AND SOLUTIONS—PRACTICE QUESTIONS

1. A	11. A	21. A	29. C	39. D	48. C
2. D	12. D	22. A	30. A	NR3. 55	49. C
3. C	13. B	NR1. 3	31. A	40. A	50. A
4. B	14. C	23. A	32. B	41. A	51. A
5. A	15. B	24. B	33. B	42. C	52. B
6. D	16. A	NR2. 12.1	34. B	43. C	53. D
7. D	17. A	25. D	35. D	44. B	WR1. See Solution
8. D	18. D	26. D	36. C	45. A	WR2. See Solution
9. B	19. B	27. D	37. B	46. B	
10. A	20. B	28. C	38. A	47. A	

1.   A

Bile is a green-yellow substance made in the liver and stored in the gall bladder. It is an emulsifier, meaning it converts large fat droplets into small fat droplets, increasing the surface area for lipase action. Bile is released into the small intestine when fat is present.

Renin secreted in the stomach functions to coagulate milk making it easier to digest. Lipases, which break down fat molecules into glycerol and fatty acids, act faster on smaller fat droplets than on large fat droplets. Glycerol and fatty acids are subsequently absorbed through cells of the microvilli, and then they pass into lacteals, branches of the lymphatic system. Hydrochloric acid (HCl), also in the stomach, converts inactive pepsinogen to active pepsin that digests proteins, sterilizes food, and denatures proteins.

2.   D

The reaction shown in the diagram involves the joining of two reactant molecules with the resultant production of a water molecule. The hydrogen atom of the hydroxyl (–OH) group on one molecule combines with the complete hydroxyl group on the other molecule, producing water. The valence vacated by the loss of hydrogen forms a bond with the valence vacated by the hydroxyl group linking the two reactant molecules. This removal of a water molecule between the two compounds (dehydration) results in the production (or synthesis) of a larger molecule. Dehydration synthesis is a mechanism common to the synthesis of many biological macromolecules from smaller compounds. For example, polysaccharides such as starches or glycogen are produced by the dehydration synthesis of many monosaccharide molecules. Amino acids are similarly assembled to form proteins by this mechanism.

Hydrolysis, the reverse reaction of dehydration synthesis, involves the breaking apart of a molecule through the addition of water. As the reaction illustrated in the diagram does not involve the simple transfer of charged groups, this is not a neutralization reaction. Catalysts are neither produced nor consumed in the reactions they facilitate, so this diagram does not represent a reaction involving the formation of a catalyst.

3. C

Sequence II depicts a reaction in which the substrate (1) is split to form two products. The hydrolysis of a disaccharide (with the help of a disaccharidase enzyme) into two monosaccharides is an example of such a reaction.

Anabolic reactions (like dehydration synthesis) make larger molecules out of smaller ones. The emulsification of fat is not an enzymatic reaction; it is a physical process in which fat is simply made into little bubbles that are suspended in a watery medium. This occurs in the small intestine so that there is more surface area of fat for lipase enzymes to lock onto, increasing the speed of digestion. Dehydration synthesis is the exact opposite type of reaction as what is seen in sequence II. It would involve an anabolic joining of two amino acid molecules to make a dipeptide.

4. B

The terms that describe the degradation of glycogen to glucose are hydrolysis and catabolism. The reaction that breaks down glycogen is known as hydrolysis. Since glycogen is being broken down into smaller monosaccharide units, the process is catabolic, not anabolic.

Anabolism refers to the assembly of smaller subunits into a larger product. Dehydration synthesis reactions are anabolic reactions.

5. A

The tube-within-a-tube structure of the vertebrate digestive system is composed of two tubes. The inner tube represents the digestive tract (equivalent to the alimentary canal). The inner lining of the digestive tract is the barrier that divides the digestive tract from the body cavity. The outer tube of the model represents the body itself. The inner tube begins at the mouth and ends at the anus. Throughout the length of the digestive tube, food is processed and absorbed in a specific sequence that is relatively common among all vertebrates.

6. D

The appendix is located directly after the junction between the small intestine and the large intestine.

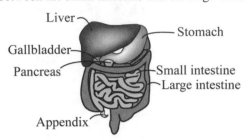

The ileocecal valve, a sphincter, regulates the passage of material from the ileum to the ascending colon. The cecum is a small pouch that hangs below the ascending colon. The appendix is a closed tube that extends from the cecum.

Fluid (chyme) containing hydrochloric acid (HCl) enters the small intestine from the stomach. This fluid is neutralized in the first part of the small intestine (duodenum) by pancreatic juice, which is alkaline (basic) because of the presence of sodium bicarbonate.

7. D

The pyloric sphincter is located at the junction between the stomach and the small intestine (duodenum) and helps to regulate the passage of chyme (digested food) from the stomach to the small intestine. The pyloric sphincter is a stronger muscle than the cardiac sphincter because when closed, it must hold the chyme in the stomach against gravity. This sphincter also contracts to aid the mechanical breakdown of food in the stomach.

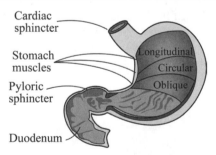

The cardiac or esophageal sphincter is located at the junction between the esophagus and the stomach. It regulates the amount of food entering the stomach and prevents food from travelling backward from the stomach to the esophagus. The tricuspid (atrioventricular) valve is located in the heart between the right atrium and ventricle. The ileocecal valve (also a sphincter) regulates the passage of food from the small intestine (ileum) to the large intestine.

8. D

The epiglottis is located at the lower end of the pharynx. The trachea (the opening to the lungs) moves up against the epiglottis during swallowing to prevent food from entering the respiratory tract. Stimulation of the epiglottis normally activates the gag reflex. The gag reflex works to prevent suffocation that could be caused by the lodging of large food particles in the trachea.

When food has reached the proper consistency after chewing, the tongue forms the food into a ball called a bolus and pushes the bolus to the rear of the mouth. When swallowing is initiated, the bolus is passed to the pharynx. The uvula (an extension of the soft palate) then closes off the opening to the nasal passage.

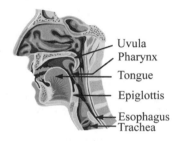

Uvula
Pharynx
Tongue
Epiglottis
Esophagus
Trachea

9. B

Proteins are composed of chains of various amino acids bonded together through dehydration synthesis. Formed between the $-COOH$ groups and the $-NH_2$ groups of the amino acids, the resulting covalent $CO-NH$ linkages are termed peptide bonds.

Ionic bonds are weak, non-covalent bonds characterized by the complete transfer of an electron from one compound to another, resulting in a significant mutual electrostatic attraction between the two ions formed from this transfer. Hydrogen bonds are weak, non-covalent bonds resulting from electrostatic attraction between oppositely charged regions of polar molecules, such as H_2O. Phosphodiester bonds are formed between adjacent bases of a DNA molecule.

10. A

Amino acids are the repeating subunits of proteins. Each amino acid has an amino functional group and an acid functional group. In the given diagram I represents an amino group (NH_2) and II represents a carboxyl ($-COOH$) or acid group. The rectangle between the amino and acid group represents a central carbon with a variable group that is unique for each amino acid.

11. A

Proteins are not two-dimensional. The polypeptide chain composed of amino acids twists into a three-dimensional shape that gives the protein its specific function.

12. D

The dehydration synthesis or joining of two amino acids is accomplished by the formation of a peptide bond. The C of the carboxylic acid ($-COOH$) group of one amino acid and the N of the amino ($-NH_2$) group of the other amino acid join together, eliminating a water molecule.

13. B

The description most likely refers to the jaw of an omnivore. Since omnivores eat both vegetation and meat, their teeth are less specialized than either the teeth of carnivores or herbivores. In omnivores, the two incisors are adapted for biting, the canine teeth function in tearing (as they do in carnivores), the two premolars are used for grinding, and the molars are adapted for crushing.

The teeth and jaws of carnivores are adapted for capturing and killing prey and for ripping and tearing flesh. Meat eaters typically have pointed incisors and long, sharp canines (which hinder jaw rotation) specialized for ripping and tearing, as well as jagged premolars and molars adapted for shredding and crushing. The teeth described do not fit this description. Herbivores exclusively consume vegetation. Their incisors and canines usually are modified for grinding. For efficient grinding of fibrous plants, herbivores have broad molars with an extensively ridged surface.

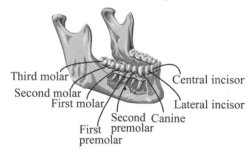

Third molar
Second molar
First molar
Central incisor
Lateral incisor
Second Canine
First premolar
First premolar

14. C

Primary protein structure
is the sequence of amino acids within the amino acid chain.

Secondary protein structure
is the region-specific conformation of the amino acid chain created by hydrogen bonds between different amino acids.

Tertiary protein structure
is the bundled-up shape that the protein forms because of attractions between pleated sheets and alpha helixes.

Quaternary protein structure
is the structure that proteins composed of more than one amino acid chain form.

When a protein loses its three dimensional (tertiary) structure it is said to be denatured and no longer functional. Extremes in pH and high temperatures are likely to denature protein permanently. Low temperature is the least disruptive to tertiary structure. Cooling proteins actually stabilizes many proteins. Freezing proteins can temporarily cause denaturation which is often reversed upon thawing. This is why some cells can continue to be active after being frozen and thawed.

15. B

Carbohydrates are molecules composed of carbon, hydrogen, and oxygen. The ratio of H:O in carbohydrates is always 2:1.

16. A

Glucose is a monosaccharide. Maltose is a disaccharide composed of two glucose subunits. Starches are branched polysaccharides consisting of hundreds of glucose monomers.

17. A

The correct sequence of the flow of blood through the cardiopulmonary system is as follows:

vena cava → right atrium → right ventricle → pulmonary artery → pulmonary vein → left atrium → left ventricle → aorta

18. D

When the skin is exposed to cold temperatures, the arterioles leading to the skin undergo vasoconstriction, which is a reduction in diameter. Vasoconstriction results in less blood flow to the skin, reducing the amount of heat lost to the environment

19. B

All dissolved nutrients (amino acids, glucose, etc.) must be returned to the blood by reabsorption. If they were not, they would pass out of the body with the urine, resulting in starvation. Nutrients are actively transported from the proximal tubule into the efferent arteriole. This requires much ATP, which is supplied by the many mitochondria in the cells that line the proximal tubule. The presence of the nutrients in the efferent arteriole makes the blood very hypertonic with a high osmotic pull. Water in the proximal tubule is pulled by osmosis into the bloodstream. About 80% of the water in the filtrate is returned to the blood in this way.

20. B

CF sufferers experience blockages in the normal flow of enzymes and secretions because of the accumulation of sticky mucus. If mucus plugs the common bile duct, pancreatic juice will not reach the small intestine. Pancreatic enzymes and sodium bicarbonate are essential for digestion of food.

Fat is not absorbed; it is hydrolyzed to fatty acids and glycerol, both of which are absorbed from the small intestine. Gastric juices are secreted from the stomach, not the large intestine. Food is not absorbed from the stomach, only the small intestine.

21. A

An ulcer is a hole or sore in the wall of the stomach. An ulcer is caused in part by the absence of the thick mucus that normally lines the stomach wall and protects it from the highly acidic gastric juices. The hydrochloric acid in gastric juice can burn through unprotected tissue (similarly causing the burning sensation in the throat and esophagus after vomiting). Untreated, the tissue damage may progress to become a hole (perforation) in the stomach wall (called a perforated ulcer), which can become life threatening because bacteria from food is then able to enter the body cavity. Since CF patients have higher than normal amounts of mucus in the stomach, intestines, and respiratory tract, more mucus would provide the stomach with more protection from acidic gastric juices.

22. A

Pancreatic juice contains components that digest the three major food groups: carbohydrates, fats, and protein. Trypsin digests small peptides and proteins into shorter peptide chains. Lipase breaks down lipids (fats). There are three types of lipases. Amylase hydrolyzes starch (a complex sugar-carbohydrate) into maltose, a disaccharide.

Vitamins are usually absorbed directly either in the stomach or in the small or large intestine. Cellulose cannot be broken down by any enzymes of the human body.

NR 1   3

Gastrin is present at pathway 3.

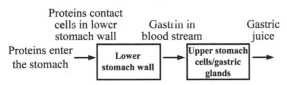

The flow chart shows that proteins in the stomach (and the stretching of the stomach wall) cause cells of the lower stomach (structure 2) to secrete the hormone gastrin. Gastrin is secreted into the bloodstream. When the gastrin reaches the upper cells of the stomach, the gastric glands (gastrin target cells) are stimulated to release gastric juice.

23. A

The main function of the large intestine is water reabsorption. Water is reabsorbed from fecal matter and eventually shunted back into the blood. Shortening the length of the large intestine by surgically removing a portion of it would decrease the amount of time and surface area available for water reabsorption. Therefore, the patient would experience less water reabsorption, resulting in more watery feces.

24. B

The small intestine is one long tube that is folded numerous times, but it is not branched. Surface area is provided by the significant length of the intestine, the presence of villi lining the intestine, and the presence of microvilli on the surface of villi. The more intestinal surface area the faster digestion and absorption will occur.

NR 2   12.1

Jorge and Ruby consumed the same amount of energy at lunch because they ate the same meal. Calculate the amount of energy they consumed during their meal.

300 g protein (steak)
20 g carbohydrate (toast)
1 g fat (butter)
Energy consumed
= (300 g)(17.2 kJ/g) + (20 g)(17.2 kJ/g)
   + (1 g)(38.9 kJ/g)
= 5 542.9 kJ of energy consumed at lunch

Calculate the time it will take to work off the energy consumed for each person.

Because of their different intensity levels following lunch, Jorge and Ruby will work off the energy consumed at lunch over different times.

Ruby climbed the stairs, so it will take her 5 542.9 kJ ÷ 4 602 kJ/h = 1.2 h to burn off the energy.

Since Jorge sat on the sofa, he will take 5 542.9 kJ ÷ 418 kJ/h = 13.3 h to burn off the energy.

Calculate the difference between their times.

The difference is 13.3 h − 1.2 h = 12.1 h.

It will take Jorge 12.1 h more to burn off the energy consumed at lunch.

25. D

Nicotine in cigarettes causes arteries in the brain and skeletal muscles of the mother to dilate and all other arteries to constrict. Dilated arteries are expanded, so they allow a greater volume of blood to flow through. Pregnant women who smoke have a greater blood supply in the brain and skeletal muscles but insufficient blood flow to the uterus, where the baby is dependent on receiving nutrients and oxygen from the mother's blood via the placenta.

26. D

Nicotine causes the dilation of the arteries supplying the brain and skeletal muscle with blood. In other arteries, such as those in the skin, nicotine causes the arteries to constrict, reducing the flow of blood to these tissues. Outwardly, the reduced flow of blood through the capillaries in the skin (for instance, in the face) is apparent from the increased pallor of the skin.

27. D

Veins return blood to the heart. In most veins blood is flowing against the force of gravity. Two adaptations of veins that assist in venous return are pocket valves and skeletal muscle pressure. Pocket valves that are similar to semilunar and aortic valves allow blood to move upwards towards the heart, but prevent blood from moving backwards toward the feet. These valves do not squeeze the blood. The second adaptation is that most large veins flow through the middle of large skeletal muscles. When these skeletal muscles contract, the veins are squeezed. Valves prevent backflow so blood is pushed upwards towards the heart.

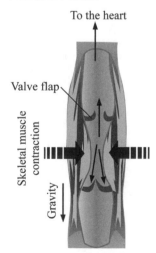

28. C

Hypertension is a medical condition where blood pressure is too high. The diagram shows that the aorta and the arteries are the blood vessels containing the highest blood pressure. There is a danger that the pressure within the blood vessel can cause the vessel to rupture. If this occurs in the brain, the haemorrhage that results is called a stroke. Because arteries have the highest blood pressure, the vessels most likely to rupture are arteries.

29. C

Good health is associated with low LDL and high HDL levels. Conversely, blockage of an artery is more likely if LDL levels are high and HDL levels are low.

30. A

Platelets are not a type of white blood cell. Platelets are small, thin-membraned blood cell fragments necessary for the clotting reaction.

31. A

When the ventricles relax between contractions, the pressure in the arteries is at its minimum. This period of time is called diastole.

When the ventricles contract, the pressure in the arteries is at its maximum. This period of time is referred to as systole. Blood pressure is reported as a ratio of systolic pressure over diastolic pressure. Normal blood pressure is 120/80 mm Hg.

32. B

In the donor, always consider the antigens that are attacking. In the recipient, consider the antibodies that are defending. Agglutination can only occur when antigens of one type meet antibodies of the same type. When type B blood is donated to an individual with type O blood, the B antigens from the donor will react with the anti-B antibodies in the recipient causing agglutination of the recipient's blood. A type O donor cannot cause agglutination because their blood contains no antigens. Agglutination cannot occur in a type AB recipient because they have no antibodies.

33. B

Hemoglobin is an oxygen carrier that either binds or releases oxygen depending on the surrounding conditions. Under the conditions present in the lungs (cool temperature, neutral pH, high pO_2 and low pCO_2) haemoglobin binds to oxygen to form oxyhemoglobin ($HgbO_2$). Under the conditions found in the capillaries and tissues (high temperature, low pH, low pO_2 and high pCO_2) haemoglobin releases oxygen.

34. B

The clotting reaction is a step-wise cascade that proceeds according to the given diagram. It begins when a platelet is torn on the ragged edge of a wound, releasing its contents of thromboplastin into the blood.

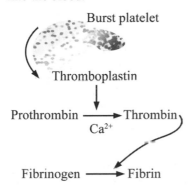

Fibrinogen, synthesized in the liver, is a soluble plasma protein that is always present in the blood. Thrombin converts fibrinogen to fibrin, a thread-like protein which is insoluble in plasma .The fibrin threads trap passing red blood cells which form a clot preventing further bleeding.

35. D

Calcium plays a part in the clotting cascade of reactions. Thromboplastin will catalyze the reaction of prothrombin to thrombin only if calcium ions (Ca^{2+}).are present in the blood. For this reason calcium must be found in the diet.

36. C

This chart shows the blood drops that have agglutinated.

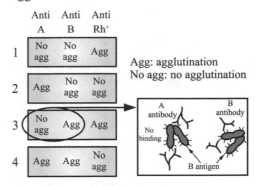

In blood type testing, a drop of the individual's blood is mixed with anti-A antibody, anti-B antibody, and anti-Rh antibody. If agglutination occurs in any of the drops then an antigen/antibody reaction has occurred. Individual 3 is B^+. Blood cells of a B^+ individual possess the B antigen and the Rh antigen so they have been bound and become agglutinated in the presence of the anti-B antibody and the anti-Rh antibody. Because no agglutination occurred in the presence of Anti-A antibody, it is certain that the individual's blood does not contain an A antigen.

Individual 1 is type O^+ because there were no antigens to agglutinate anti-A and anti-B antibodies. Anti-Rh antibody did react, so the blood does contain an Rh antigen and is therefore Rh+. Individual 2 is type A^- because agglutination occurs only in the presence of the A antibody. Individual 4 is type AB^- because agglutination occurs in the presence of both A and B antibodies but not with the Rh antibody.

37. B

The foramen ovale shunts blood directly from the right atrium to the left atrium in the fetal heart, whereas in an adult heart, the right atrium collects deoxygenated blood from the body tissues and passes it to the right ventricle.

The right ventricle then pumps the deoxygenated blood to the lungs, where blood becomes oxygenated. In a fetus, the lungs are not functional for gas exchange until birth (when the baby utters its first cry). Instead, fetal gas exchange occurs at the placenta. The placenta puts oxygen into the fetal bloodstream and removes carbon dioxide from fetal blood, thus replacing the fetus' lungs. The advantage of the foramen ovale in the fetus is that it allows blood to pass from the right side of the fetal heart to the left side, completely bypassing the lungs.

38. A

During a sprint, muscle tissue would be actively respiring, producing heat, CO_2, and possibly lactic acid if respiration is anaerobic. In the tissue capillaries accu mulating CO_2 combines with H_2O to produce carbonic acid. Under the influence of the enzyme carbonic anhydrase, carbonic acid releases protons (H^+) which drop the pH of the blood in the capillaries.
($H_2CO_3 \rightarrow HCO_3^- + H^+$)

At the same time, pCO_2 is very high and pO_2 is very low. Under these conditions (high temperature, high $pCO2$, low $pO2$, and low pH) haemoglobin in the capillaries dissociates, releasing its load of oxygen.
$HgbO_2 \rightarrow Hgb + O_2$.

Oxygen then diffuses into the muscle tissue to enhance cell respiration and ATP energy production.

39. D

In the trachea, ciliated cells produce mucus. Mucus traps debris such as dust and bacteria that have entered the lungs. Cilia are hair-like extensions of the cell membrane that transport debris trapped in mucus out of the trachea.

Alveoli, blind sacs at the ends of bronchioles filled with air and lined with moisture, function to increase the surface area for gas exchange. Water and gases are absorbed by cells lining the alveoli, from which absorbed molecules enter nearby capillaries by diffusion. Air is circulated in the lungs by the contraction of the diaphragm and external intercostal muscles. Contraction of these muscles causes air to enter the lungs. Relaxation of these muscles results in exhalation.

NR 3   55

Partial pressure (versus air pressure that represents the pressure exerted by the combination of all atmospheric gases) is the air pressure contributed by a specific gas.

In the table, the partial pressure of oxygen entering the lungs is 40 mmHg. This is lower than the partial pressure of oxygen (100 mmHg) in the alveoli, so oxygen diffuses into the blood. Since a gas diffuses from an area of high partial pressure to an area of lower partial pressure, blood leaving the lungs has a higher partial pressure of oxygen (95 mmHg).
95 mmHg – 40 mmHg = 55 mmHg

The increase in the partial pressure of blood oxygen between oxygen entering and leaving the lungs is 55 mmHg.

40. A

At high elevations the air is thinner, meaning gas molecules are further apart. At these altitudes the $pO2$ (partial pressure of oxygen) is much lower than at sea level

41. A

The pCO_2 of blood as it passes through the lungs drops from 45 to 40 mm Hg. The blood is therefore losing CO_2 to the alveoli. The pH of the blood in the lung capillaries is slightly higher because, relative to the tissues, there is so little cell respiration occurring to produce CO_2 and form carbonic acid. Under these conditions (low pCO_2, high pO_2, neutral pH, and cool temperatures) $HgbCO_2$ releases CO_2. It is able to diffuse into the alveoli from the capillaries and be exhaled out.

42. C

In the trachea, ciliated cells produce mucus. Mucus traps debris such as dust and bacteria that have entered the lungs. Cilia are hair-like extensions of the cell membrane that transport mucus with trapped debris out of the trachea. Thick, sticky mucus is not easily moved by waving cilia, so it remains in the trachea.

The pH of the blood is affected by the concentration of carbon dioxide (CO_2). CO_2 released from body tissues reacts with water in the blood plasma to form carbonic acid, which lowers the pH. To compensate for reduced gas exchange, a CF sufferer would breathe at a faster rate to avoid prolonged high concentrations of CO_2 in the blood.

Asthma is associated with inflammation of the bronchioles. Such inflammation is often associated with allergic reactions. It results in narrowing of the bronchial passage.

A collapsed lung results from piercing a hole in a pleural membrane. The lung is enclosed by two pleural membranes: the outer membrane lines the walls of the chest and diaphragm, and the inner membrane is fused to the lungs. The pressure in the interpleural space is lower than atmospheric pressure. When the chest cavity expands, the lung is also pulled open because of the adhesion of the two pleural membranes. Piercing one of the membranes causes the interpleural pressure to equalize with atmospheric pressure. As a result, expanding the chest cavity will not simultaneously expand the lungs.

43. C

Cilia line the trachea and bronchioles. The bronchioles beat upward toward the mouth, sweeping out foreign particles that have passed through the glottis by chance. (Normally, the flaps of the epiglottis close during swallowing to prevent particles from entering the respiratory tract.) Coughing occurs when a large number of cilia are stimulated by a larger particle or irritation. In the case of smoking, the cilia are disabled, so coughing is the only means to dislodge particles or respond to irritation.

The concentration of oxygen taken in and absorbed at the lungs decreases during smoking because lung cells are destroyed, decreasing the surface area available for gas exchange. The concentration of oxygen also decreases because carbon monoxide in smoke binds tightly to hemoglobin in place of oxygen and stays bound, preventing oxygen from being carried in red blood cells to the body tissues, leading to low resources for cellular respiration (low stamina). Nicotine causes arteries in the skin to constrict, causing a pale complexion. There are numerous other effects on the body caused by smoking.

44. B

Red blood cells (erythrocytes) develop in the red bone marrow and are not involved with lymph tissue.

The lymph nodes are concerned with the formation of lymphocytes, antibodies, and antitoxins and with filtering out microorganisms, phagocytes, dead cells, and cells that have been damaged by inflammation.

45. A

B cells are lymphocytes that mature in the bone marrow. They play a role in the humoral (non-cell mediated) immune response. The job of B cells is to make antibodies against foreign antigens. They eventually develop into memory B cells and are part of the adaptive immune system.

T cells are a group of lymphocytes that are involved in cell-mediated immunity. All T cells mature in the thymus gland. T-helper cells are first alerted to the presence of foreign antigens and secrete cytokines to activate the immune system. Cytotoxic B cells destroy tumor cells and virally-infected cells by punching holes in the cell membranes. Natural killer T cells secrete cytokines and are cytotoxic. Suppressor (regulator) T cells call off T-cell immune responses once the attacking antigen has been subdued. Memory T cells remember the antigen that has attacked and will activate T cell responses rapidly if the invader attacks again.

46. B

The ureter is the duct connecting the kidney and bladder. It carries urine from the kidney to the bladder. Urine is expelled out of the body through the urethra from the bladder.

47. A

The afferent arteriole in the nephron delivers blood to the glomerulus, and the efferent arteriole carries blood away from the glomerulus to the peritubular capillaries. In the glomerulus, the blood arrives at such a high pressure that the blood undergoes force filtration out of the glomerulus and into Bowman's capsule. The membrane between the glomerulus and Bowman's capsule is selective, allowing only small molecules, ions, and water to pass from the glomerulus into the Bowman's capsule and urine. Large molecules, such as large proteins and cells, cannot leave the glomerular capillaries and will be part of the contents of the efferent arteriole.

48. C

The process labelled 1 is filtration. The high blood pressure in the leaky glomerular capillaries forces small molecules, ions, and water from the glomerulus into the Bowman's capsule of the nephron. Substances in the glomerular blood that are too large to fit through the pores in the Bowman's capsule (cells, large proteins) will remain in the glomerulus and will pass into the efferent capillary

49. C

Antidiuretic hormone (ADH) and aldosterone are two hormones that regulate water balance in the body. ADH is produced in the hypothalamus of the brain and is released from the pituitary gland when osmoreceptors in the hypothalamus detect high osmotic pressure (insufficient water content in blood or high solute concentration in blood). ADH travels in the blood to the nephrons, where it targets both the distal tubule and the collecting duct, making them more permeable to water. Water can then travel by osmosis (labelled 5) to the intercellular spaces and into the bloodstream.

Aldosterone is produced in the adrenal cortex and also targets the distal tubule and collecting duct. When blood pressure is low, aldosterone secretion causes an increase in Na^+ reabsorption (labelled 4) from the collecting duct and distal tubule into the bloodstream. As more Na^+ ions are reabsorbed, the extracellular fluid and blood become hypertonic, causing water to move into the blood by osmosis. The resulting increase in blood volume raises blood pressure.

50. A

When the nephron is functioning properly, urea is filtered from the blood of the glomerulus into the urine. All the glucose is reabsorbed from the urine back into the blood by active transport from the proximal convoluted tubule. Therefore, there will be less urea and the same amount of glucose in the renal vein as there is in the renal artery.

51. A

Skeletal muscle, also called striated muscle, exists as very long cells or fibres that stretch the length of the muscle (I). Under a microscope, the muscle appears striated or striped (II). The striations are caused by the bands of thick myosin fibres and thin actin fibres. Skeletal muscles are under conscious or voluntary control (V). The individual cells of skeletal muscles are not distinguishable (VI).

Smooth muscles exist around internal organs such as arteries and the digestive system. Smooth muscles are not consciously controlled.

52. B

Muscle attached to bones, or skeletal muscle, is under voluntary control. That means that there is conscious control over its contraction. Skeletal muscle is striated or striped in appearance.

Smooth muscle that exists around internal organs is involuntary and non-striated.

53. D

Inside muscle cells, there are bundles of protein filaments called myofibrils. The myofibrils contain thick protein filaments called myosin (shown in grey) and thin protein filaments called actin (shown in black). During muscle contraction, the actin and myosin slide past each other so that the myofibril unit gets shorter, as shown in diagram W.

1.　**a)** *Identify the four valves shown in the diagram that may have been affected in the 24 women in the study.*

Valve 1 is the pulmonary semilunar valve located within the pulmonary artery. Valve 2 is the tricuspid valve, which is the right atrioventricular valve. Valve 3 is the aortic semilunar valve located within the aorta. Valve 4 is the mitral or bicuspid valve, which is the left atrioventricular valve.

b) *One reported result was mitral stenosis, where the left atrioventricular valve narrows and thickens. Predict two ways that blood flow or blood pressure in the heart or lungs might be affected. Justify your response.*

One way in which blood flow will be affected is that blood will be prevented from flowing freely into the left ventricle. This would reduce blood flow out of the aorta. One would therefore expect there to be reduced blood pressure in the systemic arteries with a lack of oxygen delivery to the tissues, resulting in fatigue and pale skin. Another way blood flow might be affected is that blood that would normally enter the left ventricle would instead back up into the left atrium and possibly into the pulmonary veins and lungs, increasing the blood pressure in these areas.

c) *Define the term hypertension.*

Hypertension is defined as elevated blood pressure. Blood pressure is the pressure exerted on the walls of the arteries by the force created by ventricular contraction. The medical definition is a consistent blood pressure of 140/90 or greater.

d) *Blood pressure is given as a ratio between two factors. Identify and describe each of the factors.*

A blood pressure reading is a ratio of systolic blood pressure over diastolic blood pressure. The systolic is the higher pressure and represents the pressure in the arteries when the heart ventricles are contracting. The diastolic reading is a measurement of the pressure in the arteries when the heart is at rest between contractions. For example, blood pressure may be read as 150 over 99 and written as 150/99.

e) *What are the lowest and highest possible blood pressures that may be observed in women taking fen-phen?*

The women in the study had blood pressures that ranged from moderate to severe. According to the information provided in the table, the lowest possible blood pressure (reading from the moderate row) is 160/100, and the highest possible blood pressure was 209/119 (reading from the severe row).

2. **a)** *What type of molecule is ADH?*

ADH is a protein that functions by increasing the speed of a specific reaction. This is indicative of an enzyme. An enzyme increases the rate of formation of products from the reactants. An enzyme does not alter any other factor in the reaction besides the reaction rate and does not alter the products. Enzymes lower the activation energy of the reaction such that it takes less energy for products to form. The enzyme itself remains unaltered by the process and can be reused.

b) *The term* induced fit *refers to the mechanism by which ADH works on its substrate. Why is this term used?*

Enzymes are specific for a particular substrate. The specificity is attributable to a fit between the shape of the active site and the substrate. The active site is not a rigidly shaped site. As the substrate enters the active site, it induces a change in the shape of the enzyme, commonly referred to as a "fit." The enzyme shape changes slightly to fit snugly with the shape of the substrate. Thus, the mechanism by which the enzyme and substrate bind can be described as an induced fit.

c) *If ALDH is labelled A, what structures or substances are represented by the labels B, C, and D, respectively?*

The substance labelled *A* is ADH, the enzyme, and the structure labelled B is the active site where the enzyme binds (typically a groove or pocket in the protein structure of the enzyme itself). Usually, only a few amino acids make up the active site, and the remaining molecule provides the framework for the active site. The substrate is labelled *C*. The substrate is the reactant on which the enzyme acts. The chemical reaction occurs when the enzyme, bound to its substrate (the enzyme-substrate complex), converts the substrate into the product, labelled *D*, of the reaction.

d) *How might the absence of ALDH be detected in a person?*

Lacking the enzyme ALDH would prohibit the conversion of acetaldehyde to acetic acid. Absence of ALDH in an individual would cause a buildup of acetaldehyde in the blood. This can be measured chemically. Buildup of acetaldehyde in the bloodstream is also toxic, causing reduced tolerance for alcohol. In a normal individual, there are no free acetaldehyde molecules in the blood.

e) *A number of antagonistic drugs exist that cause the inhibition of ALDH. These inhibitors are used to help control excess alcohol consumption. The drugs also cause nausea, flushing, and perspiration. Give one mechanism by which these drugs could inhibit ALDH.*

Certain chemicals inhibit the activity of a specific enzyme. There are two types of inhibitors: competitive inhibitors and non-competitive inhibitors.

Competitive inhibitors mimic the shape of the substrate and are able to form a complex with the enzyme. The enzyme's activity is therefore reduced because it is bound and unable to act upon the correct substrate. As a result, formation of the product is reduced. Competitive inhibitors may either be reversible or irreversible.

A non-competitive inhibitor does not bind to the active site but does bind to another portion of the enzyme. By binding to the enzyme, the inhibitor changes the shape of the active site such that it either can no longer bind the substrate or it reduces the catalytic ability of the enzyme. Either of these two types of inhibitors may be effective in preventing excess use of alcohol and causing undesirable symptoms.

UNIT TEST—HUMAN SYSTEMS

Use the following information to answer the next question.

Appendicitis occurs when the appendix becomes inflamed because of a bacterial infection. If the inflamed appendix bursts before it can be surgically removed, harmful intestinal bacteria may be released into the body cavity, with potentially fatal consequences.

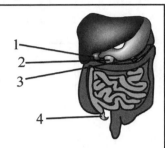

1. Which structure in the given diagram represents the appendix?

   A. 1

   B. 2

   C. 3

   D. 4

2. Proteins differ from fats and carbohydrates in that proteins

   A. contain nitrogen

   B. consist of smaller subunits

   C. are high-energy compounds

   D. are formed by dehydration synthesis

3. Which of the following statements about stomach acid is **false**?

   A. It helps to denature protein food molecules.

   B. It activates certain stomach enzymes.

   C. It is an important stomach enzyme.

   D. It kills microbes in the stomach.

4. Which of the following substances is **not** found in gastric juice?

   A. Hydrochloric acid

   B. Bile

   C. Pepsin

   D. Mucus

5. Blood flows out of the heart through the aorta and the

   A. carotid artery

   B. coronary artery

   C. subclavian artery

   D. pulmonary artery

Use the following information to answer the next question.

The Human Heart

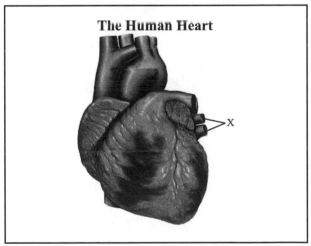

6. The function performed by the blood vessels labelled X is to carry blood from the

   A. heart to the lungs

   B. lungs to the heart

   C. head to the heart

   D. heart to the head

7. Blockage of which blood vessel would result in death of heart muscle?

   A. Aorta

   B. Carotid artery

   C. Coronary artery

   D. Pulmonary artery

Use the following information to answer the next question.

Three types of blood vessels are shown.

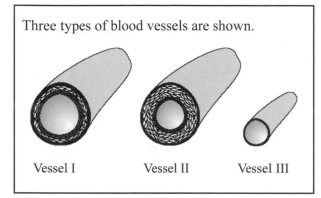

Vessel I   Vessel II   Vessel III

8. Which of the following statements about the given vessels is **true**?

   A. Vessel I is an artery, while Vessel II is a vein.

   B. Vessel II is an artery, while Vessel I is a vein.

   C. Vessel I is a capillary, while Vessel III is a vein.

   D. Vessel II is a capillary, while Vessel III is an artery.

9. Which type of blood cell is responsible for clotting?

   A. Fibrin

   B. Calcium

   C. Platelets

   D. Hemoglobin

Use the following information to answer the next question.

The foramen ovale normally closes at birth. In some cases, however, the opening between the atria fails to close, and a baby is born with a hole in his or her heart.

10. Failure of the foramen ovale to close would have which of the following effects on arterial blood gas concentration?

    A. A lower than normal concentration of oxygen and carbon dioxide in arterial blood

    B. A higher than normal concentration of oxygen and carbon dioxide in arterial blood

    C. A higher than normal concentration of oxygen and a lower than normal concentration of carbon dioxide in arterial blood

    D. A lower than normal concentration of oxygen and a higher than normal concentration of carbon dioxide in arterial blood

CHALLENGER QUESTION

11. Detection of a low blood pH by pH sensors in the medulla oblongata, carotid arteries, and aorta results in stronger and more frequent stimulation of the

    A. epiglottis and intercostal muscles

    B. epiglottis and bronchiole muscles

    C. diaphragm and intercostal muscles

    D. diaphragm and bronchiole muscles

12. Which of the following body responses would **not** occur in the event of exposure to higher altitudes?

A. Faster heart rate

B. Secretion of ADH

C. Breathing more rapidly

D. Secretion of erythropoietin

Use the following information to answer the next question.

The given figure illustrates the human venous system.

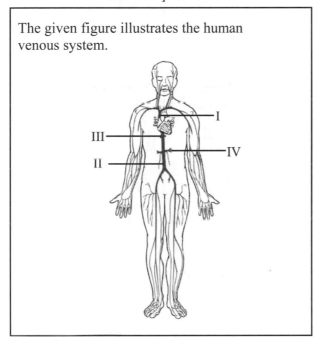

13. The inferior vena cava is labelled

A. I

B. II

C. III

D. IV

14. In the human body, urine is excreted through the

A. ureter

B. urethra

C. collecting duct

D. urinary bladder

Use the following information to answer the next question.

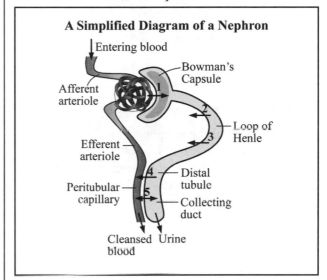

15. Which of the following substances returns to the blood at the collecting duct?

A. Urea

B. Water

C. Protein

D. Glucose

Use the following diagram to answer the next question.

Muscle Function in the Upper Arm

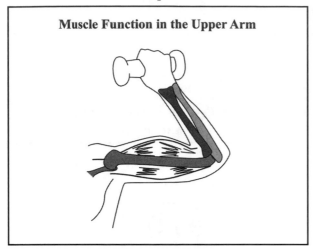

16. If the mass of the weight in the diagram were increased substantially and the position held for a prolonged period of time, which of the following substances would **most likely** accumulate?

A. Glycogen

B. Lactic acid

C. Ethyl alcohol

D. CO_2 and H_2O

17. The degree of force exerted by a muscle at any given time is determined by the

A. length of the muscle

B. length of the myofibrils

C. amount of CO_2 available

D. number of motor units stimulated

18. Which of the following tables shows the effects of the secretion of antidiuretic hormone (ADH) on urine volume and concentration?

A.

Urine Volume	Concentration of Urine
Low	Low

B.

Urine Volume	Concentration of Urine
Low	High

C.

Urine Volume	Concentration of Urine
High	High

D.

Urine Volume	Concentration of Urine
High	Low

19. Urine is produced in the nephron by the processes of

A. reabsorption and tubular secretion

B. filtration, dialysis, and tubular secretion

C. dialysis, filtration, and tubular secretion

D. filtration, reabsorption, and tubular secretion

20. In the immune response, exposure to a foreign antigen causes B cells to begin the formation of

A. antibodies

B. phagocytes

C. killer T cells

D. helper T cells

ANSWERS AND SOLUTIONS—UNIT TEST

1. D	5. D	9. C	13. C	17. D
2. A	6. B	10. D	14. B	18. B
3. C	7. C	11. C	15. B	19. D
4. B	8. B	12. B	16. B	20. A

1. D

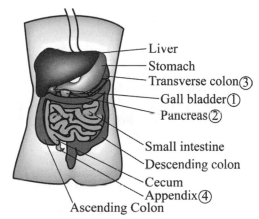

Liver
Stomach
Transverse colon③
Gall bladder①
Pancreas②
Small intestine
Descending colon
Cecum
Appendix④
Ascending Colon

The closed tube that extends from the cecum is called the appendix (structure 4). Food and bacteria can be easily lodged in the appendix, and the proliferation of harmful bacteria can lead to infection (appendicitis). Inflammation of the body cavity caused by the release of harmful bacteria from a burst appendix is called peritonitis.

Ingested food travels from the stomach through the small intestine (duodenum, jejunum, then ileum), and then through the large intestine (ascending colon, transverse colon (structure 3), then descending colon). Passage of food from the ileum to the ascending colon is regulated by the ileocecal valve. A small pouch called the cecum is located at this point.

The gallbladder is a gland that stores bile produced in the liver (structure 1). The pancreas produces a number of the enzymes required for digestive processes in the small intestine and also produces insulin (structure 3).

2. A

Proteins, carbohydrates, and fats are all composed of smaller subunits. Proteins are composed of amino acids, carbohydrates are composed of monosaccharides, and fats are composed of fatty acids and glycerol. Only proteins contain nitrogen, which is found in the amino groups of their constituent amino acids.

3. C

Hydrochloric acid (HCl), secreted as part of the gastric juices in the stomach, has a number of important functions. First, the acidic pH (between pH 2.0 and 3.0) is corrosive enough to denature protein and degrade a number of substances. Because microbes (bacteria) also are made of proteins, most bacteria are killed in the stomach's acidic environment.

The high pH of the gastric juice also activates the gastric enzyme pepsin.

Although HCl degrades numerous types of molecules to some extent, HCl is not an enzyme, but rather a chemical.

4. B

Bile is produced in the liver and stored in the gallbladder. It is released into the small intestine. There, it emulsifies fat by breaking it up into tiny droplets suspended in a watery environment. This increases the surface area for the digestive enzyme lipase to act on, increasing the speed of fat digestion.

Hydrochloric acid, pepsin, and mucus are all components of gastric juice.

5. D

During ventricular contraction, blood from the right ventricle is pushed into the pulmonary artery and taken to the lungs for oxygenation. Oxygenated blood is pushed from the left ventricle into the aorta for distribution throughout the body.

The carotid, subclavian, and coronary arteries all originate at the aortic arch.

6. B

The blood vessels labelled X are the pulmonary veins, which carry oxygenated blood from the lungs to the heart. The pulmonary veins are four little vessels that enter the left side of the heart: two come from the right lung and two come from the left lung.

The pulmonary artery carries deoxygenated blood from the heart to the lungs. It leaves out of the top of the heart. The carotid vein carries blood from the head to the heart via the anterior vena cava, and the carotid artery carries blood from the heart to the head via the aorta.

7. C

Oxygenated blood leaves the left side of the heart through the aorta. The first branch of the aorta, just as it is coming out of the heart, is the coronary artery. The coronary artery turns back, and its several branches flow over the surface of the heart, supplying the heart muscle with oxygen and nutrients. Without enough oxygen or nutrients, the heart muscle will die.

8. B

In the given illustration, Vessel I can be identified as a vein because of the presence of a broad lumen with fibrous tissue. Vessel II can be identified as an artery because of the presence of a thick, muscular wall that can resist blood pressure and yet remain elastic to respond to surges in blood. Vessel III can be identified as a capillary because of its small diameter and the presence of a thin wall compared with the walls of vessels I and II.

9. C

Platelets are commonly referred to as clotting cells because they initiate the blood-clotting reaction.

Fibrin and calcium are both involved in the clotting process, but they are not cells. Hemoglobin is neither involved in the clotting process nor is it a cell.

10. D

Blood that passes through the foramen ovale escapes the right ventricle and passes directly into the left side of the heart. This blood would therefore have bypassed the lungs.

At the lungs, gases are exchanged. Oxygen is taken up by the blood out of the lungs, and carbon dioxide is released by the blood into the lungs. Therefore, bypassing the lungs would cause blood in the arteries to have a lower concentration of oxygen and a higher concentration of carbon dioxide waste.

11. C

Low blood pH (signalling a high CO_2 concentration in the blood) activates the chemoreceptors in the medulla oblongata, which in turn signal the diaphragm and external intercostal muscles to contract. Contraction and dropping of the diaphragm and contraction of the external intercostals both serve to expand the thoracic cavity, pulling on the lungs, decreasing the air pressure within them. As a result, air enters the lungs to fill the vacuum. Exhalation is passive as relaxation of the diaphragm and intercostals decrease the lung volume, increase pressure on the lungs, and cause air to exit. The epiglottis is the flap-like structure at the opening of the trachea that prevents food from entering the respiratory tract during swallowing. The bronchiole muscles are smooth muscles in the bronchiole walls; when these muscles contract, the diameter of the bronchioles decreases, allowing less air to enter.

12. B

At higher altitudes, pO_2 (partial pressure of oxygen in the air) falls, meaning the diffusion gradient between oxygen in the environment and oxygen in the bloodstream is not as great. The result is that oxygen does not enter the blood as well.
Low blood oxygen levels will cause the heart to beat faster in an attempt to deliver more oxygen to the tissues. Breathing rate will increase to attempt to put more oxygen into the blood. The kidneys will secrete erythropoietin hormone to stimulate the bone marrow to produce more red blood cells in an attempt to carry more oxygen. What will not occur is the secretion of antidiuretic hormone (ADH). ADH is a hormone that increases the reabsorption of water from the urine into the bloodstream.

13. C

The given diagram illustrates the venous system; therefore, all the blood vessels shown contain deoxygenated blood. Vessel III is the inferior vena cava. The inferior vena cava is the largest vein of the body. It collects all deoxygenated blood from the lower body and returns it to the right ventricle of the heart.

Vessel I is the superior vena cava, which gathers deoxygenated blood from the upper body and enters the heart at the right ventricle. Vessels II and IV are too low to be the inferior vena cava.

14. B

The urine stored in the urinary bladder is discharged from the body through the urethra.

The ureter transports urine from the kidneys to the urinary bladder, and the collecting duct is the terminal section of the nephron, which empties into the renal pelvis.

15. B

Water is returned to the bloodstream from the collecting duct, particularly under the influence of ADH.

Urea is never reabsorbed from the nephron back into the bloodstream, as it is toxic. Protein is never part of the urine. The molecules of protein in the afferent arteriole are too large to be filtered from the glomerulus through the Bowman's capsule into the proximal tubule. Glucose is reabsorbed back into the bloodstream by active transport from the proximal tubule.

16. B

If a muscle is taxed for an extended period of time, all the available oxygen will be used up, and the cells will be forced to respire anaerobically in order to produce ATP. A product of anaerobic respiration in muscles is lactic acid.

Glycogen levels should decrease with activity, not increase. Ethyl alcohol is a product of anaerobic respiration, but only in yeast cells. Carbon dioxide and water are the products of aerobic cellular respiration.

17. D

The force of contraction is determined by the number of myofibrils, or motor units, that are contracted. A motor unit is composed of a nerve and the myofibrils it commands.

The amount of CO_2 available and the lengths of the muscle and myofibrils are not relevant.

18. B

ADH is a homeostatic hormone that is secreted when the water concentration of the blood is low as a result of dehydration, diarrhea, vomiting, or excessive sweating. It acts to increase the permeability of collecting ducts to water. As a result, more water is reabsorbed from the urine of the collecting duct back to the bloodstream, increasing the water concentration back to normal. However, since the urine loses water, it will be very concentrated in wastes, very yellow, and will have a low volume.

19. D

Urine is produced in the nephrons of the kidney by filtration, reabsorption, and tubular secretion. Filtration occurs when the blood is filtered from the glomerulus into the Bowman's capsule of the nephron. Filtration allows all small molecules (water, nutrients, ions, and urea) into the nephron but prevents large molecules (such as blood cells and plasma proteins) from entering. Reabsorption into the blood of precious substances that should not be excreted (such as water and nutrients) occurs by active transport from the proximal tubule and osmosis from the proximal tubule, loop of Henle, and collecting ducts. Secretion is a last-chance removal of toxic waste or drug molecules from the blood into the distal tubule of the nephron.

Dialysis is not a function of the nephron. It refers to a medical procedure in which victims of kidney failure have their blood cleaned of nitrogenous and other wastes on a regular basis.

20. A

If a B cell encounters an antigen, it responds by initiating the cloning of antibodies that are custom built to attach to the specific foreign antigen that has infected the victim. When the antibodies are released into the bloodstream, they attach to the foreign antigens, forming antigen-antibody complexes. These complexes result in the destruction of the foreign antigens.

KEY Strategies for Success on Tests

TEST PREPARATION AND TEST-TAKING SKILLS

THINGS TO CONSIDER WHEN TAKING A TEST

- It is normal to feel anxious before you write a test. You can manage this anxiety by:
  - –Thinking positive thoughts. Imagine yourself doing well on the test.
  - –Making a conscious effort to relax by taking several slow, deep, controlled breaths. Concentrate on the air going in and out of your body.

- Before you begin the test, ask questions if you are unsure of anything.

- Jot down key words or phrases from any instructions your teacher gives you.

- Look over the entire test to find out the number and kinds of questions on the test.

- Read each question closely and reread if necessary.

- Pay close attention to key vocabulary words. Sometimes these are **bolded** or *italicized*, and they are usually important words in the question.

- If you are putting your answers on an answer sheet, mark your answers carefully. Always print clearly. If you wish to change an answer, erase the mark completely and then ensure your final answer is darker than the one you have erased.

- Use highlighting to note directions, key words, and vocabulary that you find confusing or that are important to answering the question.

- Double-check to make sure you have answered everything before handing in your test.

When taking tests, students often overlook the easy words. Failure to pay close attention to these words can result in an incorrect answer. One way to avoid this is to be aware of these words and to underline, circle, or highlight them while you are taking the test.

Even though some words are easy to understand, they can change the meaning of the entire question, so it is important that you pay attention to them. Here are some examples:

all	always	most likely	probably	best	not
difference	usually	except	most	unlikely	likely

Example

1. Which of the following equations is **not** considered abiotic?

   A. wind

   B. bacteria

   C. sunlight

   D. precipitation

HELPFUL STRATEGIES FOR ANSWERING MULTIPLE-CHOICE QUESTIONS

A multiple-choice question gives you some information, and then asks you to select an answer from four choices. Each question has one correct answer. The other answers are distractors, which are incorrect. Below are some strategies to help you when answering multiple-choice questions.

- Quickly skim through the entire test. Find out how many questions there are and plan your time accordingly.

- Read and reread questions carefully. Underline key words and try to think of an answer before looking at the choices.

- If there is a graphic, look at the graphic, read the question, and go back to the graphic. Then, you may want to underline the important information from the question.

- Carefully read the choices. Read the question first and then each answer that goes with it.

- When choosing an answer, try to eliminate those choices that are clearly wrong or do not make sense.

- Some questions may ask you to select the best answer. These questions will always include words like *best*, *most appropriate*, or *most likely*. All of the answers will be correct to some degree, but one of the choices will be better than the others in some way. Carefully read all four choices before choosing the answer you think is the best.

- If you do not know the answer, or if the question does not make sense to you, it is better to guess than to leave it blank.

- Do not spend too much time on any one question. Make a mark (*) beside a difficult question and come back to it later. If you are leaving a question to come back to later, make sure you also leave the space on the answer sheet, if you are using one.

- Remember to go back to the difficult questions at the end of the test; sometimes clues are given throughout the test that will provide you with answers.

- Note any negative words like *no* or *not* and be sure your choice fits the question.

- Before changing an answer, be sure you have a very good reason to do so.

- Do not look for patterns on your answer sheet, if you are using one.

HELPFUL STRATEGIES FOR ANSWERING OPEN-RESPONSE QUESTIONS

A written response requires you to respond to a question or directive such as **explain**, **predict**, **list**, **describe**, **show your work**, **solve**, or **calculate**. In preparing for open-response tasks you may wish to:

- Read and reread the question carefully.
- Recognize and pay close attention to directing words such as *explain*, *show your work*, and *describe*.
- Underline key words and phrases that indicate what is required in your answer, such as *explain*, *estimate*, *answer*, *calculate*, or *show your work*.
- Write down rough, point-form notes regarding the information you want to include in your answer.
- Think about what you want to say and organize information and ideas in a coherent and concise manner within the time limit you have for the question.
- Be sure to answer every part of the question that is asked.
- Include as much information as you can when you are asked to explain your thinking.
- Include a picture or diagram if it will help to explain your thinking.
- Try to put your final answer to a problem in a complete sentence to be sure it is reasonable.
- Reread your response to ensure you have answered the question.
- Think: Does your answer make sense?
- Listen: Does it sound right?
- Use appropriate subject vocabulary and terms in your response.

ABOUT SCIENCE TESTS

What You Need to Know about Science Tests

To do well on a science test, you need to understand and apply your knowledge of scientific concepts. Reading skills can also make a difference in how well you perform. Reading skills can help you follow instructions and find key words, as well as read graphs, diagrams, and tables.

Science tests usually have two types of questions: knowledge questions and skill questions. Knowledge questions test for your understanding of science ideas. Skill questions test how you would use your science knowledge.

How You Can Prepare for Science Tests

Below are some strategies that are particular to preparing for and writing science tests.

- Note-taking is a good way to review and study important information from your class notes and textbook.

- Sketch a picture of the process or idea being described in a question. Drawing is helpful for learning and remembering concepts.

- Check your answer to practice questions the require formulas by working backward to the beginning. You can find the beginning by going step-by-step in reverse order.

- When answering questions with graphics (pictures, diagrams, tables, or graphs), read the test question carefully.

    –Read the title of the graphic and any key words.
    –Read the test question carefully to figure out what information you need to find in the graphic.
    –Go back to the graphic to find the information you need.

- Always pay close attention when pressing the keys on your calculator. Repeat the procedure a second time to be sure you pressed the correct keys.

TEST PREPARATION COUNTDOWN

If you develop a plan for studying and test preparation, you will perform well on tests.

Here is a general plan to follow seven days before you write a test.

Countdown: 7 Days before the Test

1. Use "Finding Out About the Test" to help you make your own personal test preparation plan.

2. Review the following information:
   - Areas to be included on the test
   - Types of test items
   - General and specific test tips

3. Start preparing for the test at least 7 days before the test. Develop your test preparation plan and set time aside to prepare and study.

Countdown: 6, 5, 4, 3, 2 Days before the Test

1. Review old homework assignments, quizzes, and tests.

2. Rework problems on quizzes and tests to make sure you still know how to solve them.

3. Correct any errors made on quizzes and tests.

4. Review key concepts, processes, formulas, and vocabulary.

5. Create practice test questions for yourself and then answer them. Work out many sample problems.

Countdown: The Night before the Test

1. The night before the test is for final preparation, which includes reviewing and gathering material needed for the test before going to bed.

2. Most important is getting a good night's rest and knowing you have done everything possible to do well on the test.

Test Day

1. Eat a healthy and nutritious breakfast.

2. Ensure you have all the necessary materials.

3. Think positive thoughts: "I can do this." "I am ready." "I know I can do well."

4. Arrive at your school early so you are not rushing, which can cause you anxiety and stress.

SUMMARY OF HOW TO BE SUCCESSFUL DURING A TEST

You may find some of the following strategies useful for writing a test.

- Take two or three deep breaths to help you relax.
- Read the directions carefully and underline, circle, or highlight any important words.
- Look over the entire test to understand what you will need to do.
- Budget your time.
- Begin with an easy question, or a question you know you can answer correctly, rather than following the numerical question order of the test.
- If you cannot remember how to answer a question, try repeating the deep breathing and physical relaxation activities first. Then, move on to visualization and positive self-talk to get yourself going.
- When answering a question with graphics (pictures, diagrams, tables, or graphs), look at the question carefully.
  - Read the title of the graphic and any key words.
  - Read the test question carefully to figure out what information you need to find in the graphic.
  - Go back to the graphic to find the information you need.
- Write down anything you remember about the subject on the reverse side of your test paper. This activity sometimes helps to remind you that you do know something and you are capable of writing the test.
- Look over your test when you have finished and double-check your answers to be sure you did not forget anything.

NOTES

PRACTICE TEST 1

Use the following information to answer the next question.

The pitcher plant is the provincial flower of Newfoundland. When filled with water, the pitcher-shaped leaves of this plant trap small insects. The plant digests the insects to obtain nitrogen. The bodies of the insects are also consumed by a number of other organisms (including micro-organisms) that live in the plant. In turn, the micro-organisms are consumed by mosquito larvae.

1. The pitcher plant and the other organisms that live in it comprise a small ecosystem. Which of the following definitions **best** describes an ecosystem?

   A. Includes only the living organisms in an area and the interactions between those organisms

   B. Includes all the living organisms in an area and all the abiotic factors with which those organisms interact

   C. A system in which materials, but not energy, are transferred between living organisms and their environment

   D. A system that is regulated by the external environment and involves transfer of both energy and matter between biotic and abiotic factors

Use the following information to answer the next question.

The acidity of a bog prevents decay, such that the surface of a bog covers thousands of years of non-decomposed sphagnum moss. When a dam is built and bogs are flooded, the acidity is rinsed away, and the sphagnum moss begins to decompose. Methane, an important greenhouse gas, is released when the sphagnum moss decays.

2. The flooding of bogs contributes to

   A. increased skin cancer

   B. climate change

   C. soil erosion

   D. ozone loss

Use the following information to answer the next question.

Animal cells rely only on cellular respiration for energy production. Plant cells, however, contain both mitochondria and chloroplasts, so they undergo both cellular respiration and photosynthesis.

3. Which of the following statements about cellular respiration and photosynthesis is **false**?

   A. Photosynthesis produces oxygen, which is required for cellular respiration.

   B. Photosynthesis produces glucose, which is required for cellular respiration.

   C. The CO_2 given off during cellular respiration is required for photosynthesis.

   D. The net chemical reactions for photosynthesis and cellular respiration are the same.

Use the following information to answer the next four questions.

Photosynthesis begins with the capture of light energy and its conversion to chemical energy. This occurs in the chloroplast thylakoid membrane. First, light energy hits chlorophyll *a*, boosting electrons into a higher or excited energy state. The electrons enter the electron transport systems (ETS) of photosystem II. Acceptors in the ETS pass the excited electrons along, extracting energy chemiosmotically to make ATP, which will be used to drive the reduction of carbon in the light-independent reactions. Chlorophyll *a* replaces its lost electrons by splitting a water molecule using light (photolysis). The oxygen is released as waste, the hydrogen protons (H^+) are pumped to the stroma for chemiosmosis, and the electrons replace the lost electrons of chlorophyll *a*. The exhausted electrons leaving photosystem II are re-excited by light hitting chlorophyll *a* in photosystem I. The excited electrons are added to $NADP^+$ to make NADPH, which will provide reducing power in the light-independent reactions.

The given diagram illustrates the photosystems.

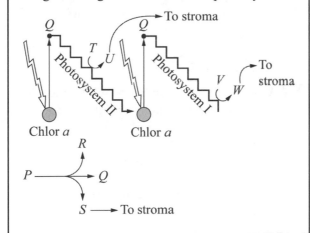

4. The photosystems occur on a membrane
   A. on the outside of mitochondria
   B. on the outside of chloroplasts
   C. inside mitochondria
   D. inside chloroplasts

5. In the given diagram, $NADP^+$ and NADPH are labelled, respectively,
   A. *P* and *Q*   B. *R* and *S*
   C. *T* and *U*   D. *V* and *W*

6. In the given diagram, ADP + P and ATP are labelled, respectively,
   A. *P* and *Q*   B. *R* and *S*
   C. *T* and *U*   D. *V* and *W*

7. In the given diagram, oxygen and hydrogen protons are labelled, respectively,
   A. *P* and *Q*   B. *R* and *S*
   C. *T* and *U*   D. *V* and *W*

Use the following information to answer the next question.

Theodor Engelmann shone different wavelengths (colours) of light onto photosynthesizing algae. He released oxygen-loving bacteria onto a plate and noticed that the bacteria clustered around the algae only where the algae were exposed to red and blue light.

8. One reasonable conclusion from Engleman's experiment is that
   A. photosynthesizing algae use oxygen
   B. photosynthesis uses red and blue light
   C. the bacteria were using the algae as a source of glucose
   D. the bacteria were attracted by the green light emitted by the chloroplasts

9. The source of high-energy electrons needed for assembling glucose is
   A. light
   B. ATP
   C. water
   D. the thylakoid membrane

Use the following information to answer the next question.

Before the time of Jan Baptiste van Helmont, most people believed that as plants grew, they obtained their food from the soil. Van Helmont planted a young willow tree weighing 11 kg in a tub containing 440 kg of soil. After five years, the willow tree weighed 361 kg, and the soil still weighed almost exactly 440 kg. Van Helmont concluded that the increased weight of the tree was caused by the water he added to the soil. He was only partly correct.

10. Van Helmont did **not** account for which of the following factors that adds significant mass to a plant?

   A. Light

   B. CO_2 in the air

   C. Minerals in the soil

   D. Decomposers in the soil

Use the following information to answer the next two questions.

Oxidation involves the loss of electrons; reduction involves the gain of electrons. In photosynthesis, oxidation and reduction involve the loss and gain of hydrogen electrons.

11. The respective chemical reactions acting upon CO_2 and H_2O in photosynthesis are

   A. oxidation and oxidation

   B. oxidation and reduction

   C. reduction and oxidation

   D. reduction and reduction

12. During respiration, energy is released as

   A. CO_2 and H_2O

   B. ATP and heat

   C. glucose and O_2

   D. $FADH_2$ and NADH

13. The removal of NH_2 from a molecule such as an amino acid is called

   A. excretion

   B. glycolysis

   C. anabolism

   D. deamination

Use the following information to answer the next question.

During the chemiosmosis portion of cell respiration, one ATP molecule is synthesized from the energy of two protons. Each NADH contains the energy of six protons. Each $FADH_2$ contains the energy of four protons. The breakdown of one glucose molecule results in the assembly of eight NADH and four $FADH_2$. Two NADH from glycolysis are converted to $FADH_2$.

Numerical Response

14. What is the total number of ATP molecules that can be produced by chemiosmosis following the breakdown of one glucose molecule? _____
(Record your answer to **two** digits.)

15. What is the primary function of the Krebs Cycle?

   A. Release oxygen

   B. Produce 36 ATP

   C. Produce NADH and $FADH_2$

   D. Fix carbon dioxide with hydrogen

Use the following information to answer the next question.

Fermentation (a process used in making beer and wine) is a form of anaerobic respiration. In winemaking, glucose derived from grapes is used by yeast to produce CO_2 and ethanol (alcohol).

16. To ensure that fermentation occurs, a winemaker must ensure that the winemaking ingredients

   A. contain alcohol-producing bacteria

   B. maintain a 37°C temperature

   C. are exposed to light

   D. are free of oxygen

Use the following information to answer the next question.

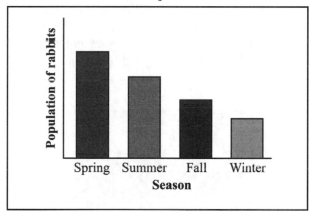

17. Which limiting factor most likely affects the rabbit population during the winter?

   A. Food

   B. Space

   C. Oxygen

   D. Sunlight

Use the following graphs to answer the next four questions.

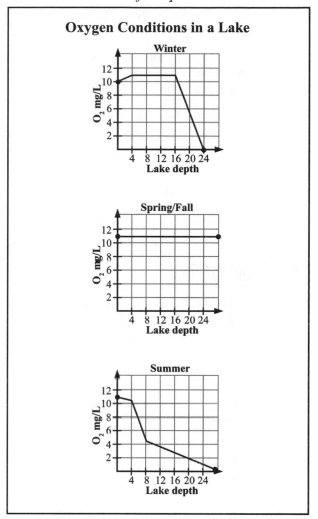

Numerical Response

18. A fish in the lake would experience what concentration of O_2 at a 12 m depth during the summer? _____ mg/L
(Record your answer to the nearest **whole** number.)

19. Trout require a minimum of 10 mg/L of O_2 to be healthy. During which season would trout have the **greatest** difficulty surviving in this lake?

   A. Summer

   B. Winter

   C. Spring

   D. Fall

20. One possible explanation for the unusual O_2 profile in the lake during spring and fall is that

A. without floating vegetation, consumers are evenly distributed throughout the lake

B. during these seasons, many organisms have moved into rivers to spawn, reducing demand for O_2 in the lake

C. during these seasons, temperature is roughly uniform from top to bottom, so the diffusion rate is equal throughout the lake

D. as the temperature changes, the surface water becomes denser than the deeper water. The surface water then rolls over and mixes the lake water

Numerical Response

21. Regardless of the season, the densest water is found at the bottom of the lake.
What temperature would you expect the lake bottom to be? ____°C
(Record your answer to **one** digit.)

22. Most energy transferred from one organisms to another is the form of

A. solar energy

B. kinetic energy

C. thermal energy

D. chemical energy

23. A farmer's field that contains only one kind of plant is an example of a

A. monoculture

B. grassland

C. biome

D. niche

24. The ability of hydrogen sulfide-converting bacteria to synthesize glucose without the use of light is called

A. mutualism

B. chemiosmosis

C. decomposition

D. chemosynthesis

Use the following information to answer the next question.

The quantity of biomass (living matter) decreases at each successive trophic level because organic matter is converted to inorganic matter at each step through the process of cellular respiration.

25. In living organisms, organic matter is converted to

A. H_2O and O_2

B. CO_2 and H_2O

C. decaying matter

D. glucose and starch

Use the following information to answer the next question.

A small and isolated population of lions live in the Olduvai Gorge of East Africa. Despite the favourable climate and ample food supply in the gorge, the lions are not healthy. The lions have a low fertility rate and are susceptible to disease.

26. Based on the given information, the **most likely** reason for the poor health of the Olduvai lion population is their

A. degraded habitat

B. low genetic variability

C. inadequately varied diet

D. over-competitive environment

For a long time it was thought that blood type (A, B, AB, and O) was not related to the human survival rate. However, recently it has been shown that for Caucasian males, life expectancy is greatest for type O individuals and lowest for type B individuals. For Caucasian females, exactly the opposite is true: females with type B blood have the greatest life expectancy and females with type O have the lowest life expectancy. Also, both males and females with type A blood are more likely to contract the Asian flu.

27. The information above has little value for the study of evolution because

   A. blood type does not relate to fitness

   B. blood types do not affect environmental interactions

   C. blood type does not affect the reproductive rate

   D. the relationship between life expectancy and blood type may not be true for other racial groups

28. Fossils provide important evidence about evolution. The age of a dinosaur fossil could be determined relatively by

   A. measuring the depth of the layer of rock in which it is buried, and absolutely by measuring the radioactive decay of uranium 235

   B. measuring the depth of the layer of rock in which it is buried, and absolutely by measuring the radioactive decay of carbon 14

   C. examining its features, and absolutely by measuring the radioactive decay of uranium 235

   D. examining its features, and absolutely by measuring the radioactive decay of carbon 14

29. A whale's fin and a human hand are homologous organs. This indicates that

   A. a common ancestor had both fins and hands

   B. both species underwent the same mutations

   C. both species are descended from a common ancestor

   D. both organs evolved under the same set of environmental pressures, but does not indicate common ancestry

30. One example of the phenomenon of overproduction in nature that Darwin observed is when

   A. plants produce more food than is consumed in food chains

   B. organisms produce more offspring than can survive

   C. more organic matter is produced than can be supported by the environment

   D. organisms develop structures that are of better quality and function than required

31. Another of Darwin's observations was that, for all things, there exists a struggle for existence. In this struggle, organisms compete for

   A. breeding rights

   B. all resources

   C. territory

   D. energy

Use the following information to answer the next five questions.

Egg whites are rich in protein; egg yolks are rich in fat and cholesterol. To determine what is required to digest an egg, tubes containing different chemical reagents were set up.
Two mL of raw egg was then added to each test tube. All test tubes were incubated for four hours at room temperature (22°C) and shaken regularly in order to mix the contents.
The concentrations of the other additives were kept constant among all tubes.

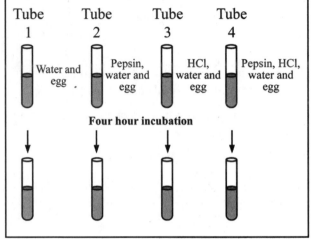

| Tube 1 | Tube 2 | Tube 3 | Tube 4 |
| Water and egg | Pepsin, water and egg | HCl, water and egg | Pepsin, HCl, water and egg |

Four hour incubation

32. In which row are the expected results for test tubes 1 through 4 found?

Row	Tube 1	Tube 2	Tube 3	Tube 4
A.	No digestion	Digestion of egg white	No digestion	Digestion of egg white
B.	No digestion	No digestion	No digestion	Digestion of egg white
C.	No digestion	Digestion of egg white	Digestion of egg yolk	No digestion
D.	No digestion	No digestion	Emulsific-ation of egg yolk	Digestion of egg yolk

33. The part of the digestive system that is modelled in test tube 4 is the

A. mouth

B. jejunum

C. stomach

D. duodenum

Use the following additional information to answer the next three questions.

Four additional test tubes were set up, as outlined in the table below.

Test Tube	Contents	After Four Hours Incubation
5	Bile, water, egg	No digestion— small yolk fat droplets formed
6	Pepsin, bile, water, egg	No digestion— small yolk fat droplets formed
7	Lipase, HCL, water, egg	No digestion
8	Egg, water, + ?	Complete digestion of yolk fat

34. To obtain the result shown for test tube 8, what ingredients were added to the test tube?

A. Pepsin, bile, and HCl

B. Pepsin and HCl

C. Lipase and bile

D. Bile and HCl

35. What could be modified in the experiments involving test tubes 1 to 8 to increase the efficiency of protein and fat digestion?

A. Maintain a constant pH of 7.5

B. Increase the temperature by 15ºC

C. Decrease the incubation time by half

D. Increase the incubation time by 8 hours

Use the following additional information to answer the next question.

Sudan IV is an indicator for fat. It is a red powder that is insoluble in water but produces a bright red solution in the presence of lipid. Similarly, the biuret assay can be used to test for the presence of proteins. Biuret reagent produces a blue solution in the absence of protein and a violet/purple solution in the presence of protein. At the end of the four hour incubation period, the biuret assay was performed using half of the solution in test tube 8. Sudan IV was added to the other half of the solution in test tube 8.

36. Which of the following rows shows the expected results from each test?

Row	Biuret Assay	Sudan IV Assay
A.	Violet/purple	Insoluble
B.	Violet/purple	Bright red solution
C.	Blue	Bright red solution
D.	Blue	Insoluble

Use the following information to answer the next question.

Digested material moves through the intestines by peristalsis. Movement of feces is promoted by physical activity, adequate water intake, and a diet high in fibre. Constipation, or the inability to defecate, is a fairly common problem in our society, and is associated with bowel cancer. Many North Americans seek relief by using laxatives containing fibre.

37. The fibre present in laxatives is composed of
   A. proteins
   B. vitamins
   C. cellulose
   D. water

Use the following information to answer the next question.

It is estimated that half of all fecal matter is composed of *E. coli* bacteria. In the large intestine, these bacteria consume food matter that cannot be digested. In the process, *E. coli* releases vitamins and other nutrients that are absorbed by the intestine.

38. For various reasons, *E. coli* bacteria flourish in the anaerobic environment of the large intestine but are not present in the remainder of the digestive tract. Which of the following is **most crucial** in allowing *E. coli* to survive in the large intestine?

   A. The pH of the large intestine is fairly neutral.

   B. There is an adequate supply of oxygen in the large intestine.

   C. There are almost no digestive enzymes in the large intestine.

   D. Material moves through the large intestine relatively slowly.

Use the following information to answer the next question.

Irritant laxatives irritate the smooth muscle of the large intestine, stimulating it to expel its contents. Many of the irritant laxatives that are available as over-the-counter medications contain senna herbal extract. Senna is a plant that has been used for centuries as a herbal laxative. The chemical irritant phenolphthalein was also a common ingredient in many commercial laxatives, but has now been banned because it is linked to cancer.

39. Irritant laxatives work by stimulating
   A. acid production
   B. peristaltic movements
   C. contraction of skeletal muscles
   D. the secretion of water into the intestine

40. How are lymph vessels similar to blood vessels?

   A. Both lymph capillaries and blood capillaries connect arteries to veins.

   B. Both lymph vessels and arteries have a thick muscular wall.

   C. Both lymph vessels and blood vessels carry red blood cells.

   D. Both lymph vessels and blood veins contain valves.

Use the following chart to answer the next two questions.

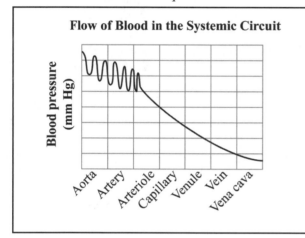

Flow of Blood in the Systemic Circuit

41. The pulsing nature of blood pressure in the aorta, arteries, and arterioles is caused by the contraction of the

   A. left ventricle

   B. right ventricle

   C. semilunar valves

   D. atrioventricular valves

42. The part of the graph that represents the section of the circulatory system with the **greatest** surface area is the

   A. capillaries

   B. vena cava

   C. arteries

   D. aorta

Use the following information to answer the next four questions.

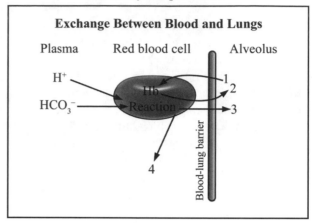

Exchange Between Blood and Lungs

Numerical Response

43. In the given diagram, which two numbers represent carbon dioxide?
Answer: _____
(Record your answer in ascending numerical order.)

Use the following additional information to answer the next question.

Heart rate is regulated in part by the pH of the blood. A low pH stimulates the heart to beat faster.

44. Which of the substances in the given diagram is responsible for lowering blood pH?

   A. H^+ **B.** Hb

   C. HCO_3^- **D.** Plasma

Use the additional information to answer the next question.

At the capillaries near body tissues, the reaction that occurs in red blood cells is the reverse of the reaction shown in the diagram.

45. The enzyme that catalyzes the reverse reaction is

   A. amylase

   B. carbonic acid

   C. carbonic anhydrase

   D. carbaminohemoglobin

46. The red blood cells leave the right side of the heart through the

   A. superior vena cava

   B. pulmonary artery

   C. pulmonary vein

   D. aorta

Use the following information to answer the next two questions.

After breathing normally, Jolene took two deep breaths that filled her lungs to the maximum volume. After the first breath, she exhaled normally. After the second breath, she exhaled as much air as she could force out of her lungs. Jolene then continued breathing normally. Her breathing pattern is illustrated in the graph below.

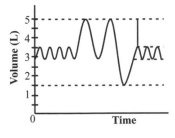

Numerical Response

47. Inspiratory reserve is the volume of air that can be inhaled beyond the volume inhaled during normal breathing. What is Jolene's inspiratory reserve? _____ L
(Record your answer to **one** decimal place.)

Use this additional information to answer the next question.

The fact that humans cannot entirely collapse their lungs during breathing is one factor that contributes to the inefficiency of the human respiratory system. There is always some air left in the lungs following exhalation. The stale air remaining in the lungs after maximum exhalation is called the residual air.

Numerical Response

48. Jolene's volume of residual air is _____ L.
(Record your answer to **one** decimal place.)

Use the following information to answer the next three questions.

Ammonia (NH_3) is produced during the deamination of amino acids. Ammonia is highly toxic even at low concentrations. Fish excrete much of their nitrogenous waste as ammonia, but mammals convert ammonia to urea before excretion. Urea is also toxic, but can be tolerated at a much higher concentration than ammonia. Birds and reptiles go one step further, converting their nitrogen waste to insoluble uric acid. A small amount of uric acid is produced by mammals.

49. Which combination correctly states the human organ that deaminates amino acids, and the organ that removes urea from the bloodstream, respectively?

   A. Kidney, liver

   B. Liver, kidney

   C. Pancreas, liver

   D. Stomach, pancreas

50. Greater amounts of ammonia would be produced if more of which of the following types of food were eaten?

A. Fat　　　　　　B. Sugar

C. Starch　　　　D. Protein

Use the following additional information to answer the next question.

Researchers at the University of Alberta have discovered a build-up of uric crystals in the fossils of the *Tyrannosaurus rex* species of dinosaur. The scientists found that the fossils of these dinosaurs had erosions on the bone similar to bone erosion in humans with gout. Gout is a metabolic disorder in humans caused by high levels of uric acid in blood. In high concentrations, uric acid precipitates out of blood and accumulates in the joints of the skeleton. The uric acid crystals cause swelling, redness, and pain.

51. Which of the following foods would a person with gout be advised to avoid?

A. potatoes　　　B. broccoli

C. butter　　　　D. meat

52. Cardiac muscle produces very little lactic acid. Therefore, it can be assumed that cardiac muscle

A. always contracts at the same rate

B. uses large amounts of glucose

C. functions mainly aerobically

D. lacks mitochondria

53. Because muscle contractions require large amounts of ATP,

A. chloroplasts are found in high numbers in most muscle cells.

B. a high density of mitochondria are found in myofibrils

C. ribosomes occur in large numbers in myofibrils

D. myofibrils secrete ATP

54. The conditions under which hemoglobin releases oxygen include

A. high pCO_2, low pO_2, warmer temperatures, neutral pH

B. low pCO_2, high pO_2, cool temperatures, low pH

C. high pCO_2, low pO_2, warm temperatures, low pH

D. low pCO_2, high pO_2, cool temperatures, neutral pH

Use the following information to answer the next question.

Recipient / Donor	O $a + b$	A b	B a	AB o
O $a + b$	—	—	—	—
A b	●	—	●	—
B a	●	●	—	—
AB o	●	●	●	—

Key — No agglutination　　● Agglutination

55. The given table shows that agglutination takes place when the recipient has blood type O and the donor has blood type A. The reason for this is that

A. the recipient has anti-A antibodies and the donor has A antigens.

B. the recipient has O antibodies and the donor has A antigens

C. the recipient has O antigens and the donor has anti-O antibodies

D. the recipient has O antigens and the donor has anti-A antibodies

Written Response

Use the following information to answer the next question

Heavy metals (HM) are defined as metals that have a specific gravity (density) of over 4.0 or 5.0 g/mL. Such metals include lead, nickel, mercury, cadmium, and aluminum.

These metals could become contaminants in the environment and could cause harmful results (see the given table). Sources of HM are mainly anthropogenic (human caused) activities that leak HM into the environment and into the human food chain. Some activities that leak HM are the mining of ores, the use of fertilizers, and the manufacture of goods. Fine metal particulates become airborne and can travel long distances, only to then be rained down into the soil and water. Run-off is also a means by which HM enter bodies of water, and depending on pH and redox conditions, HM can enter the food chain.

In the soil, HM are found in the form of cations. Some will be tightly bound and remain for many years; others are less tightly bound and may enter the roots of plants. If a safe limit is exceeded, contamination of the food source occurs. Because HM are fat-soluble, they biomagnify through the food web, causing the most devastation in the top trophic levels. Heavy metals are known to damage cell membranes, and to enter the nucleus, causing mutations. HM also compete with essential elements and metabolites and replace them in the organism.

Animals have metal-binding proteins called metallothioneins, which bind metals and take them out of circulation to help prevent damage. Plants have developed tolerance mechanisms to deal effectively with HM, such as actively pumping out the cations or removing them through plant vacuoles.

Heavy Metals—Sources and Effects

Metal	Source	Effects on Humans
Lead (Pb)	• Paint in older houses • Lead pipes	• Central nervous system damage • Children born with brain disorders
Cadmium (Cd)	• Fertilizers • Batteries	• Accumulates in kidneys and liver causing disease • Interferes with calcium uptake, contributing to bone degeneration
Mercury (Hg)	• Scientific equipment • Fungicides and germicides • Dentistry equipment	• Central nervous system damage

1. Using a food chain pathway, outline how fertilizer in the soil may cause toxic effects in humans. Follow an example food chain and state how the level of toxicity will change with each step. Define the term biomagnification and predict how it affects the food chain you have described. Explain how setting a specific guideline limit to the amount of contaminant that is allowed to be in soil may not prevent biomagnification.

(8 marks)

Use the following information to answer the next question.

Complications of diabetes is one of the leading causes of death in North America. In Type II diabetes, insufficient levels of insulin are released from the pancreas. Symptoms include thirst, hunger, excess urination, and glucose in the urine. This type of diabetes usually occurs after the age of 40 and becomes more prevalent with age. In some cases, blood sugar can be managed by exercise and adequate diet; in more severe cases, injections of insulin are necessary.

2. **a)** Identify each of the labelled parts.

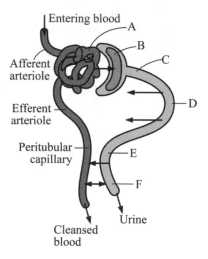

b) Explain the mechanism by which nutrients (glucose, amino acids) and water are reabsorbed from the proximal tubule into the bloodstream.

d) If the structure labelled *F* were malfunctioning, predict how the composition of urine would change. Explain your answer.

c) Many people with untreated diabetes complain of weight loss and low energy levels. From the given information, suggest a possible reason for these symptoms.

ANSWERS AND SOLUTIONS—PRACTICE TEST 1

1. B	11. C	NR21. 4	31. B	41. A	51. D
2. B	12. B	22. D	32. B	42. A	52. C
3. D	13. D	23. A	33. C	NR43. 23	53. B
4. D	NR14. 32	24. D	34. C	44. A	54. C
5. D	15. C	25. B	35. B	45. C	55. A
6. C	16. D	26. B	36. A	46. B	WR1. See Solution
7. B	17. A	27. C	37. C	NR47. 1.5	WR2. See Solution
8. B	NR18. 4	28. A	38. C	NR48. 1.5	
9. C	19. A	29. C	39. B	49. B	
10. B	20. D	30. B	40. D	50. D	

1. B

The pitcher plant is an example of an aquatic ecosystem. An ecosystem includes all of the living organisms (biotic factors) in an area and the non-living (abiotic) factors with which the biotic factors interact. The interaction between biotic and abiotic factors involves exchange of both materials (e.g., nitrogen) and energy (e.g., the mosquito larvae consume the micro-organisms to obtain energy to grow). The pattern and rate of exchange of matter and energy is **self-regulated** by the ecosystem. For example, the number of micro-organisms living in one pitcher plant is dependent on the number and frequency of insects trapped in the pitcher-shaped leaves. The survival and growth of mosquito larvae is similarly affected by the population of micro-organisms. The volume and nutrient content of the trapped water are examples of abiotic factors in this ecosystem. If the interaction of biotic and abiotic factors in an area is sufficient to support survival of the organisms, then the factors together comprise an ecosystem.

2. B

The given information describes how flooding rinses away the acidic bog, an environment in which the sphagnum moss remains preserved. When the bog is washed away, moss decays and releases the greenhouse gas methane

Greenhouse gases are responsible for the greenhouse effect—a name given to the general increase in temperatures at Earth's surface because of the insulating properties of the greenhouse gases in the atmosphere.

Depletion of ozone in the upper atmosphere (where an ozone layer protects Earth from the harmful and cancer-causing rays of the sun) is also an environmental concern. Ozone depletion is caused in part by chlorofluorocarbons (CFCs, which are present in aerosol sprays, refrigerator and air-conditioner coolant, and released during plastic production) released into the atmosphere. The major cause of soil erosion is mass deforestation.

3. D

The net chemical reactions for photosynthesis are not the same—they are the reverse of each other. The net chemical reaction for photosynthesis is $6CO_2 + 6H_2O \rightarrow C_6H_{12}O_6 + 6O_2$.

The net chemical reaction for cellular respiration is $C_6H_{12}O_6 + 6O_2 \rightarrow 6CO_2 + 6H_2O$.

The products of photosynthesis are the reactants for cellular respiration. The balance of photosynthesis and cellular respiration partly determines the amount of free atmospheric $O_{2(g)}$ and $CO_{2(g)}$ on Earth. As such, the two processes also regulate each other, comprising a major portion of the regulatory mechanism that controls life-supporting conditions on Earth.

4. D

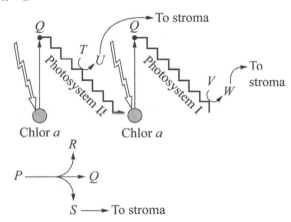

Photosystems II and I function in chloroplasts to capture energy from sunlight during *the light-dependent reactions* of photosynthesis. The mitochondria function to convert glucose into ATP during cellular respiration. Chlorophyll and its attached photosystems are embedded in the membrane of thylakoids, which are green, hollow, coin-like structures stacked within a chloroplast.

5. D

$NADP^+$ (V) is converted to NADPH (W) during electron transport in photosystem I. During photosystem II, electron transfer results in conversion of $ADP + P_i$ (T) to ATP (U). Label Q represents an electron in the excited state. Label P represents water. Some light energy absorbed by chlorophyll is used for **photolysis** ("splitting") of water into O^{2-} (R), $2H^+$ (S), and 2 hydrogen electrons (Q).

6. C

During photosystem II, electron transfer results in conversion of $ADP + P_i$ (T) to ATP (U). $NADP^+$ (V) is converted to NADPH (W) during electron transport in photosystem I. Label Q represents an electron in the excited state. Label P represents water (H_2O). Some energy absorbed by chlorophyll is used for **photolysis** ("splitting") of water into O^{2-} (R), $2H^+$ (S), and 2 hydrogen electrons (Q).

7. B

At the beginning of the light-dependent reaction, light energy is used for **photolysis** ("splitting") of water (P) into O^{2-} (R), $2H^+$ (S), and 2 hydrogen electrons (Q). The electrons (Q) released when water is split enter photosystem II to replace the excited electrons lost by chlorophyll to the electron transport chain. Electron transfer through the ET chain results in conversion of $ADP + P_i$ (T) to ATP (U). $NADP^+$ (V) is converted to NADPH (W) during electron transport in photosystem I.

8. B

Engelman deduced that the photosynthesizing algae preferred blue and red light. The evidence for this is that photosynthesis produces oxygen, and oxygen-loving bacteria congregated where the oxygen was being produced. Therefore, photosynthesis uses red and blue light preferentially.

9. C

Light absorbed by chlorophyll energizes a chlorophyll electron, which is then transferred to an electron transport system. The electron lost from chlorophyll is replaced by an electron liberated during the splitting of water (photolysis) into H^+, O_2^-, and H electrons. If electrons from water were not continually replacing chlorophyll electrons, then the photosystems, and therefore all photosynthesis, would stop. This is one reason why water is essential for photosynthesis.

10. B

The net formula for photosynthesis is
$6CO_2 + 6H_2O + \text{solar energy} \rightarrow C_6H_{12}O_6 + 6O_2$
(carbon dioxide and water combine to form glucose and oxygen).

Van Helmont was partly correct in that water is a reactant (input) in the equation, and it contributes mass to the plant in the form of hydrogen and oxygen atoms. What Van Helmont did not know is that plants also take in carbon dioxide. The carbon and oxygen atoms are fixed into sugars (e.g., glucose) and other organic compounds in the plant, where they contribute to the mass of the plant.

Carbon dioxide adds the most mass to the plant. A plant does take up minerals from the soil, but only in minute quantities. Decomposers are not taken up by the plant; they remain in the soil, where they break down organic matter. Light transmits energy to a plant, and energy is of negligible mass.

11. C

According to the given information,
Oxidation—H and e^- are lost
Reduction—H and e^- are gained

The photosynthetic reaction is summarized as
$6CO_2 + 6H_2O + \text{light} \rightarrow C_6H_{12}O_6 + 6O_2$.

The carbon molecule in the reactants (CO_2) becomes $C_6H_{12}O_6$ in the products, meaning that CO_2 has gained hydrogen in the reaction. Therefore, CO_2 has been reduced. The water molecule in the reactants (H_2O) loses hydrogen during the reaction to become O_2 in the products. Therefore, water is oxidized in photosynthesis.

12. B

The ultimate goal of respiration is to release stored energy from organic molecules (e.g., sugars) by converting them to a useable form. ATP is a universal form of useable energy. The chemical reactions of respiration result in the release of energy from glucose; energy is released as ATP. However, as during any energy conversion, some energy is lost, usually in the form of heat.

According to the net formula for cellular respiration, CO_2 and H_2O are also products, but they are not used as a major source of energy.

$C_6H_{12}O_6 + 6O_2$
$\rightarrow 6CO_2 + 6H_2O + 36 \text{ ATP}$

Glucose is a reactant, not a product, of respiration. Both $FADH_2$ and NADH, although released as forms of energy during the Krebs cycle, are eventually oxidized during the electron transport chain, during which the majority of ATP is produced by transfer of energy from $FADH_2$ and NADH.

13. D

Removal of an $-NH_2$ (*amino*) group from a molecule is called *deamination*. The remainder of the molecule is composed of C, H, and O, and it enters the respiratory pathway.

Excretion is the process in which the body removes nitrogen-containing chemicals by converting them to urine. Excretion also regulates water content in a multicellular organism.

Anabolism is the process that builds larger molecules from smaller molecules (the opposite of *catabolism,* during which molecules are broken down) in a biological system.

Glycolysis is the set of reactions that break down glucose (a six-carbon sugar) into two molecules of pyruvate (a three-carbon sugar) in the first steps of cellular respiration.

NR 14   32

One NADH contains six protons, resulting in three ATP. Eight NADH results in $3 \times 8 = 24$ ATP.

One $FADH_2$ contains four electrons, resulting in two ATP. Four $FADH_2$ results in $2 \times 4 = 8$ ATP.

$24 + 8 = 32$ ATP—the maximum generated from the chemiosmosis of one glucose molecule

15. C

The Krebs cycle uses carbon derived from glucose to generate NADH and $FADH_2$. These proton carriers are the reduced forms of NAD^+ and FAD. These carriers transfer protons and electrons to the electron transport chain which produced the proton gradient necessary to carry out oxidative phosphorylation.

16. D

Oxygen could result in aerobic respiration, producing CO_2 and water (not ethanol). For maximum ethanol production, the system must be kept anaerobic (free of oxygen). The alcohol is produced by yeast, which are fungi, not bacteria. Even though heat does increase the rate of biological reactions up to a point, yeast are not endothermic organisms, so they do not have to be kept at a very warm temperature. Yeast are heterotrophic; they get their energy from the sugar in the grapes, so there is no need for light.

17. A

Rabbits are herbivores, which means that they eat plants. Since very few plants survive during the winter, rabbit's food availability decreases during the winter season. Therefore, food is a limiting factor during the winter for the rabbit population. The correct answer is a.

The change of seasons does not affect the space or oxygen available. Also, rabbits do not need sunlight to survive.

NR 18   4

Read the graph for oxygen conditions of the lake in the summer. Look from the depth of 12 m on the vertical axis across to the line, then up to the horizontal axis to determine the answer, 4 mg/L.

19. A

Trout require a lot of oxygen, and there is not an abundance of oxygen in this lake at any time of the year. Some lakes may have periods with oxygen as high as 20 mg/L, but oxygen levels in this lake rarely exceed 9 mg/L during the summer.

Spring and fall show an oxygen level uniformly of 11 mg/L, which is quite high. During the winter, oxygen is low at the bottom of the lake, but in the top half, there is ample oxygen.

20. D

Water is most dense (heaviest) at 4°C. In the spring and fall, it is possible for the surface water to be 4°C and deeper water to be warmer, hence less dense. As a result the heavier surface water, which contains a lot of oxygen, sinks to the bottom. Less dense deeper water moves to the surface where it can absorb oxygen. Therefore, during the spring and fall, oxygen can be evenly distributed throughout the lake.

Consumers deplete the oxygen supply, so if they are evenly distributed they should use up the oxygen in the deep parts of the lake.

Temperature is roughly uniform from top to bottom, but diffusion of oxygen from air occurs only at the surface.

Many organisms remain in the lake throughout the year, including bacteria, so the migration of organisms cannot account for the high level of oxygen in the deep part of the lake.

NR 21   4

Water is densest at 4°C , therefore we would expect the lake bottom to be this temperature.

22. D

Energy contained in organic compounds is stored as chemical energy. When animals eat, they take in organic compounds. Solar energy is light, which is not transferred from one organism to another. Kinetic energy is movement. Thermal energy is heat. When a carnivore eats a bird or mammal, it may take in some heat, but this makes up a very small percentage of the energy transferred from one organism to another.

23. A

A monoculture is dominated by only one kind of organism, such as only one type of plant grown in a farmer's field. Natural grassland has a rich array of different types of plants and animals.

A biome refers to a large ecological region, such as boreal forest. It may encompass several different ecosystems, including lakes, bogs, coniferous forest, and deciduous forest. A niche is a role played by a type of organism—what it eats, what eats it, and what relationships it has with other organisms.

24. D

Chemosynthesis involves using the chemical energy of inorganic compounds rather than light energy to produce organic compounds. Mutualism is a relationship between two or more types of organisms in which all the organisms benefit. Chemiosmosis refers to the production of ATP in electron transport chains, using an electrochemical gradient of H^+ to drive ATP-synthase molecules. Decomposition refers to the breakdown of organic matter into inorganic matter.

25. B

All organisms gain ATP energy through respiration. The waste products of respiration are CO_2 and H_2O. Glucose and starch are organic matter. O_2 is consumed during respiration and only produced during photosynthesis. Decaying matter is organic.

26. B

The information indicates that the Olduvai lions have a low fertility rate, which indicates that the small population size and the isolation of this group limits their breeding opportunities. Because the population is isolated there is likely to be inbreeding leading to reduced genetic variability. The lack of genetic variation in the population increases the lions' susceptibility to changing environmental conditions, such as the introduction of disease.

Lions are carnivorous, so an inadequately varied diet is an unlikely cause of their poor health.

Competition in a small isolated group of lions is not likely to be great enough to affect the fertility rates of the group or to increase their susceptibility to disease.

Habitat degradation could potentially impact the fertility rates and disease susceptibility of a group of lions, but there is no indication of habitat degradation in the given information, so it is not the most likely cause of the poor health of the Olduvai population.

27. C

A characteristic is only significant to evolution if it affects the ability of an organism to leave offspring. Since the information provided does not necessarily imply an influence on the reproductive capability of a person, it has no bearing on evolution.

Blood type may relate to fitness if it affects the survival rate of individuals.

This information may or may not relate to other racial groups, but further tests would be needed to determine this. Apparently, blood types do affect environmental interactions if they influence the rate at which people get the Asian flu.

28. A

Relative dating refers to the fact that fossils in deeper layers are older than fossils in shallower layers. Radioactive uranium 235 can be used to determine the absolute age of the rock that a fossil is in.

Carbon 14 can be used to determine the age of the fossil itself, but it is only accurate for fossils younger than 50 000 years old. Since dinosaurs went extinct about 65 million years ago, carbon 14 would not be useful for finding the age of a dinosaur fossil.

Examining features is not a good way to estimate the age of a fossil. For example, there are animals alive now that have some of the same features that dinosaurs had.

29. C

Homology refers to the fact that species that have common ancestors will have similar structures. Examples are the wing of a bat, the arm of a primate, the fin of a whale, and the paw of a cat. Homology is contrasted with analogy, which refers to two structures that perform the same function but evolved independently along different ancestral lines, such as the fin of a fish and the fin of a whale, or the wing of a bird and the wing of an insect.

30. B

Darwin noticed that organisms have many more offspring than the environment can support. This is called overproduction.

Plants may produce more food than they can consume, but this is not significant to Darwin's natural selection.

Darwin thought that organisms produced structures exactly as they were required.

The environment has to support life, but it does not have to support organic matter.

31. B

Darwin's theory is applicable to all organisms. Every organism is born with certain characteristics. Whether that organism survives is dependent on its ability to survive in a particular environment. Those individuals in the population that possess the most appropriate characteristics for survival in that environment are the most likely to survive and have offspring. Appropriate characteristics are features that allow an organism to better deal with factors such as food and water availability, extreme temperatures, and territory. The struggle for existence is won by organisms that are able to overcome challenges provided by the environment, survive, and produce future generations with the same favourable characteristics.

Organisms do compete for all resources (e.g., water, space, food). Breeding rights, territory, and energy are each only some factors faced by an organism.

32. B

Egg whites are rich in protein, and egg yolks are rich in fat and cholesterol. Because no additional chemicals or enzymes are added to tube 1, no digestion of the egg should occur after four hours of incubation. All the rows are correct for tube 1.

Pepsin is added in addition to water and egg in tube 2. Pepsin is a gastric enzyme (secreted in the stomach) that breaks down proteins into small peptides. Pepsin functions best at an acidic pH similar to that in the lumen of the stomach, which has a pH between 2 and 3. Therefore, little to no digestion should occur at the neutral pH of the solution in test tube 2.

Although the pH of test tube 3 is low because of HCl, no pepsin is present, and HCl alone cannot digest the egg. Therefore, no digestion should occur in test tube 3.

Digestion of protein (the egg white) should occur in tube 4; however, because pepsin is present, HCl (hydrochloric acid) is added to lower the pH for pepsin to be active. Other factors that affect enzyme function include the following:

(i) The temperature—room temperature (roughly 22°C) is warm enough for digestive enzymes to function.

(ii) Time allowed for the reaction to occur—four hours should be sufficient because food normally leaves the stomach within three hours of ingestion when pepsin has digested most of the protein. Fats and cholesterol are not broken down by either HCl or pepsin, so the egg yolk remains undigested in tubes 1–4.

33. C

Test tube 4 models the stomach. Both pepsin (a hydrolytic enzyme that digests protein) and HCl (hydrochloric acid—secreted in the stomach and responsible for the acidic pH of gastric juice) are major components of gastric juice. None of the other digestive organs normally secrete and possess high concentrations of these two substances.

34. C

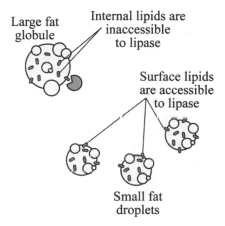

The results of the experiments are shown for tubes 5–8. In both tubes 5 and 6, small yolk fat droplets are formed. Breaking up large globules of fat into small fat droplets is called emulsification—the same physical change (not chemical change in which chemical bonds are broken) occurs when dish detergent is added to a sink of greasy water. In the body, fats are emulsified by bile salts that are produced in the liver and stored and secreted by the gall bladder. Fats present in the small intestine trigger the release of a hormone that is carried in the blood to the gallbladder, in turn signalling bile secretion.

Emulsification creates a larger surface area for the chemical digestion of fats (see diagram). Pancreatic lipase acts along the surface of fat droplets, chemically breaking down fats into fatty acids and glycerol. Providing a larger accessible surface area for lipase allows more efficient fat digestion.

Therefore, to obtain the result in tube 8 in which the yolk fat was digested, both bile and lipase must be added (in addition to water and egg) prior to incubation. Although lipase is present in tube 7, it is probably non-functional because the addition of HCl causes the solution to be acidic. Lipase normally functions in the small intestine that has an alkaline pH (up to a pH of 9). Both pepsin and HCl are components of gastric juice; together, they begin the digestion of proteins in the stomach.

35. B

The original experiment describes the following experimental conditions.

- Incubation at room temperature (22°C)
- Four hour digestion time
- Regular shaking to mix the tube contents

The shaking of the tube contents is designed to mimic peristalsis and mixing of food in the stomach and intestine. The four hour digestion time is slightly longer than the time that food would normally remain in the stomach (about three hours). Decreasing the time might decrease the efficiency of digestion, and increasing the time probably would not affect the efficiency of digestion. Maintaining a constant pH of 7.5 (neutral pH) would decrease the efficiency of digestion because pepsin (gastric enzyme that hydrolyzes proteins into small peptides) functions at an acidic pH.

Increasing the temperature by 15°C is the correct response. The experiment could, therefore, be made more efficient if the tubes were incubated at or close to human body temperature, 37°C. Given that room temperature is about 22°C, then 22 + 15 = 37°C. Normal body temperature at which human digestive enzymes are most active is 37°C.

36. A

The results for test tube 8 show that the yolk fat was digested. (In order for the yolk fat to be digested, bile and lipase must have been added to the egg and water. Lipase breaks down fats into fatty acids and glycerol.) Therefore, little or no fat molecules should be remaining in the solution, and the Sudan IV dye should be insoluble and stay pink. The results do not indicate that any protein was digested. (Protein is broken down into small peptides in the stomach by gastric juice that contains HCl and the enzyme pepsin. Proteins are further digested in the small intestine by trypsin and pepsin.) The addition of biuret reagent to a sample of the solution in tube 8 should therefore produce a violet/purple colour.

37. C

Laxatives contain fibre—complex carbohydrates or cellulose. Although fibre is not digested by the human digestive system, it is an essential part of the human diet for two reasons. First, fibre attracts water that softens stool, thereby preventing constipation. Second, fibre stretches the colon, causing reflex contraction of the smooth muscles of the digestive tract. Proteins and vitamins do not perform the same function as cellulose. Vitamins are absorbed directly, and proteins are digested and absorbed in the small intestine. Water, although helpful for constipation is not a major active ingredient in laxative medication.

38. C

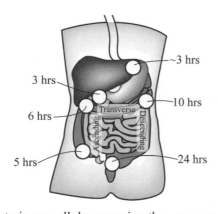

Bacteria are cellular, meaning they are composed of proteins, lipids, and carbohydrates. Therefore, the most crucial element of the large intestine is that no digestive enzymes are present here. If enzymes existed here, the bacteria would be digested. There is no information regarding the importance of a neutral pH. If the bacteria are anaerobic, then an adequate supply of oxygen will kill *E. coli*. There is no reason to believe that the speed of transit through the large intestine is a factor.

39. B

Fecal matter normally is moved through the large intestine by contraction of the smooth muscles of the intestinal wall. The regular muscular contraction of the intestine and other parts of the digestive tube is called **peristalsis.**

The muscles of organs, including the organs of digestion, are composed of smooth muscle. They are not striated like the skeletal muscles are (muscles of the arms, legs, back, etc.).

Acid is secreted in the stomach, not the intestines.

The intestine does not actively secrete water into the intestinal lumen. Water must be absorbed from the tissues by the fecal matter (i.e., water must move down a concentration gradient into the intestinal lumen).

40. D

Veins return deoxygenated blood from the capillaries to the heart against gravity. Lymph vessels collect fluid from the interstitial space and return it to the blood stream. Because both vessels are under low pressure they need valves to help prevent backflow. The valves are pocket (semi-lunar) valves similar to the pulmonary and aortic valves.

41. A

Pulses or surges of blood pass through arteries and veins about 72 times a minute. These surges through the systemic system are caused by the rhythmic contraction of the left ventricle. The right ventricle only pumps blood to the lungs, not into the systemic circuit. Valves do not contract. Semilunar valves (aortic and pulmonary) are cups that snap open when blood backflows from the aorta and pulmonary artery back toward the ventricles. This snapping produces the second heart sound (dub) heard through a stethoscope. The snapping closed of the cusps of the atrioventricular valves makes the first heart sound (lub) and occurs when the ventricles contract.

42. A

A large surface area is required in the circulatory system to facilitate gas exchange and to transport nutrients and wastes into and out of tissues. These functions occur in the capillaries. Moreover, capillary walls are composed of a single cell layer and have a diameter just wide enough for red blood cells to travel in single file. Each cell in the body is no more than two cells away from a capillary. Capillaries are therefore designed for efficient exchange of material across membranes. The aorta and vena cava (superior and inferior) are the largest of arteries and veins, respectively. The aorta conducts blood directly from the powerful left ventricle of the heart and, like all arteries, is built to withstand high fluid pressure and volume.

The vena cavae conduct deoxygenated venous blood back to the heart (right atrium).

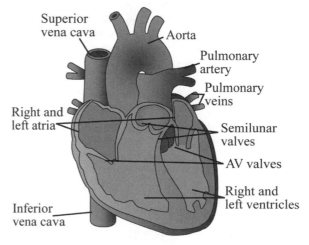

NR 43 23

Numbers 2 and 3 represent carbon dioxide because they are diffusing from the blood into the alveolus to be exhaled.

Number 4 represents water, which is produced when hydrogen ions and bicarbonate ions combine.

Number 1 represents oxygen that diffuses from the alveolus into the red blood cell.

Carbon dioxide is collected from respiring body cells and transported back to the heart in the venous system in three different ways:

1. A very small proportion of carbon dioxide produced by body tissue dissolves in blood plasma. CO_2 and H_2O form carbonic acid (H_2CO_3), which drops the pH of the blood. Therefore, very little CO_2 travels this way.

2. More of the carbon dioxide returns to the blood as carbaminohemoglobin. When $HgbO_2$ (oxyhemoglobin) disassociates in the tissues, CO_2 attaches to the empty binding sites on hemoglobin, and is thus carried back to the lungs.

3. Most of the carbon dioxide returning to the heart travels as HCO_3^- (bicarbonate ion). CO_2 reacts with water in the plasma to form carbonic acid (H_2CO_3). Carbonic acid is unstable and breaks down readily into H^+ ions and bicarbonate ions. The H^+ ions enter and hide in the red blood cell cytoplasm, remaining there while being transported to the lungs. This prevents a dangerous drop in pH in the plasma. The bicarbonate ions contain the CO_2, and they remain in the plasma. When the blood reaches the lungs, the reactions are reversed. H+ comes out of the cytoplasm and joins with HCO_3^- in the plasma to form carbonic acid (H_2CO_3). Carbonic acid is immediately broken down to H_2O and CO_2, which diffuses into the alveoli and is exhaled out of the lungs.

44. A

Lowering pH indicates that a solution is becoming more acidic, and results from **increasing** the relative concentration of hydrogen ions (H^+). H^+ is released into blood when CO_2 accumulates as a result of cellular respiration. CO_2 combines with water to form carbonic acid. (This reaction is catalyzed by the enzyme carbonic anhydrase.)

$H_2O + CO_2 \rightarrow H_2CO_3$ (carbonic acid)

Carbonic acid is unstable and breaks down into H^+ ions and bicarbonate ions (HCO_3^-).

$H_2CO_3 \rightarrow H^+ + HCO_3^-$

It is H^+ that drops the pH of the blood.

Hemoblogin helps buffer the blood from too great a drop in pH. Hb binds H^+ ions, producing reduced Hb. At the lungs, oxygen binding to Hb causes the H^+ ions to be released. Therefore, Hb has a net effect of increasing the pH by removing H^+ ions from plasma.

45. C

The reverse reaction to the one in the diagram occurs at the capillaries near body tissues where CO_2 is picked up from the tissues and brought into the capillaries for the return trip to the lungs. CO_2 released during cellular respiration diffuses into the blood and reacts with water (H_2O) to form carbonic acid.

$H_2O + CO_2 \rightarrow H_2CO_3$ (carbonic acid)

Carbonic acid is unstable and breaks down into H^+ ions and bicarbonate ions (HCO_3^-). This reaction is catalyzed by carbonic anhydrase. A small amount of this H^+ remains in the blood (dropping the pH slightly). The rest enters the red blood cell where it is bound to hemoglobin as HHb. In this way, the venous blood is prevented from becoming too acidic.

Carbaminohemoglobin is hemoglobin bound to carbon dioxide. About 40% of the CO_2 that returns to the lungs is carried as carbaminohemoglobin ($HgbCO_2$)

CO_2 binds to hemoglobin in red blood cells at capillaries near body tissues. Amylase is an enzyme in the digestive system that breaks down starch.

46. B

The deoxygenated red blood cells leave the right ventricle through the pulmonary artery. Recall that arteries carry blood *away* from the heart and veins carry blood *to* the heart.

NR 47 1.5

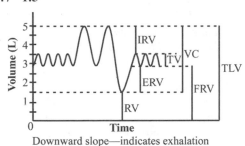

Downward slope—indicates exhalation
Upward slope—indicates inhalation

The graph shown is a **spirogram** and is produced by an instrument called a **spirometer.** A spirometer measures two things: (i) how fast air moves in and out of the lungs, and (ii) the volume of air that moves. In a single normal breath, the volume of air inhaled or exhaled is called the **tidal volume** (labelled TV on the graph) and is about 500 mL. IRV is inspiratory reserve volume—the volume of air that can be forcibly inhaled after a normal breath in. ERV is expiratory reserve volume—the amount of air that can be forcibly exhaled after a normal exhalation. The amount of air that remains in the lungs and airways after a forced exhalation is called the residual volume (RV). An individual's vital capacity (VC) consists of IRV + TV + ERV. Based on the graph, the IRV is about 1.5 L.

NR 48 1.5

The residual volume is the volume of air remaining in the lungs after a forced, exhalation. On the graph in the solution to the previous question, the residual volume is labelled *RV*. The correct answer is therefore 1.5 L.

49. B

Deamination occurs in the liver. Here, the amino end of an amino acid is removed, forming ammonia (NH_3). The remainder of the amino acid is metabolized in cell respiration as fuel, or stored as fat. The kidney's job is to filter urea (formed from ammonia) from the bloodstream and deposit it in the urine. The pancreas is involved with the secretion of pancreatic enzymes. The stomach begins the hydrolysis of proteins into amino acids.

50. D

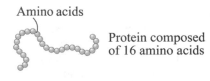

Amino acids

Protein composed of 16 amino acids

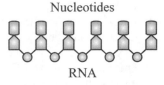

Nucleotides

RNA

Ammonia is derived from the **deamination** of amino acids that occurs in the liver. Deamination is a process by which hydrogen and nitrogen atoms are removed from amino acids, the building blocks of proteins. Therefore, proteins will increase ammonia concentrations in the blood.

51. D

The information given states that uric acid forms from urea which forms from ammonia which forms from the deamination of amino acids. Amino acids are the building blocks of protein. Meat is the only protein listed in the distractors

52. C

Lactic acid is produced when cells respire anaerobically. When no oxygen is available, there is no Krebs cycle or ETS. Glycolysis occurs and the pyruvate is converted to the waste lactic acid. Lactic acid causes the sensation of tiredness. If the heart does not generate much lactic acid, it must be respiring with oxygen—aerobically.

53. B

ATP is generated in the process of cellular respiration. ATP is necessary for muscular contraction. The ATP produced in cellular respiration is formed in the ETS that occurs inside the mitochondria. The more mitochondria a cell has (assuming glucose and oxygen are unlimited), the more ATP the cell is capable of producing.

54. C

Hemoglobin binds to oxygen or carbon dioxide depending on the conditions around it. Oxyhemoglobin ($HgbO_2$) is carried in red blood cells from the lungs to the capillary beds that intertwine among respiring tissues. In the warm temperature, high pCO_2, low pO_2, and low pH conditions found in the tissues, hemoglobin releases oxygen and instead binds to CO_2. The released oxygen diffuses into the waiting cells for use in cell respiration, and $HgbCO_2$ is carried back to the lungs. In the lungs, the conditions are the opposite of what they were in the tissues. The temperature is cooler, pH is neutral, pO_2 is high, and pCO_2 is low. In these conditions hemoglobin releases CO_2 and binds to inhaled oxygen. The released CO_2 crosses into the alveoli and is exhaled. The $HgbO_2$ is carried back to the tissues, completing the cycle.

55. A

Agglutination (clumping) of the blood occurs when an antigen-antibody complex is formed. When an antigen of one type meets an antibody of the same time, they physically combine, causing agglutination. In the donor, the focus is on the antigens that are attacking. In the recipient, the focus is on the antibodies that are defending. The donor has type A blood, meaning it contains A antigens. The recipient has type O blood, meaning it has no antigens, but it does have antibodies to defend against both kinds of antigens. Type O blood contains both anti-A antibodies and anti-B antibodies. The A antigens from the type A blood of the donor will combine with the anti-A antibodies in the recipient, causing agglutination.

---

1. *Using a food chain pathway, outline how fertilizer in the soil may cause toxic effects in humans. Follow an example food chain and state how the level of toxicity will change with each step. Include four homeostatic responses that may occur to help prevent any accumulation of HM. Define the term biomagnification and predict how it affects the food chain you have described. Explain how setting a specific guideline limit to the amount of contaminant that is allowed to be in soil may not prevent biomagnification.*

Two examples of possible food chains in which there is contamination are provided below. The beginning of the food chain should involve the soil. Use table 1 for the HM in fertilizers.

1. Cadmium (Cd) in fertilizer is the HM that has contaminated the soil → crops or grasses grown on soil absorb Cd → grazers or herbivores consume plants and are thus contaminated → grazers such as cattle are consumed by humans, thus there is human contamination.

In the soil, the roots of the plant may selectively take up cadmium.

2. Fertilizer → oil → crops → humans

Definition of biomagnification:
Biomagnification is a phenomenon in which fat-soluble substances accumulate in food chains. Because these substances are not excreted, each organism carries with it all the toxins it has been exposed to in its environment, plus all the toxins in each of the organisms that it has eaten. Each level of the food chain will contain higher levels of contaminant than the level below it. The top trophic levels will have many times higher concentrations of the toxin in their tissues than the environment (soil). Because humans who eat meat take the position of top predator in the food chain, human tissue will contain high concentrations of these toxic substances.

Setting a specific guideline limit to the amount of contaminant that is allowed to be in soil may not prevent biomagnification. Some plants, depending on species and conditions, absorb more HM than others, introducing higher concentrations into the food chain. Unless a food chain is prevented from being established, the toxin will biomagnify. An ecosystem with longer food chains will have higher concentrations of toxins in their top predators.

2. **a)** *Identify each of the labelled parts.*

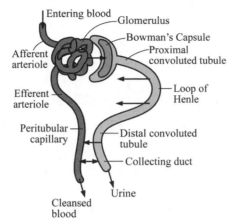

A – Glomerulus
B – Bowman's capsule
C – Proximal convoluted tubule
D – Loop of Henle
E – Distal convoluted tubule
F – Collecting duct

b) *Explain the mechanism by which nutrients (glucose, amino acids) and water are reabsorbed from the proximal tubule into the bloodstream.*

The nephric filtrate consists of small molecules from the blood that were able to pass through the sieve-like Bowman's capsule into the proximal tubule. In the filtrate are wastes such as urea that need to remain in the urine and be excreted. The filtrate also contains small molecules such as glucose, amino acids, and other nutrients that are far too precious to be excreted and must be reabsorbed back into the bloodstream into the efferent arteriole. Similarly, most of the water in the filtrate must be returned to the blood to prevent dehydration. The function of the proximal tubule is to return these needed substances to the blood. The walls of the proximal tubule are lined with cells with many mitochondria capable of producing large amounts of ATP. The ATP is used to actively transport nutrients back into the efferent arteriole. This creates a very hypertonic, syrupy efferent arteriole with high osmotic potential. As a result, water follows by osmosis from the proximal tubule into the blood. By the end of the proximal tubule, all nutrients (glucose, amino acids, etc.) should have been reabsorbed, as well as most of the water. Water reabsorption continues in the loop of Henle and collecting duct.

c) *Many people with untreated diabetes complain of weight loss and low energy levels. From the given information, suggest a possible reason for these symptoms.*

In a normal person, all glucose is reabsorbed from the proximal tubule back into the blood, so there is no glucose in the excreted urine. The given information indicates that in diabetics glucose is found in the urine. If glucose from meals is being excreted into the urine instead of being reabsorbed, then the victim will lose weight and will suffer from low energy levels caused by the lack of fuel for cell respiration. There is another reason for the symptoms, which is not related to the given information. Insulin has two functions. One is to allow excess blood glucose to be laid down as storage glycogen in the liver, lowering blood glucose. The other function is to increase the permeability of cells to glucose so that glucose can enter cells, supplying fuel for cell respiration and ATP energy production. In a diabetic, there is not enough insulin to allow adequate glucose into cells. Thus, cell respiration and energy production are reduced, resulting in fatigue.

d) *If the structure labelled* F *were malfunctioning, predict how the composition of urine would change. Explain your answer.*

The structure labelled *F* is the collecting duct of the nephron. Because its cells are permeable to water, its normal function is to complete the reabsorption of water from the urine back into the bloodstream. (Any water that remains in the urine after this point is not needed for body functions.) ADH (antidiuretic hormone or vasopressin) is a hormone secreted by the posterior pituitary when there is low water concentration in the blood because of dehydration. ADH acts on the walls of the collecting duct, increasing their permeability to water, allowing even more water to be reabsorbed back into the blood. In this way, ADH allows water to be borrowed from the urine to solve the dehydration problem. In summary, malfunction of the collecting duct would mean that not enough water would be reabsorbed back into the blood, leaving the urine more dilute, less concentrated in wastes, a lighter colour of yellow, and of a higher volume.

PRACTICE TEST 2

Use the following information to answer the next question.

The release of compounds containing excessive amounts of phosphates can have a devastating effect on the environment.

1. Which of the following situations would have a negative effect on the environment **most similar** to the release of compounds containing excessive phosphates?

   A. The excess use of fertilizers, which contain nitrates

   B. The burning of fossil fuels, which releases excess atmospheric carbon dioxide

   C. The burning of fossil fuels, which releases excess nitrogen gas into the environment

   D. The clear-cutting of forests, which causes an increase in atmospheric carbon dioxide

Use the following information to answer the next question.

In 1941, Samuel Rubin and Martin Kamen carried out two experiments using radioactive oxygen. In the first experiment, plants were provided with water containing radioactive oxygen atoms. The gas that was released as waste from photosynthesis contained radioactive oxygen. In the second experiment, plants were provided with CO_2 that contained radioactive oxygen atoms.

2. The **most likely** results of the second experiment performed by Rubin and Kamen was that the

   A. oxygen released was radioactive

   B. radioactive oxygen atoms were transferred to water

   C. radioactive oxygen atoms remained in carbon dioxide

   D. glucose produced contained radioactive oxygen atoms

Use the following graph to answer the next question.

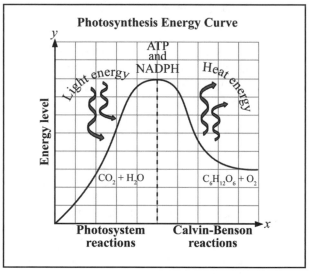

3. Which of the following statements describes a conclusion that can be drawn from the given graph?

   A. The chemical energy at the end of photosynthesis is greater than chemical energy at the beginning of photosynthesis.

   B. The energy of ATP and NADPH exceeds both the input energy and the output energy.

   C. The total energy at the end of photosynthesis exceeds the total input energy.

   D. The light energy absorbed is equal to heat energy released.

Use the following information to answer the next two questions.

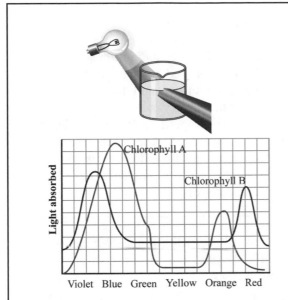

Violet Blue Green Yellow Orange Red

A scientist isolated chlorophyll A, dissolved it in a beaker of water, and then shone visible light on the beaker. The percentage of input light that passed through the beaker and out the other side was measured.

4. The scientist **most likely** observed that most of the

    A. green, yellow, and red light was absorbed by the chlorophyll

    B. violet, blue, and orange light was absorbed by the chlorophyll

    C. green, yellow, and red light passed through

    D. violet, blue, and orange light passed through

5. If the light were made brighter, it would be reasonable to assume that

    A. more energy would be absorbed

    B. all colours of light would be absorbed

    C. the peaks in the graph would occur at different colours of light

    D. less light would pass through the beaker than would if the light was less bright

6. Splitting a water molecule results in the production of

    A. H_2 and O

    B. H_2 and O_2

    C. H^+ and OH^-

    D. H^+, H^+, and O_2^-

7. The fact that a candle burns longer in a sealed jar containing a sunlit live plant than it does in a sealed jar with no live plant is because of the

    A. energy stored by the plant

    B. oxygen produced by the plant

    C. carbon dioxide removed by the plant

    D. moisture from the air removed by the plant

Use the following information to answer the next question.

In the 1930s, people thought that during photosynthesis, carbon was removed from CO_2 and was added to water to make CH_2O. This was later proven to be incorrect.

Numerical Response

8. How many molecules of CH_2O would be needed to make one glucose molecule? _____ (Record your answer to the nearest **whole** number.)

Use the following information to answer the next two questions.

Marathon runners sometimes talk of "hitting the wall." Around kilometre 30, some runners suddenly stumble, fall, and are unable to continue. One theory explaining the phenomenon is that the store of glucose in the muscles is used up, and the runner's body begins to break down fat for cellular respiration. During fat metabolism, blood pH lowers, causing the stressful effects that lead to collapse.

9. Normally, glucose is stored in muscles in the form of

   A. ATP

   B. protein

   C. sucrose

   D. glycogen

10. To avoid "hitting the wall," for a few days prior to the run, a runner would be wise to consume large quantities of

    A. water

    B. proteins

    C. vitamins

    D. carbohydrates

11. During the process of cellular respiration, NADH and $FADH_2$ both act as

    A. electron carriers

    B. forms of stored ATP

    C. the sites of ATP synthesis

    D. sources of energy for chemiosmosis

12. Heat released during fermentation can be explained by the

    A. electron transport system

    B. first law of thermodynamics

    C. second law of thermodynamics

    D. flow of energy through an organism

Use the following information to answer the next three questions.

The Indonesian rainforests are the some of the largest tropical rainforests on Earth. Unfortunately, Indonesian rainforests are currently being burned down at an alarming rate. Tropical rainforests are home to an amazing quantity and variety of organisms. For plants, the competition for light is fierce. Some small plants called epiphytes grow on the upper branches (canopy) of tall trees where they have access to light and their roots can absorb water from the moist air.

13. The role that epiphytes play as canopy-dwelling plants in a rainforest would be described as their

    A. range

    B. niche

    C. habitat

    D. community

Use the following additional information to answer the next question.

Some of the canopy-dwelling plants in a rainforest form their leaves into a bowl that holds water. Insects such as mosquito larvae live in the tiny pools. When the larvae become adults, they leave behind their larval skin and feces.

14. From the remaining skin and feces of the mosquito larvae, the canopy-dwelling plants gain

    A. water

    B. CO_2 and O_2

    C. organic nutrients

    D. necessary minerals

Use the following additional information to answer the next question.

Tree frogs will sometimes lay eggs in one of the small leaf pools in the forest canopy.

15. The relationship between these plants and the tree frogs is an example of

   A. parasitism

   B. mutualism

   C. communalism

   D. commensalism

Use the following information to answer the next question.

The density of organisms that can exist within an area depends on biotic and abiotic factors.

16. One abiotic factor affecting a rabbit population is the

   A. availability of food

   B. number of parasites

   C. availability of water

   D. number of predators

Use the following information to answer the next question.

Pollution often results in a drop in O_2 concentration in lakes and rivers. When this occurs, bottom feeders such as suckers and leeches generally are favoured for survival.

17. Bottom feeders have the greatest chance of survival when O_2 levels in a lake drop because

   A. there is a higher concentration of oxygen at the bottom, so these animals are able to thrive

   B. bottom feeders are adapted to living in a low-O_2 environment

   C. pollution has less effect in the colder water of a lake bottom

   D. pollutants settle to the bottom, and these animals are well-adapted to pollution

Use the following information to answer the next two questions.

Coyotes have a varied diet. In the spring, they eat grass, while in the summer, they eat berries, beetles, and bird eggs. They also will scavenge any dead animal they  encounter. All year round, mice make up an important part of the coyote food supply. Assume that 5 coyotes hunt in a 5 km^2 area. On average, a coyote catches a mouse every three days. Of course, they do not catch every mouse available—mice are also hunted by owls, hawks, and weasels. Assume that coyotes only consume 20% of the number of mice caught by predators each year. Also, many mice escape, or avoid predators. Assume that the total mouse population is four times the number caught.

Numerical Response

18. What is the size of the mouse population per km^2? _____ (Record your answer to the nearest **whole** number.)

19. The given description of coyotes, mice, and plants illustrates the concept of

   A. succession

   B. a food web

   C. a pyramid of numbers

   D. a biogeochemical cycle

Use the following graphs to answer the next question.

Lake Oxygen Conditions

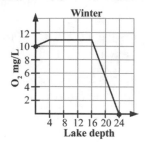

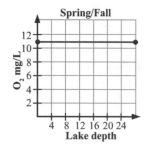

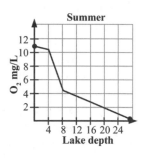

20. The low level of O_2 in the lake in the summer is **most likely** caused by

   A. animals that increase their activity and therefore consume more O_2

   B. thriving plants that take O_2 from the water

   C. a higher rate of bacterial decomposition

   D. a higher water temperature

Use the following information to answer the next question.

Micro-evolution is defined as the evolution of a species in response to its changing environment.

21. One example of micro-evolution is

   A. antibiotic resistance in bacteria

   B. a forest regrowing following a fire

   C. an owl catching the slowest mouse

   D. a person tanning during exposure to the sun

Numerical Response

22. A radioactive isotope that is two half-lives old possesses what percentage of its original mass? ____%
(Record your answer to the nearest **whole** number.)

23. Analogous structures can be defined as having similar

   A. anatomy and evolutionary ancestry

   B. development but different functions

   C. evolutionary ancestry and development

   D. functions but a different anatomical origin

Use the following information to answer the next question.

When first presented, Darwin's theory was not popular for the additional reason that the theory challenged Aristotle's view of a fixed hierarchy of organisms.

24. Aristotle's supporters would have opposed Darwin's idea that

   A. as organisms evolve, they can move up and down the hierarchy

   B. humans hold the top position in the hierarchy of evolution of successful species

   C. all species that exist are survivors, therefore all existing species are equally successful

   D. more primitive organisms have survived longer than less primitive organisms, so they should be at the top of the hierarchy

Use the following information to answer the next three questions.

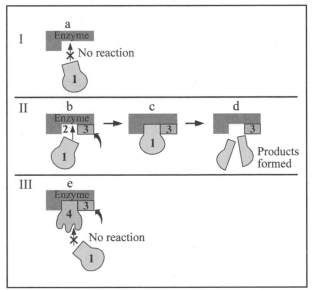

25. In the given diagram, 1 and 2, respectively, represent the

   A. coenzyme and the active site

   B. substrate and the active site

   C. substrate and the coenzyme

   D. active site and the substrate

26. Without the addition of structure 3, the enzyme is **not** able to function properly. The structure labelled as 3 in the given diagram is

   A. a protein made by a ribosome

   B. ATP, produced through respiration

   C. a substrate, processed by the enzyme

   D. a coenzyme, likely obtained as a vitamin

27. The structure labelled as 4 in the given diagram is a

   A. buffer

   B. molecule of ATP

   C. receptor molecule

   D. competitive inhibitor

Use the following information to answer the next question.

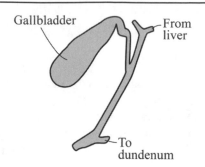

Gallblladder

From liver

To dundenum

The liver removes many waste products from the blood. Some waste products are added to the bile. Bile is stored in the gallbladder before being secreted into the duodenum. Insoluble molecules, such as cholesterol, form solid chunks in bile and sometimes plug the gallbladder. As a result, bile that cannot be stored in the gallbladder enters the bloodstream, causing an affected person to develop yellowish skin colour.

28. A gallbladder that is plugged by gallstones would most likely affect the digestion of

A. fats

B. proteins

C. nucleic acids

D. carbohydrates

Use the following information to answer the next question.

Researchers at the University of Alberta have been studying the genetics and resistance mechanisms of *Helicobacter pylori*. Recently, *H. pylori* has 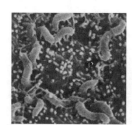 been shown to be the main cause of ulcers. The bacterium *H. pylori* lives in the stomach and the duodenum. It infects about 20% of people below the age of 40 years, and 50% of the people over the age of 60.

29. At first, researchers were reluctant to believe that bacteria cause ulcers because

A. bacteria have difficulty entering the stomach

B. the pH of the stomach should kill most bacteria

C. there is an inadequate supply of oxygen in the stomach to support bacteria

D. the contraction of stomach muscles during digestion should flush out all bacteria

30. The enzyme enterokinase activates the pancreatic enzyme trypsinogen, converting it to trypsin. The method by which enterokinase activates trypsinogen is by

A. acidifying the duodenum

B. altering the shape of the substrate

C. providing trypsinogen with energy

D. removing a segment of the trypsinogen protein

31. Trypsin must be produced in an inactive form because it

A. could consume too much ATP before it left the pancreas

B. could be degraded in the pancreatic environment

C. could be used up before it entered the duodenum

D. could damage the cells of the pancreas

Use the following information to answer the next two questions.

A capillary bed is shown in the given diagram.

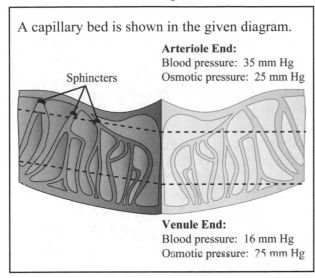

Arteriole End:
Blood pressure: 35 mm Hg
Osmotic pressure: 25 mm Hg

Sphincters

Venule End:
Blood pressure: 16 mm Hg
Osmotic pressure: 25 mm Hg

32. What is the function of the precapillary sphincters?

A. The precapillary sphincters monitor the blood for antigens.

B. The precapillary sphincters prevent back flow of blood in the arteries.

C. The precapillary sphincters adjust blood supply to each region of the body.

D. The precapillary sphincters contract regularly to pump blood through the capillary bed.

Use the following additional information to answer the next question.

Fluid movement between capillaries and extracellular fluid will move __*i*__ capillaries at the arteriole end and __*ii*__ capillaries at the venule end.

33. Which of the following rows correctly completes the given sentence?

Row	*i*	*ii*
A.	out of	out of
B.	out of	into
C.	into	into
D.	into	out of

34. One important feature of capillaries that is crucial for them to function is their

A. length

B. large diameter

C. moderately thick walls

D. collectively large surface area

35. Lymph vessels that are close to capillary beds

A. monitor the tissues for antigens

B. drain away excess fluid in tissue

C. transport antibodies into the tissue

D. collect blood that has leaked into the interstitial spaces

Use the following diagram to answer the next five questions.

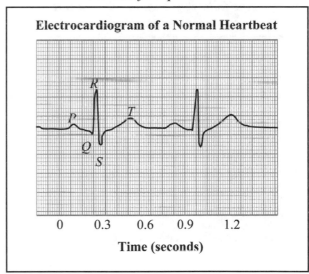

Electrocardiogram of a Normal Heartbeat

Time (seconds)

36. The sound of a heartbeat, as detected with a stethoscope, is often described as a "lubb-dubb" sound. On the electrocardiogram, the "lubb" and "dubb" noises, respectively, are at points

A. *R* and *P*

B. *P* and *R*

C. *S* and *Q*

D. *Q* and *T*

37. If accidental damage inflicted during open-heart surgery inactivated the atrioventricular node of the patient, the parts of the electrocardiogram that would be affected would be

A. *P* and *Q*

B. *P* and *R*

C. *Q, R, S,* and *T*

D. *P, Q, R, S,* and *T*

Numerical Response

38. The stroke volume of the patient whose electrocardiogram is shown in the given diagram is 66 ml/ beat. What is the patient's cardiac output? _____ ml/minute (Record your answer to **four** digits.)

Use the following additional information to answer the next question.

A significant electric shock can cause temporary tachycardia (an abnormally rapid heartbeat).

39. In comparison with the normal electrocardiogram shown, if a person did indeed have tachycardia resulting from an electric shock, the electrocardiogram would probably differ in that the

A. peak at *P* would be narrower

B. distance between *P* and *Q* would be longer

C. distance between one *P* and the next *P* would be shorter

D. *QRS* curve would be wider, and the *T* curve would be narrower

40. A heartbeat has two phases: systole and diastole. Which phase of the given electrocardiogram represents ventricular systole?

A. *P*

B. *T*

C. *QRS*

D. *QRST*

Use the following information to answer the next question.

Lung cancer is the most rapidly increasing form of cancer in the United States. The death rate from lung cancer tripled between 1950 and 1985. For people who develop lung cancer, there is an 85% mortality rate within five years. Besides being the major cause of **(1)** lung cancer, smoking causes **(2)** larynx cancer, **(3)** mouth cancer, **(4)** esophageal cancer, **(5)** bladder cancer, **(6)** pancreatic cancer, **(7)** heart disease, and **(8)** emphysema. On average, a 25-year-old male who smokes two packages of cigarettes per day cuts his lifespan by 8.3 years over that of a non-smoker.

Numerical Response

41. Which of the listed illnesses linked to smoking indicate that toxins from cigarette smoke move beyond the respiratory system and throughout the body? _____ (Record your answer as a number with digits in ascending numerical order.)

42. The loop of Henle returns which of the following substances to the blood?

A. Water and salt

B. ADH and aldosterone

C. Glucose and Na$^+$ ions

D. Amino acids and vitamins

43. If a person had severe burn damage to much of their skin, the person would **not** have a problem

A. resisting certain pathogens

B. regulating body temperature

C. maintaining correct blood pH

D. excreting certain metabolic wastes

Use the following information to answer the next question.

In the United States, a blood transfusion takes place roughly once every three seconds. Because the proportion of elderly people (who require the most transfusions) in the North American population is increasing, and blood donation is simultaneously decreasing, experts predict that there will be a shortage of four million units of blood by the year 2030. As a result, scientists are attempting to develop artificial blood. Besides alleviating a blood shortage, artificial blood would not transmit disease and would not be prone to rejection caused by an immune reaction in the recipient.

44. Cells that would mediate an immune reaction against transfused blood are **most often**

   A. platelets
   B. red blood cells
   C. B lymphocytes
   D. T lymphocytes

45. Unlike most protein molecules, hemoglobin contains four atoms of the element

   A. iron   B. iodine
   C. calcium   D. nitrogen

Use the following graph to answer the next question

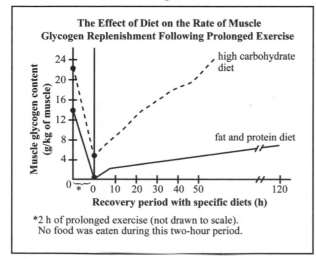

46. Athletes who consume foods rich in starches following prolonged exercise replenish their energy reserves in approximately

   A. 5 h
   B. 15 h
   C. 50 h
   D. 120 h

47. A muscle capable of rapid contraction is compared structurally with one incapable of rapid contraction. Such a comparison would reveal

   A. few observable differences between muscles
   B. more mitochondria in the muscle capable of rapid contraction
   C. more actin than myosin in the muscle capable of rapid contraction
   D. higher levels of oxygen in the muscle incapable of rapid contraction

Use the following diagram to answer the next question.

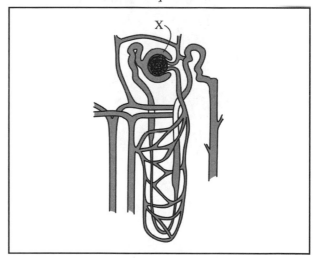

48. Which of the following molecules is **not** normally found at label X?

   A. Urea
   B. Protein
   C. Sodium
   D. Glucose

49. Which of the following descriptions best characterizes the habitat of the photic zone in oceans?

   A. High dissolved oxygen, warmer temperature, low water pressure

   B. High dissolved oxygen, cold temperatures, low turbidity

   C. Low dissolved oxygen, low solar-energy levels, colder temperature

   D. Low salinity, high carbon dioxide concentrations, low oxygen concentrations

Numerical Response

50. If a deoxygenated red blood cell enters the heart, in what order does the red blood cell travel through the following four heart structures?

   1 Right atrium
   2 Right ventricle
   3 Right semilunar valve
   4 Right atrioventricular valve

   Answer: ____, ____, ____, and ____.
   (Record your answer as a **four-digit** number.)

Written Response

Use the following information to answer the next question.

During a 2 000 m rowing race, athletes need rapid rates of cellular respiration to produce enough ATP to keep up powerful muscular contractions in their arms and legs. The muscle cells rely on glucose and oxygen delivered by the lungs and heart in order to carry out aerobic cell respiration. Since heart and lungs require time to increase their rates, aerobic respiration is slow to start. Therefore, the first minute or so of intense activity depends on anaerobic respiration to supply ATP. The initial sensation of burning caused by lactic acid accumulation begins, but will not last long because by about 1.5 to 2 minutes, aerobic respiration begins to take over. Muscles continue in aerobic respiration as long as enough ATP can be provided. If a surge in speed is required at the end of the race, the heart and lungs cannot provide enough oxygen, and the muscle cells again begin anaerobic respiration to make the extra ATP needed. As the finish line is crossed, muscles burn because of the accumulation of lactic acid. The athletes continue to gasp for oxygen long after the race is over as they re-pay their oxygen debt. During this period, the toxic lactic acid in the muscle is converted, with the help of ATP, into glycogen.

1. In a unified essay, describe and name the main processes involved in ATP yield from both types of respiration. (**Note**: No specific biochemistry is required, only the main molecules involved, e.g., glucose). Explain the difference between anaerobic and aerobic respiration, the difference in energy yield between the two, and which is a better source of energy?

   (**12 marks**)

Use the following information to answer the next question.

In 1984, Robert Gallo and Luc Montagnier independently identified what is known today as HIV. Worldwide, 17 million people suffer from HIV, a virus that attacks human T lymphocytes. The T lymphocytes, a crucial part of the immune system, mature in the thymus. As a result of HIV, B cell lymphocytes also decrease in number. Most HIV patients die because of diseases like tuberculosis and cancers such as Kaposi's sarcoma. Once an infected individual's lymphocyte count reaches less than 200 per cubic millimetre of blood (normal is from 500–1 100 T-cells/mm^3), susceptibility increases, and levels below 10 can be fatal.

2. **a)** What are the types of lymphocytes that mature in the thymus?

b) A decrease in B cell lymphocytes would affect the immune system in what way?

c) How would a decrease in thymus lymphocytes cause susceptibility to disease?

Use the following additional information to answer parts d) and e).

Immune deficiency disorders may also be hereditary, as is the case with DiGeorge's syndrome. In this disorder, no T lymphocytes are produced at all. Those afflicted can mount only limited immune responses. In a severe disorder, SCID (severe combined immunodeficiency) individuals have no immune system, and must live in a completely sterile environment.

d) In individuals with DiGeorge's syndrome, what may be the cause of missing T lymphocytes?

e) A normal response to a foreign antigen in the body would set off which chain of events that would not occur in a SCID sufferer?

ANSWERS AND SOLUTIONS—PRACTICE TEST 2

1. A	12. C	23. D	34. D	45. A
2. D	13. B	24. C	35. B	46. C
3. A	14. D	25. B	36. D	47. B
4. C	15. B	26. D	37. C	48. B
5. A	16. C	27. D	NR38. 6 600	49. A
6. C	17. B	28. A	39. C	NR50. 1423
7. B	NR18. 2 434	29. B	40. C	WR1. See Solution
NR8. 6	19. C	30. D	NR41. 4567	WR2. See Solution
9. D	20. D	31. D	42. A	
10. D	21. A	32. C	43. C	
11. A	NR22. 25	33. B	44. D	

1. A

Soil and water contain limited quantities of both phosphates and nitrates, which are common components of fertilizers used to enhance plant growth. Although crop plant production benefits from the fertilizers, increasing both phosphate and nitrate quantities in soil and water can cause overgrowth of algae and plants in waterways. Increased crop growth also removes other valuable and essential nutrients from the soil. Many of these nutrients are never replaced, creating poor-quality, non-fertile soil.

Nitrates are also derived from burning fossil fuels. However, most of the nitrates released into the atmosphere during combustion react chemically with moisture in the air to form nitric acid—a component of acid rain. Carbon dioxide, although used by plants for photosynthesis, is not a limiting factor for plant growth in most areas on Earth. Carbon dioxide is more limited in deep-water aquatic environments. Moreover, an increase in carbon dioxide has other effects on the environment that are not similar to the effects of an increase in phosphorus.

2. D

Both water and carbon dioxide are reactants/substrates for the photosynthesis reactions performed by plants. H_2O enters photosynthesis during the light-dependent reactions. Absorption of sunlight excites electrons in chlorophyll. The energy of these high-energy electrons is used for *photolysis* (splitting) of water into hydrogen and oxygen atoms. The H^+ atoms ions are used for ATP synthesis; oxygen is released by the plant as $O_{2(g)}$. Thus, radioactively labelled oxygen atoms within water are released as radioactive gaseous oxygen, as described for the first experiment performed by Rubin and Karmen. Carbon dioxide enters photosynthesis during the carbon fixation reactions (Calvin–Benson cycle). These reactions produce a three-carbon sugar called phosphoglyceraldehyde (PGAL). Two molecules of PGAL can join to form one six-carbon molecule (glucose). Thus, CO_2 is incorporated into glucose (as well as into other sugars, such as starch and sucrose), and a radioactive oxygen atom within CO_2 would therefore be incorporated into glucose.

The release of radioactive oxygen gas by the plant would require that the radioactive oxygen atom was originally incorporated in water molecules. Carbon dioxide is taken up by photosynthesizing plants. If the radioactivity remained as part of CO_2, a researcher might suspect that the plant is either dead or not performing photosynthesis.

3. A

Photosynthesis Energy Curve

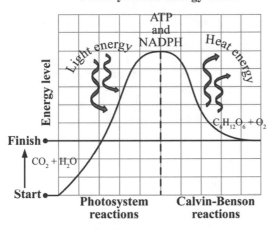

The given graph shows the energy transfer that occurs during photosynthesis. During the light-dependent reactions of photosynthesis (during photosystems I and II), light energy is converted to high-energy chemical bonds within ATP and NADPH molecules. During the carbon-fixing reactions (Calvin–Benson cycle) that follow, some of the energy stored in ATP and NADPH is used to produce glucose ($C_6H_{12}O_6$) from carbon dioxide and precursor carbon chains of the Calvin Benson cycle. According to the graph, the endpoint energy level is higher than the energy level of the plant before photosynthesis. Although plants must use some of the energy they gain form the sun to produce glucose and fuel cellular respiration, plants are able to store excess energy in the form of sugars such as glucose, sucrose, and starch. According to the graph, absorption of light energy is responsible for the upward slope of the graph, and the release of heat energy is responsible for the downward slope.

The start and end points of the line graph do not have the same energy level (value on the y-axis). If the heat energy released were equal to the light energy absorbed, the start and end points should be equal.

The line graph only represents the energy level within the plant. Light energy from the sun in this case is not measured and assumed to be non-limiting.

Energy can be neither created nor destroyed, only converted from one form to another. It is therefore impossible for ATP and NADPH to possess more energy than the input energy and the output energy. Input and output energy are all equal.

4. C

Visible light contains wavelengths of light corresponding to all the possible colours of the rainbow. Correspondingly, if an object appears green to the eye, the object must absorb all the colours of light except green; green light is reflected by the object and the eye therefore sees the object as green. For example, because plants appear green, plants must reflect green light. Chlorophyll *a* and *b* are pigments found in chloroplasts of plant cells. *The absorption spectra* (which show the colours of light absorbed by the pigment) of both chlorophyll *a* and *b* are given in the graph. Note that chlorophyll *a* absorbs mainly blue to blue-green light (the highest peak on the line graph) and some orange light (the lower peak). All the remaining colours (including violet, green, yellow, and red) are reflected by chlorophyll *a*. Therefore, blue to blue-green light and some orange light are absorbed by the solution of chlorophyll *a* in the beaker, while the reflected colours pass through the beaker.

5. A

Light is composed of particles of energy (called photons). The brighter the light, the more photons are travelling in the beam of light, and thus the more energy within the beam of light. As long as the maximum absorption capacity of the chlorophyll molecules in the solution has not been reached, brighter light should result in more absorption of light energy by chlorophyll *a*—more chlorophyll *a* molecules in solution will have absorbed light energy. If anything, *more* light might pass through the beaker once all the chlorophyll *a* molecules in solution have absorbed light.

The colours (wavelengths) of light absorbed by chlorophyll *a* always remain the same. Which colours of light are absorbed by the chlorophyll-a molecule is dependent on chlorophyll *a*'s chemical structure. The reason that chlorophyll *a* and *b* have different absorption spectra is because they have different chemical structures.

6. C

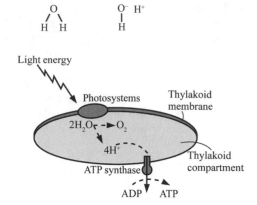

Under normal circumstances, a water molecule splits into a hydrogen ion (H^+) and a hydroxide ion (OH^-). Splitting of water occurs under special circumstances (involving a group of manganese atoms belonging to a special water-splitting enzyme) during *photolysis*—energy absorbed by chlorophyll during photosynthesis is used to split two molecules of water simultaneously, releasing two electrons and producing O_2 and four H^+ ions. The electrons replace high-energy electrons transferred from chlorophyll to the photosystems of the light-dependent photosynthesis reactions. The hydrogen ions, which build up within the thylakoid compartment, are eventually pumped out into the stroma through ATP synthase, thereby generating ATP. Oxygen is released by the plant as a waste gas.

7. B

A candle flame, like any fire, requires oxygen to burn. When a substance burns (combusts), the elements in the substance are combining with oxygen. For example, carbon combines with oxygen to form carbon dioxide. $(C + O_2 \rightarrow CO_2)$

In an empty jar, the candle (wick) will burn until all the oxygen is consumed (as a reactant in the equation), then be extinguished. In an empty sealed jar, there exists a finite amount of oxygen (the amount that was in the jar immediately after it was sealed). The candle burns longer in the jar with the plant because the plant releases oxygen by the process of photosynthesis. The photosynthesis equation is as follows:

$$6CO_2 + 6HO_2 \xrightarrow{\text{solar energy}} C_6H_{12}O_6 + 6O_2$$

Although plants do use CO_2 for photosynthesis, removing the product (CO_2) of the combustion reaction does not help the reaction to proceed faster or for a longer time if one of the reactants (O_2) is limiting.

Moisture and energy used and stored by the plant are irrelevant to the question. Plants do store energy in the form of starches and other sugars. The also remove moisture (water) from their environment through the roots.

NR 8   6

The formula for glucose is as follows: $C_6H_{12}O_6$

Using only molecules of CH_2O to assemble glucose, it would require $6CH_2O$ to produce glucose. Multiply the each of the individual elements in CH_2O (C, H, and O) by 6 to get the chemical formula of glucose.

9. D

Glycogen is a complex molecule composed of branching chains of glucose. Insulin stimulates liver and muscle cells to absorb glucose from the blood and convert it to glycogen.

Muscle cells contain a lot of protein, but this is not a form in which glucose is stored. ATP is produced when glucose is broken down, but could not be considered a storage form of glucose. Sucrose is table sugar, made by plants, not by muscle cells.

10. D

Carbohydrates (starch and various sugars) are complex molecules composed of glucose molecules. As a result, carbohydrates are a rich source of glucose.

Vitamins are necessary for enzyme mediated reactions, but are not a source of energy. Proteins are a source of energy but are not broken down as easily as glucose is. Water provides no energy.

11. A

NADH and $FADH_2$ are important for respiration. They transfer protons and high energy electrons from glycolysis and the Krebs cycle to the electron transport system for ATP production.

NADH and $FADH_2$ are transport molecules. ATP synthesis occurs mainly on the inner membrane of mitochondria. Chemiosmosis is the process of ATP production that occurs on the inner membrane of mitochondria. NADH and $FADH_2$ provide chemiosmosis with electrons for ATP production but not the energy needed to carry out the process.

12. C

The second law of thermodynamics states that during any energy conversion, some energy is lost in the form of heat. During fermentation, some of the chemical energy in glucose is converted to ATP energy, but most of the energy in glucose is lost as unusable heat. This is why anaerobic respiration (fermentation) is considered to be so inefficient.

13. B

The role of an organism in its environment is known as its niche. The epiphytes occupy the niche of small canopy-dwelling plants, and monkeys would similarly occupy the niche of small canopy-dwelling primates. The trees they live on occupy the niche of tall ground-dwelling plants.

14. D

Decay of the animal remains leaves nitrogen, phosphorous, potassium, and other compounds that a plant needs.

Almost all plants are autotrophs that make their own organic compounds. CO_2 and O_2 are gases that a plant can absorb from air. Water can be gathered from rain—insects do not provide water for the plant.

15. B

Mutualism is a relationship in which all parties benefit. Frogs benefit by having water in which to lay eggs. The tadpoles later leave animal wastes that provide the plant with mineral nutrients.

In a commensal relationship, only one side benefits. In a parasitic relationship, one side is harmed. Communalism involves several members of one type of animal working together, perhaps to secure territory.

16. C

Abiotic factors are non-living influences, such as climate and other components of the physical environment.

Food is predominantly organic matter, either living or formerly living. Predators are a living influence, as are parasites.

17. B

Bottom-feeding organisms live farthest from the surface where diffusion from air and floating plants add oxygen to the water. As a result, bottom feeders are adapted for life in low oxygen conditions.

Not all pollutants do settle. The temperature of the water will have nothing to do with the effect of pollution. It is more likely to find plants growing near and at the surface of lakes and rivers, so there is not a higher concentration of oxygen at the bottom.

NR 18   2 434

5 coyotes in 5 km^2 = 1 coyote per km^2

One coyote consumes one mouse per three days. There are 365 days in one year. Thus, there are 121.7 mice. Because this is only 20% of the total number of mice consumed, this number must be multiplied by 5 to equal 100%.
$121.7 \times 5 = 608.5$

The total number of mice consumed is 608.5. To get the total mouse population, multiply this number by four.
$608.5 \times 4 = 2434$

There are 2434 mice per km^2.

19. C

The massive number of plants that support a smaller number of mice, which in turn can support a very small number of coyotes, is an example of a pyramid of numbers.

A food web involves a large number of interconnected energy transfers. A biogeochemical cycle illustrates the recycling of matter within an ecosystem. Succession refers to the changes that occur over time within a community.

20. D

The higher the temperature of a liquid, the less gas that can be dissolved in it.

There may be more active animals, but there are also more plants undergoing photosynthesis. Thriving plants put more oxygen into the water during photosynthesis than they remove during respiration.

21. A

When bacteria first were exposed to antibiotics, the antibiotics were deadly to the bacteria. However, over time, they adapted to the presence of antibiotics in their environment. The environment changed and the bacteria evolved in response to this change.

The owl catching the slowest mouse is an example of survival of the fittest and does not necessarily reflect evolution. A forest re-growing after a fire is an example of secondary succession, the changes that can occur in a community, not the evolution of a species. A person tanning is an individual adapting to his or her environment, not a species evolving.

NR 22 25

After one half life, 50% of the original mass remains. After the second half life, this new mass is reduced a further 50%, leaving only 25% of the original mass.

23. D

The gills of a crayfish, which grow as extensions of legs, and the gills of fish, which grow as extensions of pouches in the neck, are both analogous structures. They have a similar function, but how they developed in the organism differs.

Structures with similar development but different functions are homologous structures. Often, analogous structures share similar anatomy, but their evolutionary ancestry is very different

24. C

Aristotle thought that some organisms such as humans were superior to others and formed the top rung of the ladder of life, so the idea that all organisms were equally fit would have been opposed by supporters of Aristotle's theories.

Darwin did not place primitive organisms at the top of a hierarchy. Darwin did not envision a hierarchy of organisms.

25. B

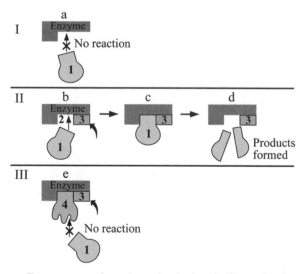

Enzymes catalyze (speed up) chemical reactions. To do this, the enzyme binds with the molecule that it acts upon (the substrate, structure 1) to form an enzyme-substrate complex—labelled C in reaction II.

Because each enzyme is specialized in shape and function for a specific substrate and reaction, the enzyme-substrate interaction is also very specific (represented in the diagram by the complementary shapes of the enzyme and substrate). Sometimes, this interaction requires an additional molecule, a coenzyme (structure 3). The coenzyme is required for the substrate and enzyme to bind. (See reaction I, in which no reaction occurs.)

In a complete reaction (reaction II), the substrate undergoes a change (is split in two) to form the products. Neither the enzyme nor the coenzyme are altered by this process. Reaction III shows a situation in which the active site is blocked by another molecule (structure 4—a competitive inhibitor) to prevent the reaction.

26. D

Enzymes, coenzymes, and cofactors are not changed during their interactions with substrates. Only the substrate (structure 2) is altered, whereas the enzyme (structure 1) and coenzyme (structure 3) remain intact. Cofactors are inorganic molecules including iron, zinc, potassium, and some compounds that contain copper. Coenzymes are organic molecules that are made from vitamins.

Structure 3 alters the active site (2) of the enzyme so that it can bind with the substrate (structure 1, the component that is altered as a result of forming the complex shown in sequence II). Without the addition of structure 3, the enzyme does not bind the substrate (as shown in sequence I).
Both cofactors and coenzymes help enzymes bind to a substrate by altering the active site of the enzyme. Neither coenzymes nor cofactors are proteins. (Proteins are synthesized within a cell by ribosomes.) ATP (adenosine triphosphate) is generated during cellular respiration when glucose is converted into a form of energy that is readily useable. ATP may be required for chemical reactions that are catalyzed by enzymes, but not in the capacity of a coenzyme/cofactor.

27. D

Structure 4 is shown in sequence III where the active site (label 2) is blocked by structure 4. Blocking the active site prevents the enzyme from interacting with the part of the normal substrate that is necessary for catalyzing the reaction. (The normal reaction is shown in sequence II.) Structure 4 is also unaffected by binding to the enzyme. That is, the enzyme simply binds to structure 4, usually with high affinity, without altering structure 4 chemically. Structure 4 inhibits the normal substrate from binding with the enzyme and is therefore also in competition with the substrate for binding the enzyme. Consequently, structure 4 is called a **competitive inhibitor**.

ATP molecules are sources of immediate energy for reactions that require energy input. Buffers are used to maintain the pH of a solution. Receptor molecules are used to receive signals in signalling pathways in the nervous system and endocrine system.

28. A

The gallbladder stores and releases bile, which emulsifies fats for digestion. If the gallbladder was plugged and bile could not be released into the small intestine, the digestion of fats would be affected.

29. B

One of the functions of gastric acid is to lower the pH enough to kill any pathogenic bacteria that enter the digestive tract in our food. The corrosive nature of gastric juice was believed to prevent survival of all bacterial cells. This is now known to be false. Oxygen supply is not an issue because bacteria can be aerobic or anaerobic. Peristaltic contractions would not result all bacteria being removed from the digestive tract.

30. D

Enterokinase is an enzyme present in the wall of the small intestine. When the pancreatic enzyme trypsinogen has entered the small intestine through the pancreatic duct, it is converted to the active form, trypsin, by enterokinase. Enterokinase is a protease that actually removes part of the inactive trypsinogen protein to convert it to active trypsin.

Secreting inactive forms of enzymes is a protective mechanism—if trypsin were present in an active form within the pancreas, it would probably digest pancreatic tissue. A clue to the function of enterokinase is in its name: the *-ase* ending indicates that enterokin*ase* is an enzyme.

Pepsinogen is converted to the active enzyme, pepsin, by the acidic environment of the stomach. The acidic environment is caused by the presence of hydrochloric acid, not an enzyme. Similarly, providing energy for a chemical reaction is usually the job of ATP molecules, or heat, or some other form of readily useable energy. Altering the shape of a *substrate* (the molecule that undergoes a change as a result of the chemical reaction catalyzed by the enzyme) would not affect the activity of the enzyme itself. The enzyme can only become activated by undergoing a structural change. Most often, the structural change exposes the active site of the enzyme to the substrate.

31. D

Trypsin is a protein-digesting enzyme. Much of the cellular structure of the pancreas is made of protein that could be digested by trypsin. In order to avoid digesting pancreatic tissue, enzymes such as trypsin (other examples include pepsinogen, which is converted to pepsin, and chymotrypsinogen, which is converted to chymotrypsin) are secreted in an inactive form and activated only when they reach the appropriate environment (e.g., trypsin is activated in the small intestine).

A second line of defense against self-digestion in the pancreas does exist. A trypsin inhibitor protein in the pancreas binds and inhibits active trypsin if it happens to be present. The interaction is similar to binding of a competitive inhibitor that prevents interaction of the enzyme with its normal substrate.

The concentration of most enzymes in the body is regulated carefully. For example, feedback systems signal more enzymes to be produced or secreted when more food needs to be digested. It is therefore not very likely that an enzyme would be used up. Similarly, stores of ATP are also regulated in the body according to need. Given that one enzyme uses an extremely small portion of the total ATP available in the body, it is highly unlikely that too much ATP is consumed by one enzyme. Although degradation of the active enzyme in the pancreas is a plausible explanation and an effective defense under the circumstances, it does not occur in the pancreas.

32. C

Sphincters are circular muscles. When the precapillary sphincter muscles contract, they close off the opening that connects the arteriole to the capillaries. Relaxation of the sphincter muscle opens the passage, allowing blood to flow from the arteriole into the capillaries that supply a particular body tissue with blood. Blood supply to the different tissues is also regulated by the nervous system, which regulates the diameter of arterioles. The middle layer of arteriole walls is composed of smooth muscle and elastic fibres. Contraction of the muscles decreases the diameter of (constricts) the arteriole, thereby decreasing the volume of blood that flows through. Relaxation of the muscles widens (dilates) the arteriole, allowing more blood to flow through. Constriction and dilation of the arterioles are also called, *vasoconstriction* and *vasodilation,* respectively.

The heart is responsible for pumping the blood throughout the body. Preventing back flow (flow of blood in the wrong direction) of blood is important in veins, which return blood to the heart from the body's tissues. Blood pressure at the end of a capillary bed is very low—insufficient to push blood to the heart. In fact, veins (but not arteries) have valves that allow blood to flow in one direction only—back to the heart. Antigens are detected in the blood by white blood cells, not sphincters.

33. B

Blood pressure is the fluid pressure in the lumen of the arteriole and capillaries that pushes outward against the capillary wall. High blood pressure at the entrance to a capillary bed causes fluid containing gases, nutrients, and small proteins to travel from the capillary to the extracellular fluid (ECF) that bathes tissues. Very few small proteins pass through the capillary wall freely; most proteins are trapped inside the capillary. Fluid movement out of capillaries is called **filtration**. **Osmotic pressure** is the water pressure in the extracellular fluid (ECF) that drives fluid from the tissues back into the capillaries by osmosis. The presence of large proteins inside the capillary but absent outside, in the ECF, creates a concentration gradient at the venule end of the capillary. As a result, water moves from the ECF, where water is present in a higher concentration, to the capillary, where water is present in a lower relative concentration. Movement of fluid back into the capillaries is called **absorption**. According to the diagram in the preamble, at the arteriole end blood pressure is higher than the osmotic pressure, so fluid moves *out of* the capillary into the ECF. At the venule end, the osmotic pressure is greater than the blood pressure, so fluid moves into the capillary from the ECF.

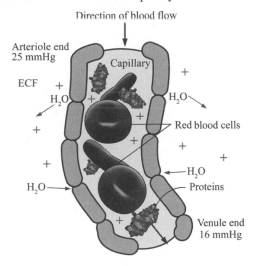

34. D

The smallest blood vessels in the body, capillaries, connect arteries to veins and are the site of gas and fluid exchange between blood and body tissues. The capillary wall is composed of only a single layer of cells through which gases, ions, minerals, amino acids, and small proteins can diffuse. For optimal exchange of fluid and gases, capillaries must have a large surface area. Collectively, the cells that form the surface of the capillaries comprise a huge membrane across which nutrients, gases, and waste are exchanged. Moreover, capillaries are so numerous that any cell is never more than a few cell lengths away from a capillary.

The diameter of a capillary is roughly 0.005 mm, just wide enough for red blood cells to squeeze through in single file. Arteries and veins are the widest blood vessels. The length of a capillary varies between 0.4 mm and 1.0 mm—very short in comparison with arteries and veins that carry blood to and from the heart to the furthest extremities of the body, and also in comparison to arterioles (and venules), which supply a localized region with blood.

35. B

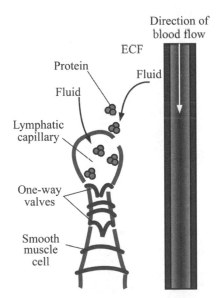

Lymph vessels close to capillaries are called lymph capillaries. Lymph capillaries are unique vessels in that they are closed at one end. Near the closed end, interstitial fluid (or extracellular fluid, ECF) diffuses from the tissue into the lymph capillary.

The pale, yellowish fluid collected by a lymph vessel is called lymph, which is similar to blood plasma except that lymph contains very few plasma proteins. Plasma proteins are generally too large to escape blood capillaries, so very few proteins end up in the ECF. Moreover, the red blood cells do not exit the blood capillaries. All the components that compose blood are not present in the ECF or in lymph.

Numerous lymph capillaries join to form progressively larger lymph veins, which are similar in structure to blood veins in that both vessels contain valves that prevent flow in the wrong direction. Both types of vessel also are dependent on skeletal muscle contraction to pump blood or lymph and maintain flow.

Lymph travelling in *lymph veins* passes through a number of *lymph nodes,* where white blood cells (some of which make and carry antibodies) monitor the fluid for foreign particles (antigens) (e.g., bacteria, damaged cells and cellular debris). White blood cells also can leave blood capillaries to monitor tissue for antigens or infection. Lymph veins join to form lymph ducts, the largest of which are the *thoracic duct* (which empties lymph into the venous system on the upper left side of the body) and the *right lymphatic duct* (which empties lymph into blood veins of the upper right side of the body).

36. D

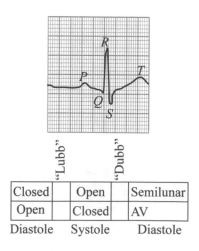

Closed		Open		Semilunar
Open		Closed		AV

Diastole   Systole   Diastole

The "lubb-dubb" sounds heard with a stethoscope are the noises of the vibrations in the heart and chest as a result of the snapping shut of heart valves. The "lubb" noise is the sound of the atrioventricular (AV) valves, between the atria and corresponding ventricle closing. When the ventricles contract (during **systole**), some blood is forced against the AV valve flaps, pushing them shut. (The heart chambers contract in unison: the right and left atria contract together, followed by synchronous contraction of the ventricles.)

The "dubb" noise is the sound of the semilunar valves (between the ventricle and the corresponding artery) closing. The semilunar valves close just after ventricular contraction (end of systole) to ensure that blood flows into the artery and away from the heart, not back into the ventricle. Presence of a heart murmur, caused by improper closing of the heart valves, can be detected by a slushy sound after the "lubb."

On the given electrocardiogram (ECG), the letter symbols correspond with the cardiac cycle as shown in the diagram. *P* represents the atrial contraction, *Q*, *R*, and *S* represent ventricular contraction, and *T* represents recovery of the ventricles. Notice that the transition of the AV valve from open to closed occurs at point *Q*. The transition of the semilunar valves from open to closed occurs just after point *T*.

37. C

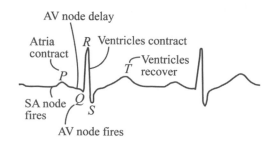

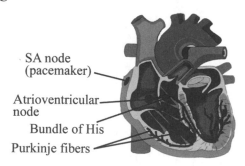

There are two nodes in the heart that regulate when the heart chambers contract. The **sinoatrial node** (SA node), also called the **pacemaker**, is where the nerve stimulus for contraction arises. The SA node regulates the rhythm of the heartbeat. The nerve impulse originating at the SA node travels first to the two atria, causing them to contract, pushing blood into the ventricles. The **atrioventricular node** (AV node) is located in the lower half of the right atrium. The AV node conducts a *delayed* impulse (so that the atria can finish their contraction before the ventricles contract) to the **bundle of His**, and then to the **Purkinje fibres**.

The Purkinje fibres conduct impulses to the ventricle muscles, signalling them to contract. The points on the ECG where the preceding events occur are labelled in the diagram. If the AV node were inactivated, all the points on the ECG beginning at point Q would be affected.

Atrial contraction at P would not be affected because it is controlled by the SA node.

NR 38   6 600

Stroke volume is the volume of blood that is pumped with each beat of one ventricle, and is therefore measured in units of mL per beat. **Cardiac output** is the volume of blood that flows from each ventricle per minute, expressed in units of ml per minute.

Heart rate is the number of times the heart contracts per minute, expressed in units of beats per minute. The formula that relates these three measurements is as follows:
cardiac output = heart rate × stroke volume

For this question, the stroke volume (66 mL/beat) is provided, and the heart rate can be inferred from the electrocardiogram (ECG). On an ECG, one heartbeat begins when the sinoatrial node (pacemaker) initiates a nerve impulse at the base of the P wave. The P wave represents the resulting contraction of the atria. The heartbeat ends when the ventricles are fully recovered at the end of the T wave. In the given electrocardiogram, there are two full beats per 1.2 seconds, which represents the heart rate. Plugging the heart rate and stroke volume into the equation (and converting seconds to minutes), you get

$$\frac{2\,\text{beats}}{1.2\,\text{seconds}} \times \frac{60\,\text{seconds}}{\text{minute}} \times \frac{66\,\text{mL}}{\text{beat}} = \frac{6\,600\,\text{mL}}{\text{minute}}$$

The solution to this question can also be derived by solving for the correct units of mL/minute.

$$\frac{\text{beats}}{\text{second}} \times \frac{\text{seconds}}{\text{minute}} \times \frac{\text{mL}}{\text{beat}} = \frac{\text{mL}}{\text{minute}}$$

39. C

Electrocardiogram of a Normal Heartbeat

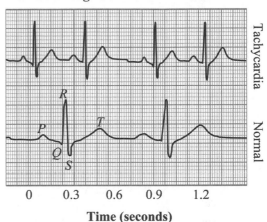

Time (seconds)

Tachycardia is a condition in which the heart rate exceeds 100 beats per minute. (**Bradycardia** is a condition in which the heart rate is abnormally slow.) On the given electrocardiogram (ECG), tachycardia would cause the $PQRST$ pattern to repeat more rapidly. As a result, the distance between P peaks would decrease.

A narrower peak at either P or Q, R, or S would indicate that some of the cells in the atria or ventricles, respectively, are slow to contract. Slowed contraction may occur because muscle cells receive abnormally delayed impulses from the relevant nerve fibres connected with either the SA or AV node. A longer than normal distance between P and Q indicates that the conduction of the nerve impulse from the SA node to the AV node is slow. Normally, the AV node will fire shortly after (although not immediately after to ensure that the atria have completed their contraction prior to ventricular contraction) it receives a nerve impulse from the SA node.

40. C

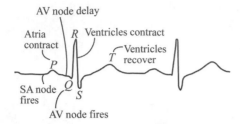

Systole refers to the contraction phase of the ventricles. (The left and right ventricles contract simultaneously, as do the two atria.)

Diastole refers to the relaxation phase of the ventricles. During ventricular diastole, the atria contract (represented by *P* on the ECG), filling the ventricles with blood.

The subsequent *QRS* wave represents the contraction of the ventricles.

T represents the recovery of the ventricles. The atria also undergo a recovery phase, but its weak signal is lost on the ECG because atrial recovery occurs during the strong *QRS* wave.

NR 41   4567

A number of diseases are listed in the given information.

Cancer—caused by uncontrolled cell division, such that a mass of cells (a tumour) invades surrounding body tissue (in some cases causing a lump that can be felt on the body's outer surface). Cancer can develop in any body tissue.

Heart disease—when the heart is at risk of failing because of insufficient blood supply from coronary arteries or a blocked artery or vein leading, respectively, from or to, the heart chambers, (e.g., in the aorta). Blockage of blood vessels can be caused by cholesterol build up caused by over-consumption of cholesterol-rich foods or a disorder in metabolizing cholesterol.

Emphysema—associated with chronic bronchitis, in which the bronchioles become narrow and mucus secretions increase, leading to blockage of the air passages. Decreasing the diameter of the bronchioles affects exhalation more than inspiration such that more air is inhaled than exhaled. As a result, air pressure in the alveoli and bronchioles increases, eventually causing the thin walls of alveoli to rupture. Reducing the number of alveoli decreases the surface available for gas exchange, so people afflicted with emphysema have a faster heart rate and breathing rate (which also becomes more laborious) to compensate. Capillaries at alveoli also rupture. Clotting and subsequent scarring of ruptured tissue over time decreases the ability of the lung to expand.

The diseases that are not related directly to the respiratory system, in ascending numerical order, are as follows:

4. Esophageal cancer—the esophagus is the tube that connects the mouth to the stomach, and is part of the digestive system.

5. Bladder cancer—the bladder is a sac-like organ that stores urine, and is part of the excretory system.

6. Pancreatic cancer—the pancreas is part of both the digestive system, because it synthesizes a number of digestive enzymes, and the endocrine system, because it synthesizes insulin.

7. Heart disease, described previously.

The correct response is **4567**.

42. A

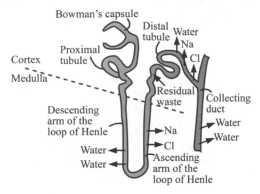

According to the diagram, water and salts are reabsorbed from the loop of Henle.

The descending arm of the loop is permeable to both water and salts, but because the extracellular environment is hypertonic, water diffuses out of the nephron. The ascending arm of the loop is impermeable to water, but salts are actively transported out of the nephron. Glucose, amino acids, and small vitamins are actively reabsorbed at the proximal tubule. Both ADH and aldosterone are hormones that target the nephron, causing the distal tubule and collecting duct to become permeable to water or salts, respectively.

43. C

Skin is the largest organ in the body. Skin is a barrier for pathogens, protects internal organs from the damaging rays of the sun, and regulates water loss and temperature (by sweating). All of these could be affected by severe burning. The skin however, does not regulate blood pH. Blood pH is maintained close to neutral by an enzyme (carbonic anhydrase) that converts carbon dioxide absorbed from respiring body tissues into carbonic acid. The carbonic acid, which would otherwise lower pH, then breaks down spontaneously into bicarbonate ions and hydrogen ions. Hemoglobin then acts as a buffer by binding the free hydrogen ions and removing them from blood plasma, where they would otherwise cause pH to decrease excessively.

44. D

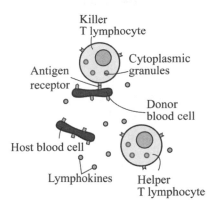

Cells that mediate immune reactions are white blood cells. Foreign (donor) blood cells have different surface antigens (or markers) than recipient cells. The T lymphocytes are responsible for recognizing non-self antigens present on the surface of cells. Helper-T lymphocytes recognize non-self antigen and respond by secreting chemicals called lymphokines that recruit other white blood cells to the site of invasion of foreign cells. Recruited killer T lymphocytes recognize and bind to the antigen on the surface of the donor blood cell and effectively punch holes in the membrane of the foreign target cell, causing it to spill its contents. Holes in the target cell are made by two mechanisms:

(i) Cytoplasmic granules are released from the killer T lymphocytes. The granules cause the target cell membrane to lose control of water transport, leading to target cell lysis.

(ii) Killer T cells secrete **cell toxins** that cause DNA degradation and the subsequent cell death of the target cell.

T lymphocytes are the major *mediators* of transfusion rejection. B lymphocytes produce antibodies, express them on the cell surface, and secrete antibodies that float freely in blood plasma.

The antibodies bind antigens, causing foreign particles and cells to clump together, inactivating them, and making them vulnerable to phagocytosis and lysis by other immune cells. Although freely floating antibodies pre-existing in plasma play a role in transfusion rejection, B lymphocytes are not major mediators of the rejection. Red blood cells contain hemoglobin, which bind and carry oxygen (and carbon dioxide). Platelets are the clotting cells. They contain thromboplastin, which initiates the blood-clotting reaction.

45. A

Hemoglobin is a protein composed of four independent polypeptide chains, each folded to produce a cavity bearing a complex prosthetic group called heme. These four heme groups are composed not only of amino acid residues (as are most proteins), but also contain an iron atom, used by hemoglobin to reversibly bind O_2.

All proteins contain nitrogen, as their constituent amino acids all by definition contain an amino group ($-NH_2$). There are no calcium or iodine atoms found in hemoglobin.

46. C

From the graph it appears that athletes who consume a diet that contains a lot of carbohydrates, such as starch, start their exercise with about 23 g/kg of muscle glycogen. Glycogen is stored carbohydrates in animals. After exercising their muscles, glycogen has reduced to about 5 g/kg. After about 50 hours, the graph indicates that those with a high carbohydrate diet again have about 23 g/kg of muscle glycogen.

47. B

Skeletal muscles, attached to bones, are capable of rapid contraction. Smooth muscles, surrounding internal organs, are not capable of rapid contractions. Muscle contraction consumes ATP. The ATP are assembled inside mitochondria. So, if muscles are going to contract rapidly using a lot of ATP, they will need an abundance of mitochondria. They would also need more oxygen. Actin and myosin are both required in all types of muscles.

48. B

Label X, the Bowman's capsule, is the first part of the nephron. This is where filtrate first arrives from the blood. Because urea, sodium ions, and glucose are all small, they are forced out of the blood of the glomerulus and through the porous Bowman's capsule, forming the nephric filtrate. The filtrate then passes into the proximal tubule. Proteins are very large molecules and are not able to pass through the Bowman's capsule. Therefore, blood proteins such as the plasma proteins are not normally seen in urine. Similarly, blood cells or hemoglobin are too large to pass through the Bowman's capsule and are not normally seen in the urine.

49. A

The photic zone in the ocean extends from the surface to the depth where light no longer penetrates. Because light is present, it is here that photosynthesis and photosynthesis-based food chains occur. Photosynthesis gives off oxygen, shallower water is warmed by the sun, and water pressure is relatively low.

High dissolved oxygen, cold temperatures, and low turbidity describe a fast-moving freshwater mountain stream. The remaining alternatives describe the aphotic or benthic zone found near the ocean bottom. Little light or warmth penetrates this region so photosynthetic plants are not present to produce oxygen. Oxygen is consumed as decomposers work on dead matter that falls to the ocean bottom. Salinity is low due to lack of evaporation.

NR 50   1423

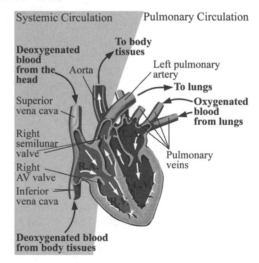

Deoxygenated blood travels in veins toward the heart. Blood from the upper body converges into the superior vena cava. Blood from the lower body converges into the inferior vena cava. Deoxygenated blood from both vena cavae enter the right atrium (RA) of the heart. Contraction of the RA forces blood through the right atrioventricular (AV) valve and into the right ventricle (RV).

The AV valves on both sides of the heart function to prevent blood from flowing the wrong way—from the ventricles back into the atria. AV valves are supported by strong connective tissue bands called chordae tendinae. Contraction of the right ventricle forces blood out of the heart and into the pulmonary arteries that carry blood to the lungs, where blood becomes oxygenated. A second set of valves, the semilunar (half-moon shaped) valves, are present at the junction between the right ventricle and the pulmonary artery (which subsequently branches into left and right pulmonary arteries).

The correct path of a deoxygenated red blood cell is therefore **1423**.

1. *In a unified essay, describe and name the main processes involved in ATP yield from both types of respiration. Explain the difference between anaerobic and aerobic respiration, the difference in energy yield between the two, and which is a better source of energy?*

The following points about the main process of ATP yield must be included.

- Glucose is the energy-yielding molecule, and cell respiration is the process by which ATP is made.

- The full aerobic breakdown of glucose involves glycolysis, which occurs in the cytoplasm, the Krebs cycle, which occurs in the mitochondrial matrix, and the electron transport chain, which occurs in the inner mitochondrial membrane.

- Glycolysis splits and activates glucose, extracting a small amount of ATP. The Krebs cycle continues the breakdown of glucose into smaller fragments, extracts high energy hydrogen pairs from the glucose fragments, and feeds them to the electron transport system, where ATP is made by chemiosmosis.

- ATP is the energy currency of the body and all activities require ATP. Anaerobic respiration involves only the reactions of glycolysis and is carried out by yeast and muscle cells deprived of oxygen.

- Each glucose molecule in aerobic respiration will yield a maximum of 36 ATP. In anaerobic respiration, glucose will yield two only ATP. Anaerobic respiration is therefore much less efficient than aerobic.

The given points are the main points of respiration; any other valid points are also acceptable.

Aerobic respiration requires oxygen, while anaerobic respiration does not require oxygen. Aerobic respiration has a high yield of energy, and is therefore more efficient per glucose molecule, whereas anaerobic respiration is stopped early and only two ATP are made. In anaerobic respiration, pyruvate does not enter the Krebs cycle. The end product is lactic acid and not CO_2 and H_2O as in aerobic respiration.

Two of the three given points will be acceptable, as are any other differences.

The better source of energy is the source that yields more ATP; therefore, when oxygen is available, the best source of energy is aerobic respiration.

2. **a)** *What are the types of lymphocytes that mature in the thymus?*

There are two sources of lymphocytes: B lymphocytes produced in bone marrow and T lymphocytes that mature in the thymus gland. The thymus is a small gland located in the upper thoracic cavity, and it produces three types of T cells: helper, killer, and suppressor T cells. Helper T cells detect a foreign antigen and signal killer T cells. The killer T cells recognize the specific antigen which triggers a chemical process that can puncture cell membranes of bacteria, destroy cells infected by viruses, or kill tumor cells. Once the have been destroyed, suppressor T cells turn off B cells in order to stop the immune response.

b) *A decrease in B cell lymphocytes would affect the immune system in what way?*

A reduction in B cells would lead to a decrease in antibody production. B cells are lymphocytes derived from the bone marrow, and their role is to produce antibodies. When a foreign antigen enters the body, B lymphocytes respond by custom-building an antibody with a specific molecular arrangement to fit the shape of the foreign antigen. The antibodies bind to cells carrying the foreign antigen and destroy them by either directly inactivating the antigen, by allowing other blood cells to engulf them (phagocytosis), or by binding to the surface of the invader and allowing other blood proteins to destroy the invader.

c) *How would a decrease in thymus lymphocytes cause susceptibility to disease?*

The body is left with no guard against an array of killer diseases, and the individual eventually succumbs to death.

The Human Immunodeficiency Virus (HIV) attacks and destroys helper T cells. Without helper T cells, the body cannot detect an attack from any type of pathogen and is unable to signal the activation of B cells and killer T cells. Without these steps there is no immune response and the person succumbs to the invading pathogen.

d) *In individuals with DiGeorge's syndrome, what may be the cause of missing T lymphocytes?*

In DiGeorge's syndrome there are no T lymphocytes produced at all, and no helper, no killer, and no suppressor T cells are found. Individuals with DiGeorge's syndrome have no thymus, and the T lymphocytes have nowhere to mature. In these individuals, only a very weak response may occur because cells that destroy other cells may still be active and can partake in immune response.

e) *A normal response to a foreign antigen in the body would set off which chain of events that would not occur in a SCID sufferer?*

Once a foreign antigen enters the body, a macrophage detects its presence and presents the antigen to a helper T cell. The helper T cell binds to it, and this stimulates cell division of the T cells, which then secrete a chemical signal that summons the lethal killer T cells to action. Besides calling on the killer T cells, phagocytes are also summoned, and signals are also sent to the spleen and the lymph nodes to release B cells. B cells produce the antibodies required, and destroy the invader. Once the invader has been effectively controlled, suppressor T cells are released, and they shut off the B cells and order the killer T cells to stop the fight. They also command helper T cells to cease.

ORDERING INFORMATION

SCHOOL ORDERS

Please contact the Learning Resource Centre (LRC) for school discount and order information.

THE KEY **Study Guides** are specifically designed to assist students in preparing for unit tests, final exams, and provincial examinations.

THE KEY **Study Guides** – $29.95 each plus G.S.T.

SENIOR HIGH		JUNIOR HIGH	ELEMENTARY
Biology 30	Biology 20	English Language Arts 9	English Language Arts 6
Chemistry 30	Chemistry 20	Math 9	Math 6
English 30-1	English 20-1	Science 9	Science 6
English 30-2	Mathematics 20-1	Social Studies 9	Social Studies 6
Applied Math 30	Physics 20	Math 8	Math 4
Pure Math 30	Social Studies 20-1		
Physics 30	English 10-1	Math 7	English Language Arts 3
Social Studies 30-1	Math 10 Combined		Math 3
Social Studies 30-2	Science 10		
	Social Studies 10-1		

Student Notes and Problems (SNAP) Workbooks contain complete explanations of curriculum concepts, examples, and exercise questions.

SNAP Workbooks – $29.95 each plus G.S.T.

SENIOR HIGH		JUNIOR HIGH	ELEMENTARY
Biology 30	Biology 20	Math 9	Math 6
Chemistry 30	Chemistry 20	Science 9	Math 5
Applied Math 30	Mathematics 20-1	Math 8	
Pure Math 30	Physics 20	Science 8	Math 4
Math 31	Math 10 Combined	Math 7	Math 3
Physics 30	Science 10	Science 7	

Visit our website for a tour of resource content and features or order resources online at
www.castlerockresearch.com

#2340, 10180 – 101 Street
Edmonton, AB Canada T5J 3S4
e-mail: learn@castlerockresearch.com

Phone: 780.448.9619
Toll-free: 1.800.840.6224
Fax: 780.426.3917

CASTLE ROCK
RESEARCH CORP

ORDER FORM

THE KEY	QUANTITY
Biology 30	
Chemistry 30	
English 30-1	
English 30-2	
Applied Math 30	
Pure Math 30	
Physics 30	
Chemistry 20	
Social Studies 30-1	
Social Studies 30-2	
Biology 20	
Chemistry 20	
English 20-1	
Mathematics 20-1	
Physics 20	
Social Studies 20-1	
English 10-1	
Math 10 Combined	
Science 10	
Social Studies 10-1	
English Language Arts 9	
Math 9	
Science 9	
Social Studies 9	
Math 8	
Math 7	
English Language Arts 6	
Math 6	
Science 6	
Social Studies 6	
Math 4	
English Language Arts 3	
Math 3	

Student Notes and Problems Workbooks	QUANTITY	
	SNAP Workbooks	Solution Manuals
Math 31		
Biology 30		
Chemistry 30		
Applied Math 30		
Pure Math 30		
Physics 30		
Biology 20		
Chemistry 20		
Mathematics 20-1		
Physics 20		
Math 10 Combined		
Science 10		
Math 9		
Science 9		
Math 8		
Science 8		
Math 7		
Science 7		
Math 6		
Math 5		
Math 4		
Math 3		

TOTALS		
KEYS		
SNAP WORKBOOKS		
SOLUTION MANUALS		
SOLUTION MANUALS		

Learning Resources Centre

Castle Rock Research is pleased to announce an exclusive distribution arrangement with the Learning Resources Centre (LRC). Under this agreement, schools can now place all their orders with LRC for order fulfillment. As well, these resources are eligible for applying the Learning Resource Credit Allocation (LRCA), which gives schools a 25% discount off LRC's selling price. Call LRC for details.

Orders may be placed with LRC by
Telephone: 780.427.2767
Fax: 780.422.9750
Internet: www.lrc.education.gov.ab.ca
Or mail: 12360 – 142 Street NW
Edmonton, AB T5L 4X9

PAYMENT AND SHIPPING INFORMATION

Name: _____

School Telephone: _____

SHIP TO

School: _____

Address: _____

City: _____ Postal Code: _____

PAYMENT
☐ by credit card
VISA/MC Number: _____
Expiry Date: _____
Name on card: _____
☐ enclosed cheque
☐ invoice school   P.O. number: _____

#2340, 10180 – 101 Street, Edmonton, AB T5J 3S4   **Phone:** 780.448.9619 Fax: 780.426.3917
Email: learn@castlerockresearch.com   **Toll-free:** 1.800.840.6224
www.castlerockresearch.com

CASTLE ROCK
RESEARCH CORP